FAITH AND PHILOSOPHICAL ANALYSIS

What tensions arise between philosophy of religion and theology? What strengths and weaknesses of analytical methods emerge in relation to strongly confessional philosophical theologies, or to Continental philosophies?

Faith and Philosophical Analysis evaluates how well philosophy of religion serves in understanding religious faith. Figures who rarely share the space of the same book – leading exponents of analytic philosophy of religion and those who question its legacy – are drawn together in this book, with their disagreements harnessed to positive effect. Figures such as Richard Swinburne and Basil Mitchell reflect on their life-long projects from a perspective which has not previously been seen in print. A wide range of approaches found in contemporary philosophy of religion are explored, including: reformed epistemology, 'traditional' metaphysical theory building, feminist methodologies, Wittgensteinian approaches, and American pragmatism.

Considering the trends in philosophy of religion as they are interacting across continents, looking particularly at philosophical influences in North America, Britain, and Continental Europe, this book will appeal to students, scholars and general readers with an interest in philosophy of religion, theology, or analytical philosophy.

HEYTHROP STUDIES
IN CONTEMPORARY PHILOSOPHY, RELIGION & THEOLOGY

Series Editor
Laurence Paul Hemming, Heythrop College, University of London, UK

Series Editorial Advisory Board
John McDade SJ; Peter Vardy; Michael Barnes SJ; James Hanvey SJ;
Philip Endean SJ; Anne Murphy SHCJ

Drawing on renewed willingness amongst theologians and philosophers to enter into critical dialogues with contemporary issues, this series is characterized by Heythrop's reputation for openness and accessibility in academic engagement. Presenting volumes from a wide international, ecumenical, and disciplinary range of authors, the series explores areas of current theological, philosophical, historical, and political interest. The series incorporates a range of titles: accessible texts, cutting-edge research monographs, and edited collections of essays. Appealing to a wide academic and intellectual community interested in philosophical, religious and theological issues, research and debate, the books in this series will also appeal to a theological readership which includes enquiring lay-people, clergy, members of religious communities, training priests, and anyone engaging broadly in the Catholic tradition and with its many dialogue partners.

Published titles
A Moral Ontology for a Theistic Ethic
Gathering the Nations in Love and Justice
Frank G. Kirkpatrick

Reading Ecclesiastes
A Literary and Cultural Exegesis
Mary E. Mills

Forthcoming titles include:
The Realist Hope
A Critique of Anti-Realist Approaches in Contemporary Philosophical Theology
Christopher Insole

God as Trinity
Patterns of Christian Discourse
James Hanvey SJ

Faith and Philosophical Analysis

The Impact of Analytical Philosophy on the
Philosophy of Religion

Edited by
HARRIET A. HARRIS

and

CHRISTOPHER J. INSOLE

ASHGATE

Published by
Ashgate Publishing Limited
Gower House
Croft Road
Aldershot
Hants GU11 3HR
England

Ashgate Publishing Company
Suite 420
101 Cherry Street
Burlington, VT 05401-4405
USA

Ashgate website: http://www.ashgate.com

British Library Cataloguing in Publication Data
Faith and philosophical analysis : the impact of analytical philosophy on the philosophy of religion. – (Heythrop studies in contemporary philosophy, religion and theology)
1. Religion – Philosophy 2. Analysis (Philosophy)
I. Harris, Harriet, A. II. Insole, Christopher J.
210.1

Library of Congress Cataloging-in-Publication Data
Faith and philosophical analysis : the impact of analytical philosophy on the philosophy of religion / edited by Harriet A. Harris and Christopher J. Insole.
    p. cm. — (Heythrop studies in contemporary philosophy, religion and theology)
    ISBN 0-7546-3141-9 (hardcover : alk. paper) — ISBN 0-7546-3144-3 (pbk. : alk. paper) 1. Philosophy and religion. 2. Christianity—Philosophy. 3. Theology. I. Harris, Harriet A. II. Insole, Christopher J. III. Series: Heythrop studies in contemporary philosophy, religion, and theology.

    B56.F35 2005
    210—dc22

                                                                    2005005008

ISBN-10: 0 7546 3141 9 (Hbk)
ISBN-10: 0 7546 3144 3 (Pbk)

Typeset by Express Typesetters Ltd, Farnham, Surrey
Printed and bound in Great Britain by MPG Books Ltd, Bodmin, Cornwall

Contents

List of Contributors

Pamela Sue Anderson is the Dean of Regent's Park College, Oxford, where she teaches philosophy as a Tutorial Fellow. She is the author of *Ricoeur and Kant* (1993) and *A Feminist Philosophy of Religion: the Rationality and Myths of Religious Belief* (1998); she has published numerous articles on philosophy of religion and feminist epistemology, and coedited *Feminist Philosophy of Religion: Critical Readings* (2004) with Beverley Clack. Her current research is on the virtues; in particular, on love and vulnerability.

Cyril Barrett (1925–2003) was co-founder of the Philosophy Department at the University of Warwick in 1965, and retired from there in 1992 as Reader. He then continued to teach and write at Campion Hall, the Jesuit house in Oxford. His main contributions to philosophy have been in aesthetics, and the study of Wittgenstein. He received permission from the executors to edit and have published Wittgenstein's *Lectures & Conversations on Aesthetics and Religious Belief* (1966), which radically altered the intellectual climate. His own appraisal, *Wittgenstein on Ethics and Religious Belief* (1991), has been translated into many languages.

Elizabeth Burns is a Lecturer in the Philosophy of Religion at Heythrop College, University of London, and Course Director for the University of London External BD. She has written on Iris Murdoch for *Religious Studies*, and produced several subject guides for the University of London External BD.

Brian R. Clack is Tutor in Philosophy at St Clare's, Oxford. He is author of *An Introduction to Wittgenstein's Philosophy of Religion* (1999) and *Wittgenstein, Frazer and Religion* (1998), and co-author of *The Philosophy of Religion: A Critical Introduction* (1998).

Giles Fraser is the Vicar of Putney and a Lecturer in Philosophy at Wadham College, Oxford. He is the author of *Christianity and Violence* (2001) and *Redeeming Nietzsche* (2002). He also writes on politics and theology for *The Guardian*.

Harriet A. Harris is Chaplain at Wadham College, Oxford, and a member of the Theology Faculty of the University of Oxford. She is an Honorary University Fellow of the University of Exeter, where she was formerly Lecturer in Theology. She has written numerous articles in philosophical theology and on Christian fundamentalism, and has a particular interest in religious epistemology. Her books include *Fundamentalism and Evangelicals* (1998).

Christopher J. Insole is a Lecturer in Philosophy of Religion and Ethics at the University of Cambridge. He is the author of *The Politics of Human Frailty: a*

Theological Defence of Political Liberalism (2004) and of *The Realist Hope: a Critique of Anti-Realist Approaches to Contemporary Philosophical Theology*.

G.W. Kimura is University Chaplain and Instructor in Religion and the Humanities at Alaska Pacific University, Anchorage, Alaska, USA. He is a Doctoral Fellow of the Episcopal Church Foundation. He has published academic work and fiction in the UK and the USA. He is completing a PhD in philosophy of religion at the University of Cambridge.

Ann Loades is Emeritus Professor of Divinity, University of Durham and President of the Society for the Study of Theology, 2005–7. She was the first woman to hold a 'personal' Chair in the University of Durham, and the first person to be awarded a CBE for 'services to theology' (2001). Her research interests have embraced theodicy in modern western European thought; theology and the significance of gender; and sacramental theology and spirituality. She is the author or coeditor of nineteen books, including *Feminist Theology: Voices from the Past* (2001), and edited (with D.W. Brown) *Christ the Sacramental Word: Incarnation, Sacrament and Poetry* (1996).

Basil Mitchell was Nolloth Professor of the Philosophy of the Christian Religion at the University of Oxford from 1968 to 1984. He has contributed not only to the philosophy of religion, but to ethics, political philosophy, theology and education. His books include *Law, Morality and Religion* (1967), *The Justification of Religious Belief* (1973), *Morality: Religious and Secular* (1980), *How to Play Theological Ping-pong* (1990), and *Faith and Criticism* (1994). He is a Fellow of the British Academy.

Richard Swinburne is a Fellow of the British Academy. From 1985 to 2002 he was Nolloth Professor of the Philosophy of the Christian Religion, University of Oxford; before that he was Professor of Philosophy at the University of Keele. He has written a trilogy of books on the justification of theism (*The Coherence of Theism*, *The Existence of God*, and *Faith and Reason*), a tetralogy of books on the philosophy of Christianity and also books on other philosophical subjects. His most recent book is *The Resurrection of God Incarnate*.

Charles Taliaferro is Professor of Philosophy, St Olaf College. He serves on the editorial board of *Religious Studies, Sophia, the Philosophical Annual, American Philosophical Quarterly* and *Ars Disputandi*, and on the Steering Committee for Philosophy of Religion in the American Academy of Religion. He is the author of *Consciousness and the Mind of God* (1994), *Contemporary Philosophy of Religion* (1998) and *Evidence and Faith; Philosophy and Religion since the Seventeenth Century* (2005). He is the coeditor of the *Blackwell Companion to Philosophy of Religion* (1997), *The Philosophy of Religion Reader* (2003) and *Cambridge Platonist Spirituality* (2005).

Acknowledgments

We would like to thank Laurence Hemming for proposing that we edit a volume together on the current state of philosophy of religion, and then for encouraging us to pursue our interest in the impact that analytical philosophy has had upon the discipline. We also thank Sarah Lloyd at Ashgate for her support and advice throughout the compilation of this volume.

This is one of the last publications to which Cyril Barrett, SJ, a philosopher, art critic and friend, has contributed. He died before the manuscript went to press, and we would like to publish it in his memory.

Verdicts on Analytical Philosophy of Religion

Harriet A. Harris and Christopher J. Insole

We have brought together a range of contributors so different and even dissonant in their approaches to philosophy and faith that one would not expect to find their names inside the covers of the same book. Our aim is to give a scholarly airing of tensions that often manifest themselves at the level of academic and departmental politics, but too rarely at the level of thoughtful and informed debate. At the level of academic politics the issues from one point of view might be expressed like this: 'the "best" philosophy departments have become those that are the most technically brilliant and have the least to say to most students' (Solomon, 1999, p.13). Robert C. Solomon, a North American philosopher specializing in Hegel and Nietzsche, sets out to save philosophy from what he sees as a thin diet of logical analysis. He warns his fellow philosophers that, unless they are willing to attend to people's heartfelt questions about divorce, serious illness, the death of a loved one, personal failure or political upheaval, then people will look elsewhere for solace: 'better the libidinal fantasies of Shirley Maclaine than the tedium of the professional skepticism that finds fault with every argument, confusions in every insight, foolishness in every good feeling, an intractable paradox hiding beneath every figure of speech' (ibid.). Yet the forerunners and champions of analytical philosophy saw themselves as rescuing philosophy from thinness and logical aridity, largely because they believed they were replacing Hegelian idealism with attention to good, solid matter (see Russell, 1975).

Of all the philosophical disciplines, one might expect philosophy of religion to attend to our most heartfelt and ultimate concerns, including death, failure and the directing of our will and emotions. Is this an expectation philosophers of religion should honour? In practice they focus more usually on the nature of justified belief, probability and proof, and how the words in our sentences function. In this volume, we hear from those who defend the rigour and clarity of analytical approaches as able to serve our thinking about religious faith, and those who regard the analytical breakdown of belief structures, arguments or sentences as thinning down our philosophical endeavour and distorting the nature of religious believing.

Analytical philosophy refers to a style or set of methods, rather than to one set way of practising philosophy. It is the term used to characterize much Anglophone philosophy of the last 100 years, philosophy that is marked by an expressed allegiance to clarity in choice of words, rigour and precision in argument, use of logical techniques (whether or not employing formal logic) and, most distinctively, the dissection of sentence structures and investigation of language as the best means of investigating concepts. The focus on language and meaning comes from a conviction that the best way of understanding ourselves and the world is to look at what we think, and the best way of getting at what we think is to analyse what we say. To 'analyse' literally means to 'break down'. Analytical philosophers vary from one another and disagree, for example, over the extent to which the philosophical task is to state definitions. But it is a sufficient generalization for now to say that they proceed by isolating beliefs for individual consideration, breaking arguments down step by step, and taking sentences apart word for word, and that they do this in order to spare us from confusion and specious argument. Analysis is believed to serve our philosophizing on matters of faith by helping us to be as clear in our thinking as possible, and so to avoid confusion and unsound reasoning. However, if the methods of breaking down and isolating various components of our belief systems gives us a distorted understanding of the nature of these components, or of how beliefs develop and operate, then analytical philosophy may be hindering more than it is helping philosophy of religion.

Why is philosophy of religion so dominated by analytical philosophy? Probably the only way of answering this question is historically. In the Anglophone world in the middle decades of the twentieth century, the challenges to religious discourse were coming from logical positivism, and philosophers of religion set about responding to these. This turned philosophy of religion into a defensive discipline. The mood of this period is recaptured for us in this volume in the essays by Basil Mitchell and Elizabeth Burns. Today the mood is different, and the sense is waning that the burden of proof rests with those philosophers who are themselves religious. Philosophers of religion are now dealing with central Christian doctrines: consider Richard Swinburne's output since the late 1980s, including books on revelation, atonement, the Trinity and the Resurrection of Christ (1989, 1992, 1994, 2003). Other philosophers are engaging in religious discourse that accepts that it does not matter whether or not we can prove or even establish the probability of God's existence: consider the developments in Wittgensteinian philosophy of religion, the influence of Reformed epistemology, and the Radical Orthodox rejection of any philosophical endeavour committed to a belief in universal reason. With the exception of Radical Orthodoxy, these philosophies of religion remain analytical, but they are not primarily defensive.

Our interest in investigating the integrity, strengths and weaknesses of analytical approaches to philosophy of religion has led necessarily and unashamedly to a focus within this volume on philosophy of religion as practised in Britain and America, and as it concerns Christianity. This focus and localization is itself expressive of a rationale for the collection: rather than simply accepting analytical philosophy's self-presentation as the neutral 'view from nowhere', we locate it within an Anglophone academic society, tradition and history. The philosophy of religion is practised vibrantly in contexts coloured by all of the world's faiths, but where the discipline is influenced by analytical philosophy it is also practised primarily in relation to Christianity. Moreover, in the Anglophone world, many philosophers of religion who are or have at some time been atheists (such as J.L. Mackie, Anthony Flew and, more recently, Brian Clack) are usually Christian atheists. It is the Christian God whom they are rejecting. Most conferences, edited volumes and textbooks in philosophy of religion assume a Christian theological framework. However they are often not explicit about this. Such reticence to acknowledge a religious tradition is part of what we wish to bring to light in considering the influence of analytical philosophy upon philosophy of religion. Many of our classic or textbook arguments concerning the existence of God or the problem of evil, for example, are conducted as though these matters could be theologically neutral, or as though the debate should not be affected until some quite advanced stage by the way theological traditions conceive God's relation to the world or divine responses to suffering. It is true that some philosophers of religion, notably Richard Swinburne, have turned their attention to matters of specifically Christian doctrine, but not before having laid a foundation in natural theology concerning the existence of a God, who is implicitly assumed to be the Christian God.

We asked contributors not to write analytical philosophy of religion, but to write about it, with a view to its historical and social context. Inasmuch as the history of the approach is more in view, the British side of the tradition, and its roots in British empiricism and Oxford philosophy, have inevitably received much attention, and more perhaps than is proportionate to their current importance in relation to exciting contemporary work in North America. Nonetheless the importance of North American approaches is recognized in most of the essays, and most explicitly in discussions by Kimura of American pragmatism, and by Harris, Insole and Loades of the 'Reformed' tradition. Ann Loades provides an extensive trans-Atlantic survey of different ways that the relationship between philosophy and theology has been configured since the 1930s, the period when philosophy of religion came increasingly to be dominated by such analytical concerns as the cognitive status and function of religious language. She notes that The American Philosophical Association keeps philosophy of religion on the agenda of philosophers to a degree not yet accomplished in the United Kingdom, and that American philosophers such as Eleonore Stump and Norman Kretzman, and we might add Marilyn McCord Adams (now Regius Professor of Divinity in Oxford), have redeployed key thinkers from the Christian tradition such as Augustine, Anselm and Aquinas.

Certain lines of consensus can be traced through contributions in the collection. Perhaps surprisingly, there is considerable agreement as to what constitutes the 'analytical tradition'. Chapters by Mitchell, Swinburne, Burns and Insole trace three stages to this tradition: the empiricist period initiated by the seventeenth-century British empiricists, the verificationist window of the 1950s centred in Oxford, and post-verificationist analytical approaches. The latter can be divided into those approaches that are happy to turn back to metaphysical questions (Mitchell and Swinburne), and revisionist approaches that seek to preserve Christian religious discourse without such metaphysical commitments (Burns and Barrett). There is also a measure of agreement that the analytical method is characterized by a commitment to conceptual clarity, rigour and transparency in argument, as well as by a respect for the discoveries of contemporary science.

The collection is more or less evenly divided between those who endorse the analytical project, those who reject it and those who have reservations mixed with some appreciation. So Basil Mitchell, Richard Swinburne and Charles Taliaferro give robust defences of the possibility and desirability of impartiality, clarity, abstraction and analytical argument; Pamela Anderson, Greg Kimura, Cyril Barrett and Giles Fraser question both the possibility and desirability of these aspirations when considering a life of Christian faith. Where the former group of thinkers see impartiality, rigour and clarity, the latter see distortion, reduction and alienation from faith. Harriet Harris, Elizabeth Burns and Christopher Insole are more ambivalent, appreciating aspects of the analytical project and the skills it instils in philosophers, while expressing anxieties about how it is currently practised and how it affects our philosophical aims and ambitions. Ann Loades's piece, which specifically addresses the relationship between philosophy and theology, provides an overview and commentary that helps to situate and make sense of these varying responses.

Varying Appropriations of Analytical Philosophy

We begin this collection with Oxford in the 1950s and the work of Basil Mitchell, who played a crucial role in keeping philosophy of religion alive in Oxford when his colleagues regarded it as a bogus discipline excelling in 'unclarity of thought' (Mitchell, quoting R.M. Hare, p.21 of this volume). Oxford philosophy of the mid-twentieth century had its heritage in the analytical philosophy of Moore and Russell in Cambridge, and the logical positivism of the Vienna Circle. We look back in various essays to both Cambridge and Vienna, and it is worth outlining their significance briefly here. Moore believed that the chief task of the philosopher was to analyse statements correctly, which involved looking for definitions of all concepts or propositions under discussion, and not merely the words used to express them. He insisted that we know a vast range of common-sense statements to be true, such as 'this is a tree' (when confronted with a tree), but that we need to master the correct analysis of statements. This involved, Moore thought, understanding that one perceives the sense-datum of a tree rather than perceiving a tree directly. Russell analysed the underlying logical structure of sentences to clarify what is being said. He shared with Wittgenstein the conviction that ordinary language concealed the logical content of complex propositions, and that we best get at their meaning by a reductive analysis, breaking propositions down into their bare logical form.

The Vienna Circle took up this conception of philosophy as reductive logical analysis, and followed Russell in taking elementary propositions to be reports of immediate experience. They then developed the principle that the ability to verify a statement in experience is the criterion of meaningfulness. It followed that theological and metaphysical statements were non-sense or at best poetry. A.J. Ayer introduced logical positivism and the verification principle to the English-speaking world in his *Language, Truth and Logic* (1936), but in the meantime Wittgenstein was changing direction and proclaiming that language is not simply fact-stating but has a multiplicity of functions and its meaning consists in the way it is used. It does not have a logical essence that the philosopher can reveal by analysis. Rather it has a history and a grammar which the philosopher is to describe. So Wittgenstein came to observe and accept ordinary language, instead of reductively analysing it into logical forms. This turn towards ordinary language gave him an affinity with Moore, who took there to be a vast body of shared convictions about the world which are shared in ordinary propositions whose meanings are perfectly clear. This philosophy of the later Wittgenstein and Moore came to be called 'linguistic philosophy', and was immensely influential from about 1945 to around 1960. Since then analytical philosophy has largely been practised in its pre-linguistic sense, but with wide-ranging variations.

Basil Mitchell recalls in this volume that not until visiting the United States did he learn that he was dealing in Oxford with what others were labelling 'analytical philosophy'. But Oxford came to have enormous influence in developing and disseminating the ideas and methods that have come to be called analytical philosophy. It has also played a key role in shaping the practice of philosophy of religion throughout the Anglophone world, not least through the Nolloth Professorship in the Philosophy of the Christian Religion. This chair was held by Ian T. Ramsey before Basil Mitchell, and then by Richard Swinburne before its current incumbent Brian Leftow. During Mitchell's time in this post, the Honour School of Philosophy and Theology was founded, thanks in large part to Mitchell's labour in building up relations between the work of philosophers and theologians in Oxford: no mean feat given the philosophers' preoccupation with logic, and the theologians' preoccupation with biblical criticism, and their distrust of one another (O'Donovan, 1987, pp.3–4). Philosophers of religion are indebted to Mitchell for maintaining the possibility of addressing big questions about ultimate reality in a climate sceptical of any such endeavour.

So Mitchell is the fitting contributor to open this volume. He writes about a time in Oxford when the assumption of Ayer and others that metaphysics was impossible was taken for granted, but also when linguistic philosophy was exercising its greatest influence. Anthony Kenny describes this period in *A Path from Rome*. Kenny arrived in Oxford in 1957 as a Roman Catholic priest sent to study philosophy. He recalls attending the Socratic Club, founded by C.S. Lewis for discussion of philosophical and theological topics:

> It was a good time for a philosophy student to be at Oxford, in the heyday of linguistic philosophy; philosophers were confident that they had discovered new philosophical methods which superannuated much of the metaphysics of the past. Wittgenstein was not long dead: the gradual publication of his works enables his genius to be appreciated not only by the small circle of his Cambridge pupils, but by the philosophical world at large. Linguistic philosophy

was in its 'ordinary language' phase; and after Wittgenstein's death Oxford came
to be regarded as the centre of this movement. It had the largest philosophy
department in the world. (Kenny, 1985, p.139)

Kenny eventually sought release from the priesthood after his initiation into the
philosophy of Wittgenstein in Oxford led, amongst other things, to his doubting that
religious experience could provide justification for the assertions of natural
theology. He already rejected the claim that it was possible to prove God's existence,
and now it came to seem that belief in God could not rest on experience either (ibid.,
pp.147–8). His estimate of Oxford philosophy remained high, unlike Iris Murdoch
or Mary Warnock's. What 'outsiders most disliked about Oxford philosophy in the
50s,' Warnock says in an interview with Andrew Brown, is the 'idea that "proper
philosophers" talked about matters removed from emotion, and the related belief
that proper moral philosophy had nothing to do with such improper subjects as right
and wrong' (Brown, 2003, p.18).

Basil Mitchell is both a moral philosopher and a philosopher of religion who in
the mid-twentieth century persevered with questions of truth and falsehood in a
positivistic climate. The dominant philosophy of the day held that statements of fact
were confined to science, and practised what Mitchell calls 'minute philosophy', in
not lifting its eyes from an analysis of words to the matters about which the words
were speaking. His essay in this volume tells of his work in keeping metaphysics
alive, and describes the life of the group he was a part of, called 'the Metaphysicals'.
He defends the rigour of analytical philosophy and its cross-cultural relevance
regardless of the historical, social or psychological conditions which may explain its
development. At the same time he resists its exclusive focus on minutiae, objecting
that philosophy that breaks everything down into a small, manageable size
consequently overlooks the wider context. He has therefore bequeathed to future
generations of philosophers of religion the legacy of a discipline honed by logical
rigour, which is unashamedly metaphysical and uses analogies and models to speak
about the divine. His philosophical method has something in common with the
natural sciences, but this does not mean it is positivistic. It means that, like natural
scientists, he uses models and theories to express what cannot be expressed in other
ways. In fact he regards his task as being more like that of an historian or literary
critic, drawing on a wide variety of evidence to build up an overall picture (Mitchell,
1973). This is a method some have come to call 'soft rationalism' (Abraham, 1985).

Mitchell's successor in Oxford, Richard Swinburne, in his contribution to this
collection, spells out for the first time explicitly and extensively how he considers
the analytical project to fit in with the Christian theological tradition. To this end he
makes an extensive and persuasive case, from the scriptures up to but not including
Kant, that the 'Christian theological tradition is very familiar indeed with the use of
the best available secular criteria to clarify and justify religious claims' (p.40).
Although most of the thinkers in this collection could agree with this sentiment,
there would be some dissent from Swinburne's claim that analytical approaches
afford the 'best available secular criteria'.

Swinburne's judgment that they provide the best criteria is stated robustly. He argues that it is an important fact whether or not there is a God who created us; if there is such a God, there are duties (such as worship) which we owe to God (p.33), and if there is not such a God, religious practice is pointless. The task is to assess, within the time available to us, the coherence of certain claims made about God, and the evidence for these claims. Analytical philosophy has particularly good tools for carrying out both these tasks, in that it has a commitment to clarity and rigour, 'features of good argument as such' (p.39), and is concerned with the discoveries of modern science, crucial for Swinburne in that 'no philosophy can hope to convince unless it takes seriously what we have learnt in recent years about neurophysiology or Quantum Theory' (p.39). The goal of the philosophical–religious life is to ensure that at any time (synchronically) one's beliefs are justified by the evidence. Over time (diachronically), inasmuch as one can, one should ensure that beliefs are properly investigated; the amount of effort we should put into this depends on the time available to us, and is proportionate to the importance of the beliefs. Being 'justified by the evidence' for Swinburne involves being a 'probable hypothesis', where a 'hypothesis is probable to the extent to which it is simple, and is such to lead you to expect the evidence, which otherwise there is no reason to expect' (p.38).

Running throughout the argument is an obvious distaste for Kant and post-Kantian philosophy. Kant's claim about the limits of human knowledge was a 'big mistake' (p.39) with Swinburne asserting that 'analytical philosophy, unlike continental philosopy, has liberated itself from that doctrine' (p.39). The liberation is made possible by the discovery of 'the atomic theory of chemistry' which by showing the unobservable causes of phenomena refutes the Kantian claim that 'investigation of the nature of the world can discover only patterns in phenomena, not their observable causes'. The confidence and frankness with which Swinburne dismisses philosophical giants and continents on the grounds of the invention of the microscope is perhaps characteristic of that which people can find either most impressive or most irritating about analytical approaches: a refusal to be intimidated by the authority of any thinker or tradition, and a preparedness to state an argument in a way which can seem unsophisticated, but which turns out to be rather hard to refute with equal simplicity. For some this is a strength, involving sufficient chutzpah and egalitarianism to declare that the Emperor has no clothes. Others consider that the analytical crowd convince themselves of the subject's nakedness, unable to bear the startling array of sequined mirrors, hidden pockets and complex folds.

Nonetheless, whether convinced or not, the reader should find much of interest in Swinburne's uncharacteristic interest in establishing the traditional credentials for his method. One of the more provocative things that emerges in this exploration is a tendency towards Catholic and Orthodox approaches, with some evident unhappiness with more Protestant positions: Protestants do not recognize the *Wisdom of Solomon* where one can find a 'sustained development of a natural theology' (p.41), helping to explain Barth's dismissal of the existence of natural theology in the scriptures. Later on in his chapter, Swinburne comments on the irrationality of Calvin's appeal 'to all humans of sixteenth century Europe to believe Scripture simply because it seems to you that it is true' (p.45).

Elizabeth Burns's piece investigates the role of analytical philosophy in the development of revisionist interpretations of Christian religious language. Such approaches seek to lessen the metaphysical commitment of religious statements by understanding them as expressive of attitudes or intentions. In a careful and scholarly treatment, Burns perceptively identifies revisionist approaches as a response to a loose verificationism: the conviction that the meaning of a statement is to be understood in terms of the way it is used. So a thinker such as Braithwaite, moved by a verificationist instinct, analyses religious statements as expressive of a certain commitment to a way of life, including a distinctive religious intention to feel in a certain sort of way.

Burns pitches Alisdair Kee against Braithwaite in making the point that this analysis can overlook the way that God-statements are really used, which after all is supposed to be the criterion of meaning. God-statements, says Kee, endorsed by Burns, are *used* to refer to a transcendent reality, and so any analysis of their use will have to incorporate this orientation to transcendence. Burns correctly points out that Kee is still under the sway of a version of verificationism in his conviction that a traditional belief in God is an unsustainable 'old supernaturalism' (p.57), needing to be replaced by a more progressive understanding of 'transcendence'. Burns's final resting point is Iris Murdoch who, she argues, manages to give a much more theologically nuanced analysis of the use of terms such as 'God', as well as retaining the use of doctrines such as original sin, prayer and grace, to express for instance our human frailty and the almost insuperable difficulties of being good (p.57). Murdoch is not completely endorsed, with Burns envisaging more of a role for the traditional terminology of 'God' than given by Murdoch. Burns also places greater emphasis on Christian distinctiveness, in that Jesus Christ is the manifestation of this 'transcendent guarantee of disinterested goodness' for the worshipping community.

Burns's piece is a valuable counterweight to the narrative given in this volume by Swinburne and Mitchell, both of whom consider that verificationist strictures on philosophy (i) hindered the consideration of religion, and (ii) were largely bankrupt by the 1970s, with the 'metaphysical turn' talked of by Swinburne. Burns's piece can be seen to respond that (i) verificationist approaches, if subtle enough, can actually capture more of the theological content of religious statements than 'metaphysical' interpretations, in that they aim to be sensitive to the use and function of that language, and (ii) that, far from finding their last expression in Braithwaite and dying out in the 1970s, such approaches lived on in thinkers such as Kee and Murdoch.

Where we might worry about Burns's argument is in her rather elusive attitude to verificationism, chiding some figures for being too bound by it (Braithwaite and Kee), but nonetheless broadly endorsing revisionist approaches (such as Murdoch's) which she identifies as motivated by verificationism. The question stands: is the loose verificationist challenge (and the turn away from metaphysics) right or wrong? Burns seems reluctant to say either, sometimes implying one, sometimes the other. It is all very well for the verificationist challenge to facilitate sensitivity to the use of religious language in prayer and thanksgiving, but of course another use for religious language has traditionally been to make metaphysical claims and arguments. If this is to be ruled out, Burns would probably need to stick her neck out and say that it is, and why it is.

There are interesting links between Burns's piece and Cyril Barrett's endorsement of the 'Wittgensteinian revolution', with Barrett demonstrating, in a more intense way, a similar deference to verificationist attitudes. Barrett explores the way in which, as he sees it, the academy and perhaps wider culture have failed to grasp the nature of the philosophical revolution promised by the thought of Wittgenstein. At the heart of this revolution is Wittgenstein's claim that religious discourse, in common with ethics and aesthetics, is neither empirically true nor false; religious discourse is not empirical or factual on any level. Barrett's positive claim about religious discourse is suggestively ambivalent between two positions: on the one hand we find the suggestion that the religious dimension is strictly nonsensical, and so one about which we must remain silent, while valuing the quality of the 'nonsense' and the motivations for the silence. On the other hand, Barrett seems to suggest that religious language is expressive of an attitude towards empirical facts, in which case it is not silence so much that is required as metaphysical modesty.

Barrett's contribution manifests all the features of Wittgensteinian approaches that can be both inviting and puzzling, flexible and yet oddly dogmatic. So, for instance, we have the usual Wittgensteinian valorization of 'ordinary words' and the 'ordinary' context for such words, at the same time as chiding people for the misuse of these 'ordinary' words, with Barrett commenting that 'most people' fail to understand properly how to 'treat words about God': 'they use ordinary words in an extraordinary way when they apply them to God and the supernatural, but they treat them as if they were using them in an ordinary way' (p.63).

The question that Wittgensteinian revolutionaries are always faced with here is this: if it is the ordinary use of words that determines their meaning, and if most people use these words with a metaphysical meaning, on what grounds is this usage being deemed reprehensible, given that the Wittgensteinian maxim is that meaning is determined by ordinary use? As with many political revolutions, the Wittgensteinian revolution is carried out in the name of the people, but with some contempt for the actual quality and understanding of those people; there is a benign, elitist and patrician attempt to speak for the people while really speaking against them. The strongly prescriptive nature of the Wittgensteinian project comes out clearly when Barrett comments that Wittgenstein attempted 'in a dramatic manner' to tell people that 'when they speak about matters religious, they are dashing themselves against the boundaries of language in thinking that they can say what remains unsayable' (pp.63–64). The contempt and pity for the people reaches a climax towards the end of the chapter, with Barrett lamenting that the prospects for the 'Wittgensteinian revolution' are 'not good': 'I cannot see that many people in this generation nor in the next (nor perhaps in any future one) will see the world as Wittgenstein saw it and wanted others to see it' (p.71).

In a lively and anecdotal fashion, Barrett proposes a sense of how a Wittgensteinian should see the world. What emerges is that, under the surface, there may be a few more metaphysical commitments to the Wittgensteinian method than meet the eye. For instance, out of respect for religious discourse the Wittgensteinian wants to steer it away from the language of empirical truth or factuality (see p.62). One suspects that, for the Wittgensteinian, straightforwardly empirical statements and facts are the only legitimate non-expressive realities (things 'out there' rather than being our attitude to what is out there). In a telling anecdote Barrett remembers a boatman on the Grand Canal in Ireland commenting of a sunset 'all I can see is a bleedin' sunset'; Barrett comments that this 'of course, was empirically and philosophically true' (p.65), as if 'philosophical' truth were reducible to the empirical. Lurking here is a perhaps unargued and unnecessary deference to verificationism, the maxim that only statements which can be empirically verified have substantial meaning. Cynical boatmen may not have the last word on sunsets, and we might reply that all we can see is 'bleedin' empiricism'.

Brian Clack writes a postscript to Cyril Barrett's piece, Cyril having sadly died before he made his finishing touches to it. Clack brings out the idiosyncracies of Barrett's own, influential, reading of Wittgenstein. He suggests that in Barrett is a desire to read Wittgenstein's late philosophy in light of the *Tractatus*, and therefore still with an eye on God as transcending the empirical. Barrett is refusing to see that Wittgenstein is denying that 'God' is the name of something or some being (just as he undermines the view that the Last Judgment is some kind of future occurrence). Wittgenstein views God and the Last Judgment as regulating pictures, but Barrett interprets Wittgenstein as saying that God is beyond our logical or empirical grasp.

Within this volume, Ann Loades offers further insight into Wittgenstein's influence upon philosophy of religion, where she discusses the work of D.Z. Phillips. Following Wittgenstein, Phillips refuses to take either an evidentialist or an anti-evidentialist approach to religious belief, but instead insists on the groundless and non-informative nature of religious belief and on the irreducible nature of religious language. He attempts to turn philosophers' minds away from science and towards literature in their quest for understanding.

Human Situatedness and the God's Eye Point of View

Charles Taliaferro and Pamela Sue Anderson have chosen in their contributions to debate with one another. They disagree over the desirability of attempting to adopt a God's eye point of view. At stake here is the validity of a particular construct of the ideal rational agent, as one who is able to possess and impartially to assess all relevant facts in a situation so as to reach a moral judgment about it. Throughout his work, Charles Taliaferro has adopted the notion of the Ideal Observer from moral philosophy and applied it to the rational agent in philosophy of religion (Taliaferro, 1988a, 1988b, 1998, 1999). He proposes that the Ideal Observer achieves the 'God's eye point of view' (Taliaferro, 1998, p.206). Analytical philosophers of religion generally assume the desirability of something like a God's eye point of view; they regard God as occupying the ideal vantage point, one that is all-seeing and disembodied, and as exercising an impartiality informed by omniscience. Notions of God and of the rational agent are interrelated: 'a theistic view of God,' Taliaferro writes, 'would more accurately be described as the portrait of what is believed to be an ideal agent' (ibid., p.210). Ideal Observer theory can find a ready home in philosophy of religion because it has so much in common with, indeed a heritage in, classical conceptions of God, as all-seeing, all-knowing, disembodied, immutable, impassable and impartial. Taliaferro applauds this. Anderson worries about it. In this respect, Anderson shares the concerns of other feminist philosophers of religion, that the 'theist's God is defined in terms of power, knowledge and detachment … [and] invulnerability … a telling picture of God made in "man's" image' (Clack and Clack, 1998, pp.120–21).

In this volume, Taliaferro sets out to defend the God's eye point of view as a desirable ideal in the face of feminist and other contemporary objections. He calls the God's eye point of view a 'divine ethic', though its ideals of objectivity and impartiality can and have been shared by secular ethicists such as David Hume, J.S. Mill and Peter Singer. He builds into his account of the God's eye point of view a significant affective element, so that he is not presenting a God who is detached and aloof, but one who is affectively appraised of the position and feelings of all involved parties. The moral agent must attempt, like God, to know what it is like to be the agents, victims and bystanders in any given situation. Taliaferro then addresses the most pressing objections to such an ethic. He defends the claim that there are such things as facts, and not only points of view; he presents his ethic as a view from everywhere rather than an attempted ahistorical and impersonal view from nowhere; he promotes impartiality as able to involve passion and desire; he denies that impartiality is always unattainable, though even where it is he insists that it functions constructively as a regulating ideal. He ends the first half of his chapter by proposing that shedding your own point of view or, rather, discovering your authentic point of view through having grappled with the points of view of others, is not a threat to moral integrity but rather part and parcel of moral development.

Then, in direct engagement with Anderson, Taliaferro takes up the objection that an Ideal Observer theory is insufficient because ideal observers could disagree with one another about a particular situation even while being equally matched in terms of knowledge, impartiality and affective identification in relation to that situation. Anderson proposes that a husband and wife might be in just this kind of disagreement over the permissibility of the wife having an extramarital affair. Taliaferro proposes three possible responses: both are ideal observers and in their different reasoning bring out good and bad aspects of the affair; both are ideal observers and disagree because the affair is morally neutral; one or both fail in being ideal observers because their judgments are clouded by self-interest, jealousy or powerful erotic desires.

Finally Taliaferro considers an existentialist objection from Jean Paul Sartre and Simone de Beauvoir, that external observation objectifies us, and diminishes or even eradicates our subjectivity. He finds connections here with Anderson's concerns that the ideal of an objective and impartial vantage point overrides proper attentiveness to our embodied, personal existence. In response, Taliaferro develops a version of the Ideal Observer theory or God's eye point of view based on a meditation on the gaze of God by the fifteenth-century German philosopher and cardinal, Nicholas of Cusa. Nicholas understands God's Absolute Sight as embracing all modes of seeing. Rather than overriding our subjectivity, the loving gaze of God apprehends our lives within God's broader vision. Moreover God's apprehension enables us to transcend our limitations and become our authentic selves. Taliaferro's solution would not reassure a Sartre or Beauvoir, but might gain the consent of those who agree that we find our true selves in God.

So why does Anderson reject even Taliaferro's Cusanian version of the ideal observer theory? Anderson was the first philosopher to produce a monograph in feminist philosophy of religion (Anderson, 1998). She is interested in religious epistemology and, like other feminist epistemologists, seeks to incorporate into epistemology the acknowledgment that 'knowledge-production is a social practice, engaged in by embodied, gendered, historically-, racially- and culturally-located knowers', so that knowledge claims 'cannot fail to bear the marks of their makers' (Code, 1992 p.141). Constructs of the rational subject as a disembodied, ahistorical, asocial individual able to perform the 'God-trick' of achieving a view from nowhere she calls 'male-neutral' (Anderson, 1998). Others working in the philosophy of religion have called them 'generic male' (Coakley, 1997) or 'masculinist' (Jantzen, 1998). Feminist epistemologists who, in all their diversity, reject ideal observer theories, hold that 'only people with the resources and power to believe that they can transcend and control their circumstances would see the detachment that the ideal demands as even a theoretical option' (Code, 1992, p.141). They insist that all enquiry comes out of, and is intricately bound up with, human purposes, and that these purposes have to be evaluated.

Anderson is not satisfied with Taliaferro's attempts to build aspects of our situatedness into his Ideal Observer theory. Her first objection is that the three elements in Taliaferro's theory sit in impossible tension with one another: that the desire to know all relevant facts while also remaining impartial implies a fact–value distinction that Taliaferro himself wishes to override. Following his academic mentor Roderick Firth, Taliaferro is committed to a philosophical position that denies there is a sharp distinction between fact and value. But Anderson argues that, if one must know all relevant facts, one must also know social and personal 'facts', which are less stable than empirical or natural facts. Knowledge of social and personal facts involves inside awareness of how context and status affect interpretation. Such knowledge would help towards omnipercipience but would threaten one's impartiality. Taliaferro believes and Anderson denies that impartiality can be made compatible with personal values and affections. How, Anderson asks, could an impartial assessment resolve differences between two people with conflicting, deeply held religious beliefs? She believes that, if such an assessment were possible, it could not depend on personal appraisal or passionate feeling because higher levels of impartial assessment involve moving beyond personal or passionate appraisals. Taliaferro, however, regards the personal and passionate as compatible with impartiality.

This essential disagreement between them fuels Anderson's second objection: that an Ideal Observer theory, even as modified by Taliaferro, is inadequate for resolving moral disputes. Anderson holds that two parties (such as a husband and wife talking through the wife's extramarital affair, or two women disagreeing about the ethics of abortion) might really share all non-moral facts, and sympathetically understand each other's feelings, values and attitudes, and seek to be impartial, and yet still disagree. Taliaferro insists that such disagreement could be explained within the terms of his theory: perhaps both sides are right, each picking out good or bad aspects of the situation; perhaps the matter over which judgment is to be reached is morally neutral; or perhaps the parties are in fact clouded in their judgment without realizing it. Anderson says that the two parties might not agree even over what constitutes genuine understanding. Moreover the manner of discourse affects the degree to which others are understood. She is suggesting that the purposes of each party, the power dynamics with which they interact with one another, the ways in which each is used to acting or being acted upon in the world, and numerous other subtle and difficult to categorize factors affect our judgments not only about whether something is good or reasonable, but about what counts as good or reasonable. She suspects that these various factors are likely to be screened out or smoothed over in any theory that promotes an all-knowing and impartial ideal. She thinks that Taliaferro glides over or does not appreciate the struggle and multiple difficulties involved in attempting to see things from the points of view of others. She holds that Ideal Observer theories work with an oversimplified view of the world, and at best can offer only a flawed aid to resolving moral dilemmas.

Anderson proposes instead a model of collective discourse in which partiality is acknowledged – such as people's differing religious beliefs – and in which the fact of people's different points of view is taken on board in the need nonetheless to arrive at a collective stage of decision making. Here agents are partial but may also be aware of their partiality and limitations. Carefully thought-out, committed positions are recognized as rational and potentially insightful, rather than cast as lesser stages on the way to a transcendent ideal. The goal is to reach a moral outcome that each party agrees 'incorporates better than any other outcome what each regards as morally significant' (p.92), rather than to achieve, in Taliaferro's words, 'a comprehensive view from everywhere'. Her case against Taliaferro turns largely on her finding inadequate his account of how partiality (such as attention to the personal and passionate) relates to impartiality. She likes the Cusanian image of the loving embrace, and argues that we should use Cusa's insights to replace Ideal Observer theories with a theory of ideal discourse.

In his essay, Basil Mitchell makes some criticism of feminist philosophy, and it would be helpful to put this in context and see how it relates to Anderson's work. By inquiring into the complex ways that power relations affect the construction of reason, feminist philosophers bring to the fore questions about who determines the criteria for rationality and goodness, and how beliefs and values are formed. Such questions could challenge the very discipline of epistemology and perhaps even of philosophy itself (Almond, 1992; Haack, 1993). They are empirical questions that could, in principle, be answered without recourse to philosophical reasoning, although this begs the question, what counts as philosophical reasoning? Grace Jantzen, who published her monograph in feminist philosophy of religion a few months after Anderson, wants to push the boundaries of philosophy so that psychological and sociological questions relating to philosophical agents do not fall outside its parameters (Jantzen, 1998). Mitchell supervised Jantzen's doctoral work and finds helpful an article in which Jantzen sets out ways in which Continental philosophers explore the unacknowledged power base of analytical philosophy (Jantzen, 1996). But he finds he cannot endorse her more recent writing in which she attempts to psychoanalyse the western philosophical tradition. Jantzen argues that western philosophy has repressed the body and the passions and privileged the soul or mind and rational activity (Jantzen, 1998). Mitchell suspects that philosophical inquiry is invalidated by a conviction that all thought is governed by psychosocial undercurrents, and that all philosophical viewpoints are culture-bound. He insists that recognizing the conditions under which philosophical advances are made does not have a bearing on the validity of these advances. In this respect he is defending the validity of analytical philosophy in the face of criticism from feminist, 'postmodern' or Continental philosophers who might be tempted to relativize and undermine its value on the grounds that they can detect the power base behind it.

Anderson's approach differs markedly from that of Grace Jantzen. Where Jantzen argues that western philosophy has typically privileged reason and repressed the passions, yearning and desire, Anderson attempts to understand reason as informed by and informing our yearning. Jantzen rejects the emphasis on epistemology in philosophy of religion and wants instead to focus on ethics and what promotes human flourishing, but Anderson is concerned to develop epistemology as something that incorporates moral desiring. Anderson draws on the philosophy of Hume and Kant, and on the work of philosophers within the analytical tradition broadly construed, notably Bernard Williams, A.W. Moore, Miranda Fricker and Onora O'Neill. She is also influenced by Continental philosophy, and particularly by the work of Michelle Le Doeuff, and finds ways of bridging insights from Continental and Anglo-American philosophy, rather than emphasizing disparity between them.

As a sub-theme of her paper, Harriet Harris proposes elements in common between feminist epistemologists and Reformed epistemologists. On the one hand, this should not surprise us in that, as Lorraine Code puts it, feminist epistemology begins where classical foundationalism ends (Code, 1992, p.141; cf. Coakley, 2002, p.103). On the other hand, it may well surprise us, for feminist and Reformed philosophers do not claim one another as allies. They have very different philosophical aims. The driving concern of Reformed epistemologists is to uphold the right of theists to believe in God even when they do not know how to defend the rationality of that belief. They also have a more general concern to defend realism. Feminist epistemologists rarely if ever engage in philosophical defences of belief in God, even if they are themselves theists and philosophers of religion, and many are wary of realism because of ways in which truth claims have been oppressive. Not that most feminist epistemologists are anti-realist; it is important for feminist and other liberationist advocates to be able to say that any claims they make about injustice are true claims, and to propose that their notions of the good reflect a true or truer way (for example, Fricker, 2000; Code, 1991, 1992; Harris, 2001; Anderson 1998). It is in efforts to combine realism with awareness of the epistemic significance of the situatedness of knowing and believing that Harris finds an overlap between feminist interests and the interests of Nicholas Wolstertorff in particular, and to lesser extent those of Alvin Plantinga. In their different ways, both feminist and Reformed epistemologists aim to uncover insights and perspectives that have been ignored or appropriated and distorted by some particular philosophical convictions about how beliefs are justified.

Harris's question is whether philosophy of religion can be practised in a way that treats as epistemically significant a person's moral and spiritual development, and nurture in religious practices. She asks whether it is a strength or a weakness of analytical philosophy to seek to operate without these variables. She acknowledges that analytical philosophers have a sensibility about the proper modesty of the philosophical task, and that they prize the intellectual virtue of rigour in breaking down arguments and propositions for careful analysis. But she would like to see other intellectual, moral and spiritual virtues taken into account in reflecting upon what equips us to become more competent religious knowers. She suspects that analytical philosophy curbs the philosophical ambition of philosophers of religion by narrowing their focus and shaping a discipline that seems detached from people's driving concerns, and which does not obviously help us to grow in wisdom for living. She is therefore interested in the Reformed epistemologists, who are critical of many aspects of the legacy of analytical philosophy while remaining firmly within that tradition. In particular, Plantinga and Wolterstorff have come to focus on the ways in which we form beliefs, and they take certain variables into account, including age and social setting, when assessing the beliefs that a person forms. This gives them some affinity with virtue epistemology, and the potential to incorporate into their epistemology consideration of how we can cultivate good habits in the formation of belief and understanding. However they do not develop their philosophy in this direction. Instead they remain primarily concerned with escaping the need for evidence, which they do not fully achieve.

One thing Harris would like to see is a more theologically developed religious epistemology from philosophers who do, after all, employ theological categories. Plantinga and Wolterstorff root their epistemology within the theological framework of the Reformer John Calvin, or at least within a version of Calvinist or Reformed tradition, which they then modify with some input from Thomas Aquinas. They hold that we are all endowed with a natural sense of the divine (the *sensus divinitatis*) which operates to make us aware of God but which is clouded by sin. They further hold that specific Christian doctrines, which are not known through any natural cognitive faculty, are specifically revealed to people through the inner testimony of the Holy Spirit. They regard both the *sensus divinitatis* and the witness of the Spirit as cognitive faculties. However they do not write into their epistemology consideration of the virtues or dispositions a person needs to develop in order to become more attuned to the *sensus divinitatis* or the workings of the Holy Spirit. Despite their interest in the variables that affect the proper functioning of cognitive faculties, they develop no discourse about growing in spiritual discernment. According to the theological framework that they deploy, there is a struggle in us to allow our God-given faculties to function properly, and to be informed by the Holy Spirit, but we cannot find that sense of struggle in their religious epistemology. This, Harris believes, is a wasted opportunity.

Locating Anglo-American Philosophy of Religion

Greg Kimura's contribution distinguishes Anglo-American philosophy from analytical philosophy, demonstrating that there is a vibrant Anglophone philosophical tradition running from British Romanticism, through American transcendentalism and pragmatism, coming to fruition in thinkers such as Richard Rorty, Stanley Cavell and Hilary Putnam. Kimura makes an almost irrefutable case for the existence of this tradition, which in many respects has more similarities with so-called 'Continental' philosophy than it does with 'analytical' approaches.

Arising from this compelling narrative are some more controversial spin-offs and claims, for example that the tradition he is drawing attention to is 'earlier and deeper' than the analytical, a claim which depends upon restricting the 'analytical tradition' to 'an historical window from the thirties to the mid-fifties'. Other contributions in the volume, from Swinburne, Burns, Insole and Mitchell, agree that this period was a crucial phase in the analytical tradition, but neither the first nor the last. So all these authors identify seventeenth-century British empiricism as the foundation of the tradition, and find from the 1970s onwards a renewed analytical interest in religion and metaphysical questions, once the strict verficationist restrictions on analytical thinking were lifted.

Kimura is explicitly developing a polemical narrative, commenting that his aim is not to be merely historical, but to be 'pragmatically speaking reconstructive' (p.120), 'to reconstruct and remythologise the notion of Anglo-American thought *via* a philosophical distinctiveness that earlier Romanticism and classical pragmatism held' (p.120). An element in this remythologizing is Kimura's gloomy prophecy concerning analytical approaches: he tells us that they are in a terminal decline, with analytical philosophy being described as 'largely defunct' (p.120). Where there are vigorous attempts to keep analytical philosphy of religion alive, as in the work of Richard Swinburne, this is not allowed as a counterexample to the narrative; instead, this is treated as 'resistance' to the inevitable decline of analysis (p.125).

Whether or not Kimura is right in his gloomy propheticism about analytical approaches, he has done a service in this chapter by showing that it is impossible to overlook a healthy alternative tradition, 'the autobiographical–literary tradition of Romanticism, specifically British Romanticism, and its current reconstructions in neopragmatism' (p.134). Kimura perhaps goes beyond what is necessary or established by his argument in making the further competitive claim against analytical philosophy that neopragmatism is *the only* living tradition of Anglo-American philosophy.

Ann Loades's contribution provides a stark contrast to Kimura's. Rather than telling a story of rise and decline between competing philosophical traditions, Loades colours in the many shades of overlapping and diverging trends in philosophy of religion as practised on both sides of the Atlantic. She attends specifically to the complex and multiple ways in which philosophers of religion since the mid-twentieth century have related their discipline to theology. She begins with a word of caution, that both 'philosophy of religion' and 'theology' are notions variously construed. However she sees analytical philosophy as having given philosophy of religion more of a uniform nature in the last half-century than theology has received from any particular mode of reflection. She also notes that theologians are very resistant to engaging in the kind of reflection that analytical philosophers of religion employ. Although Loades does not elaborate on this point, we should not assume that this is due to a sense of threat from philosophy. On the contrary, it is often because philosophers seem to theologians to take an inappropriate approach to the Bible, to religious phenomena or to articles of faith. For example, Swinburne's probability arguments for the historicity of Jesus's resurrection rely on a strongly realist view of the historicity of the Gospels arguably inappropriate to the nature of scripture and faith in the resurrection (Swinburne, 2003). With Swinburne's earlier work in mind, Maurice Wiles writes: 'I do not see how any theologian who has given serious attention to the work done by biblical scholars could begin to pursue the work of Christian theology in the way that Swinburne proposes' (Wiles, 1987, p.48). Wiles goes on: 'One of the things which as a theologian I hope to gain from philosophers of religion is some guidance as to the appropriate form that reasoning should take in the work of theology. Yet the writings of many of the ablest and most distinguished scholars in that field do not seem to have much help to offer' (ibid.).

Loades pays particular attention to those whom we might call philosophical theologians, who have been affected by the analytical climate but whose practice of philosophy goes beyond what is more usually associated with analytical philosophy, and whose work is read by theological as much as by philosophical students. Swinburne is perhaps now entering this category. Loades notes his participation in a ground-breaking conference relating biblical exegesis to philosophy of religion. At the same time, Swinburne's philosophical method, which he describes in this volume, is heavily informed by the philosophy of science, even though he stands within a Christian apologetic tradition which is at least as old as Augustine and which marshals arguments to defend the rationality of its beliefs. Others whom we might more usually consider philosophical theologians, such as Austin Farrer and David Brown, have had the very shape of their reasoning more strongly informed by strands of Christian theological tradition.

Throughout her essay, Loades disabused the reader of the notion that philosophers of religion uniformly approach their discipline non-confessionally. She acknowledges that many, such as Basil Mitchell, Anthony Kenny and Donald McKinnon, have felt committed to maintaining a professional agnosticism in practising their discipline. But she also notes differences of opinion amongst philosophers of religion over the propriety of confessionalism. A commitment to rationality expressed in argument, and to deployment of analytical tools, is shared by both those who proceed confessionally and those who proceed non-confessionally. Loades suggests that more of the former practise in the USA, and she makes particular mention of the Calvinist philosophers Alvin Plantinga and Nicholas Wolterstorff who hold that philosophical problems should be engaged from a specifically theistic and Christian point of view.

The few disparate endeavours to practise philosophy of religion in ways which do or could take in religions other than Christianity, receive mention in Loades's essay, notably the work of Keith Ward, Stephen L. Clark and the Buddhist philosopher Michael McGhee. So too do the many non-analytical approaches more usually practised in mainland Europe. Loades avoids driving an uncompromising wedge between analytical and Continental philosophy. She ends by mentioning the development of the new 'Radical Orthodoxy' movement, which came to prominence in the 1990s. This movement looks back to the heritage of Augustine and Aquinas in particular, and sideways to the work of Derrida, Irigaray and other (mostly) Francophone philosophers with which it has an ambivalent relationship. Its key thinkers are John Milbank, Graham Ward and Catherine Pickstock (Millbank, 1990, Millbank, Pickstock and Ward, 1990; Ward, 1996; Pickstock, 1993, 1998). They reject (what they fashion as) Enlightenment confidence in universal reason, and consequently reject the approaches to theism taken by most modern philosophy of religion. Their project involves seeing theology as the queen of the sciences, and as that under which philosophy, politics, the natural and social sciences and all other disciplines are to receive their true understanding. They are largely ignored by analytical philosophers of religion who regard their writing as obtuse and opaque, as is hinted at in Mitchell's comments in this book about 'postmodern' challenges to philosophy of religion. It is most frustrating to analytical philosophers that Radical Orthodox theologians disregard the virtues of impartiality, clarity and logical analysis. Theirs is a small movement that has made a big splash. It may now be waning; time will tell. But the stimulating challenges it poses to analytical philosophy over the nature of rationality will continue to be influential amongst theologians.

Giles Fraser shares some of the emphases of the Radical Orthodox in wanting to reveal to analytical philosophers their own historically and culturally shaped presuppositions. He draws imaginative parallels between analytical philosophy of religion, apophatic approaches to God and the ambition of the Modernist Art movement to create pure images, stripped of historical, narrative or figurative significance. All three movements attempt to eliminate the way in which our experience is 'embedded within a particular context' (p.157), attempting to drive towards 'a pre-linguisitic, pre-cultural' dimension (p.157). Against these movements, Fraser critiques the 'icy logic of pure modernity' (p.154), insisting that 'all experience is necessarily the experience of a particular person, in a particular place and time' (p.157). Rather than resorting to thin 'spiritualities' or the 'common theistic core' discussed by analytical philosophers such as Swinburne, Fraser wants a rich, full-blooded faith, resolutely Trinitarian, depicted throughout with Christian particularity, story and tradition.

It is unusual to draw out the way in which analytical philosophy can be seen as part of a wider modernist movement. Fraser does a fine and persuasive job, focusing on the huge canvases of Rothko, who aims to stimulate a 'characteristically Modernist' sense of pure and abstract divinity, 'a sense of the divine that can be shared by people of very different faith traditions' (p.150). In a similar way, Fraser finds analytical philosophers such as Swinburne aiming at a theism that is 'wholly abstract and empty of any suggestion of figuration or narrative' (p.150).

Fraser's suggestion hits its target well when considering the analytical project of the 1950s, with the particularly austere turn it took in Oxford. It may be less convincing when we consider more recent work in analytical philosophy of religion, liberated from the earlier verificationist strictures. So, although Swinburne does attempt to establish a general theist position, he goes on (in *The Christian God*) to argue that many points of Christian doctrine are also more probable than not, given the evidence and our a priori sense of what is probable. Fraser would not agree with the content or style of this attempt, but it is nonetheless an endeavour to come up with a more full-blooded Christianity. A philosopher such as Plantinga fits even less well into the Modernist aspiration, with his insistence on his epistemic right to believe the whole Christian package (Trinity, Fall and Redemption).

It would be rather rigorous to chide Fraser for failing to explain the work and aspirations of every philosopher of religion, when he has opened up a rarely discussed 'modernist' dimension to analytical philosophy.

Insole's contribution provides a rather unusual defence of analytical philosophy of religion. In many ways Insole agrees with Fraser, commenting upon the way in which analytical approaches attempt to bracket out tradition, authority, history and social complexity. But where Fraser sees a hubristic attempt to escape from our embeddedness and limitations, Insole sees some virtue in bracketing out factors that arise from our embeddedness, in an effort to reach mutual comprehension and peace within pluralistic frameworks, particularly where the situations are marked by mutual hostility, incomprehension and human frailty. In some respects Insole's discussion has resonances with Taliaferro's extolling of the virtues of the 'Ideal Observer'.

In making this case Insole goes back to the roots of both analytical philosophy and political liberalism, showing that for John Locke the 'clarification of words' had an important social and political dimension. Locke considered confusion about words to be responsible for the bloodshed and violence of the English Civil War and other European wars of religion. Insole traces an enduring commitment to 'clarity' as the hallmark of analytical approaches, where by 'clarity' there is intended a certain distance from any authority or tradition.

The relationship between the desire for abstraction (such as we find in Locke) and a horror of war has an interesting parallel in Fraser's 'opposing' argument. Fraser comments on how a motivation for Modernism was the horror at twentieth-century wars, and a subsequent desire to become 'free from the weight of European culture … implicated in the atrocities of two World Wars' (p.154). Fraser finds this desire hubristic and impracticable; Insole recommends the artificial exercise of attempting to abstract from one's thicker commitments in an effort to reach common understanding. There is no clear way of evaluating who is 'right' in this debate. The questions to be asked are probably more particular and context-sensitive. To Fraser we might ask: are people to be deprived of, or reprimanded for, the enrichment they feel from 'neutral' spiritual areas and Modernist art? Are we to insist on Christian distinctiveness, no matter how incomprehensible and exclusive that can be to those on the outside? To Insole we might raise the challenge: in what situations can an analytical approach achieve the fine goals he outlines of 'dealing with situations in which human diversity, plurality, conflict and frailty are to the fore'? If this amounts to little more than a few ecumenical seminars, then it might be better to concentrate instead on practical expressions of mutual coexistence (community projects and so forth). Analytical philosophers are anyway unlikely to enjoy such seminars if the value of their contribution is recognized only as an artificial attempt to abstract from their thicker commitments and embodiment, it being a feature of so many analytical thinkers to deny both these commitments and their embodiment.

CHAPTER 1

Staking a Claim for Metaphysics

Basil Mitchell

Analytical philosophy of religion has always to some extent suffered from the taint of illegitimacy. Its practitioners have felt they needed to establish its credentials. The reason is not far to seek. It is not just that, unlike logic and epistemology, it is not central to philosophy as an academic discipline, for neither are philosophy of mind, philosophy of science, philosophy of history, philosophy of law or moral and political philosophy; these do not incur the same distrust.

Before attempting to explain this let me first illustrate it. Sir Peter Strawson in *The Bounds of Sense* introduces his chapter on Kant's critique of Natural Theology thus: 'It is with very moderate enthusiasm that a twentieth century philosopher enters the field of philosophical theology, even to follow Kant's exposure of its illusions' (Strawson, 1966, p.207) and, even more explicitly, R.M. Hare, himself a practising Anglican, writes in his essay on 'The Simple Believer': 'The philosophy of religion is not a speciality of mine. It is indeed a subject which fastidious philosophers do not like to touch. This is not merely because it is a confused subject – this could be said of other branches of philosophy – but because the whole atmosphere of the subject is such as to put a premium on unclarity of thought' (Hare, 1992, p.1).

Given this distrust it is natural to ask whether philosophers of religion who wish to vindicate the intellectual respectability of their subject should seek to show its credentials within the ambit of analytical philosophy or rather should repudiate analytical philosophy altogether.

With his question in mind it may be useful to engage in a brief historical retrospect. When I first started to teach philosophy after the Second World War it was being strongly argued by A.J. Ayer, and tacitly assumed by others, that metaphysics was impossible and a fortiori so was theology. It was to combat this pervasive assumption that, in 1946, the philosophical theologian Eric Mascall gathered together a small group of philosophers and theologians in Oxford who came to call themselves 'the Metaphysicals'. The first meeting was attended by, besides Mascall himself, Austin Farrer, myself, Michael Foster, Ian Crombie, Dennis Nineham, Richard Hare and Iris Murdoch. After a few years the last two dropped out and we were joined by Ian Ramsey, Helen Oppenheimer, John Lucas and Christopher Stead, and by others as time went by. The group continued to meet until 1984.

With *Faith and Logic* (Mitchell, 1957), a collection of essays designed to illustrate how philosophy of religion might be seriously discussed, I did not in the introduction use the expression 'analytical philosophy'. Remarking that few philosophers would at that time call themselves 'Logical Positivists' I preferred the terms 'Logical Empiricism' and 'linguistic analysis'. I did not myself become familiar with 'analytical philosophy' until I went to Princeton in 1960. There I discovered that, in America, philosophy departments would as a rule contain Kantians, Hegelians, process philosophers ... and analytical philosophers, of whom I was presumed to be one.

Back in Oxford we did not think of ourselves as either attacking analytical philosophy or practising it. If we *were* to be classified, Mascall was a Neo-Thomist, deeply influenced by Maritain and Gilson, Foster was, if anything, a Hegelian with his roots in Plato, Ramsey was a somewhat eccentric empiricist and Farrer began as a Thomist who engaged increasingly with Oxford philosophy as he encountered it. The rest of us had as undergraduates gone through the Oxford mill and were seeking to come to terms with it. We would have been classified in the United States as analytical philosophers.

We found ourselves out of sympathy with various features of philosophy as it was being practised in Oxford at the time which precluded any serious interest in the philosophy of religion. Were these features essential to analytical philosophy as such?

The first of them, which may be termed 'minute philosophy', was a preference for discussing topics which could be treated with exemplary clarity and rigour. This put a premium on tight manageable themes. I have referred elsewhere to the way in which 'the prevailing orthodoxy was reinforced by gestures, tones of voice and figures of speech which served to define the boundaries of what it was acceptable to *think*!' (Mitchell, 1993, p.41). For example, a favourite gesture was one in which philosophers would, as it were, take the topic, place it in front of them, pat it into shape with precise movements and then with the right hand cut slices off it for closer inspection. This went together with a curious linguistic habit of using the demonstrative pronoun 'this' to the almost complete neglect of 'that', clearly conveying that the topic was within easy reach and suitable for careful analysis: '*This* is very interesting,' they would say, referring to the specimen before them.

This concentration on what was immediately accessible and manageable had the consequence that the wider context of the expression under examination was inevitably overlooked. As I have put it elsewhere, Michael Foster in his contribution to *Faith and Logic*

> detected unerringly the underlying weakness in the 'linguistic philosophy' of the period. The 'ordinary language' that philosophers purported to analyse and interpret in a supposedly neutral fashion was in fact deeply theory-laden, and the theories themselves involved substantive claims that it was the task of philosophy to articulate and criticize. It followed that critics of theism were not, as they liked to think, disposing of it from a position of unchallengeable neutrality, but proposing an alternative metaphysic which it was incumbent upon them to acknowledge and defend. (Ibid., p.43)

This became apparent as soon as one paid attention to the whole context in which a given linguistic expression was used. It was at the time generally accepted that philosophy was, in Gilbert Ryle's phrase, 'talk about talk'. It involved the use of a 'meta-language' and what was said in the meta-language had no implications for the truth or falsehood of what was being said in the first order language under examination. In moral philosophy, for example, much play was made with the distinction between descriptive and evaluative language, the one stating facts, the other expressing attitudes to the facts. Thus to call an act or a person 'good' was to commend that act or person on account of certain characteristics in virtue of which the act or person was commended. Whether the act or person actually possessed these characteristics was a question of fact susceptible in principle of empirical investigation; the act of commendation itself was a free exercise of individual will. Neither required or allowed of philosophical judgment.

This distinction was most plausible in the case of the most general words of commendation like 'good' and 'right'. But when attention was paid to the extended context in which such words were employed it came under strain. 'Mixed words' like those for the virtues and vices could not readily be disjoined from rather particular sets of qualities. One could not call someone 'courageous' who systematically evaded challenges of any kind nor could one call him unequivocally 'good' if he altogether lacked courage. Moreover some virtues, like humility, widely accepted in a Christian culture, were not acknowledged at all in other cultures. The more extensively moral language was explored, the more evident it became that it was profoundly influenced by pervasive conceptions of what it was to be a human being. Broad metaphysical issues could not be ignored. The point was well made by Iris Murdoch:

> In short if moral conceptions are regarded as deep moral configurations of the world rather than as lines drawn round separate factual areas, then there will be no facts 'behind them' for them to be erroneously defined in terms of. There is nothing sinister about this view; freedom here will consist, not in being able to lift the concept off the otherwise unaltered facts and lay it down elsewhere but in being able to 'deepen' or 'reorganize' the concept or change it for another one. (Murdoch, 1966, pp.214–15)

Closely associated with the descriptive/evaluative distinction in moral philosophy was the pervasive assumption that matters of fact were confined to science or common sense (thought of as vestigial science). This was a tenet of logical positivism which long outlived it. Even when the verification principle was abandoned, taking with it any hope of devising a simple formula for distinguishing between scientific and non-scientific discourse, analytical philosophers were reluctant to jettison this tenet entirely.

Accordingly the Metaphysicals were concerned to reject this assumption. If metaphysics was to be rehabilitated it was not enough to show that moral and political systems of thought had metaphysical implications; it was required to show that disputes about these were in principle capable of rational resolution and that questions of truth and falsehood were involved. In this respect the response to critics of theism was two-pronged. It was necessary, on the one hand, to question the excessively simplistic account of scientific reasoning itself which was being promulgated by such philosophers as Popper and Hempel and, on the other, to produce instances of disciplines which were such that (i) they were normally accepted as rational and as yielding conclusions that were true and false, and (ii) their methods of reasoning could not be assimilated to the Popper/Hempel pattern.

In relation to both of these our discussions were aided by developments which were entirely independent of us. In the philosophy of science, T.S. Kuhn in *The Structure of Scientific Revolutions* (1962) asserted that, while the Popper/Hempel model worked well enough for what he called 'normal science', it could not explain what took place when large-scale revolutions occurred involving change from one 'paradigm' to another. A choice had then to be made which *ex hypothesi* could not be determined by applying the rules operative in the existing paradigm. Kuhn himself was ambivalent as to whether the choices then made were rational (though I think myself that his overall argument required that they should be), but in our group John Lucas in an early paper had argued convincingly that, in many contexts, scientific as well as non-scientific, there was a need for informal as well as formal reasoning (Lucas, 1955); and Ian Crombie had propounded a distinction between 'canonical' and 'non-canonical' reasoning, which made essentially the same point.[1]

We were similarly aided, so far as the other prong was concerned, by William H. Dray in his *Laws and Explanation in History* (1957). Dray vigorously contested the Popper/Hempel thesis that historical reasoning consisted in the application of general laws to the events of the past and argued that it was *sui generis* and involved an irreducible element of historical judgment.

In pursuing this line of thought we were distancing ourselves from an alternative way of coping with the descriptive/evaluative distinction which had its attractions for philosophers and theologians alike. This was to develop the possibility of assimilating religious to moral language and to analyse the latter as essentially expressive. Hare himself was insisting that what was expressed in moral judgments was not emotions but imperatives and that, unlike emotions, imperatives could be the subject of rational argument. He never applied this analysis with any thoroughness to religious language, but his attempts to apply it at all put him in a permanent minority in our group, with the result that he eventually withdrew.

One advantage of some sort of expressive theory for Christian apologists was that it offered a tempting way of dealing with the embarrassing profusion of images and metaphors which made it so difficult to examine religious claims with the desiderated 'clarity and rigour'. If all this could be classed as 'poetry', which no-one doubted had profound emotional significance for human beings but which was not in any ordinary sense 'fact-stating', philosophers and theologians would be relieved

---

1   Crombie made this distinction in the informal discussion meetings of the Metaphysicals.

of the task of saying clearly what it meant or determining whether it was true or false. Here philosophical analysis joined hands with Rudolf Bultmann's project of 'demythologizing' the Gospel.

Traditionally the response of philosophical theologians to the problem of how we can talk intelligibly about a God who is not an object of observation or straightforwardly definable in terms of observables was by way of a doctrine of analogy. The Metaphysicals spent a lot of time discussing how this doctrine might be adapted to a defence of the objectivity of religious statements. This was especially the domain of Austin Farrer, who had explored the topic with inspired eloquence in his Bampton Lectures of 1948, published under the title of *The Glass of Vision* (1948). Farrer was undoubtedly the central figure of the Metaphysicals until his death in 1968; indeed a major reason for the rest of us in the early days to go on meeting was to make sure that Farrer continued to work seriously in philosophy and not spend too much of his time in New Testament exegesis.

Farrer held that revealed truth is conveyed in inspired images and cannot be grasped independently of a metaphysical framework which is itself analogical. Both involved what he termed 'irreducible analogy'. Given agreement on this, two problems remained. One was how to deal with the basic terms that figured in any metaphysical theism, such as 'person', 'cause' and 'know'. Were these to be treated in the same way as the 'inspired images' given in revelation? Unlike them these words had a reassuringly down-to-earth character which appeared to need no further explanation, but on closer examination they too were problematical when applied to God. This problem had surfaced in *Faith and Logic*, where Ian Crombie in his chapter on 'The possibility of theological statements' remarked in a footnote about Farrer's use of 'parable' that 'I would say, what he would not, that to speak of God as a Person is to speak in parable' (Crombie, 1957, p.70). In a subsequent paper I tried to resolve this disagreement by suggesting that one should adopt Bishop Berkeley's distinction between 'metaphysical' and 'proper' analogy. In the latter case we are using a word which bears a clear sense when applied to a human being and, when applied to God, is used 'in such a way as to denote perfection' (Mitchell, 1990c, p.192).

The other problem associated with this was how the metaphysician's analogies were to be controlled. Much time was spent by us in considering this problem. It became apparent that, in spite of the clear distinction Farrer had made between scientific and metaphysical thinking, there had to be a place for theory in the latter which was to some extent analogous to its role in the former. Here again our efforts were assisted by developments in the philosophy of science in which the part played by 'models' in scientific theories was stressed.

In all of this we were criticizing positions taken up by many, perhaps most, analytical philosophers, but were we attacking analytical philosophy as such or were we, indeed, ourselves practising analytical philosophy? It is difficult to give clear answers to these questions. In one respect we inevitably fell short of the standards routinely set by analytical philosophers in their demand for clarity and rigour. These standards favoured the small-scale problems and manageable questions which we undoubtedly complained about. We staked a claim for metaphysics as a rational discipline but, in its theistic form, it inevitably involved the employment of analogies which owed their explanatory power to a superfluity of meaning over and above what could be precisely defined. In our discussions, Farrer talked of 'the art of balancing parables' and this required the exercise of judgment which does not allow of a strict decision procedure. It is doubtless these features of our procedures which provoked Hare's allegation of unavoidable 'unclarity of thought' and helped to moderate Strawson's enthusiasm for philosophical theology. But we remained committed to saying clearly whatever could be said clearly and to formulating arguments with as much rigour as the context allowed. In addition we embraced two further features of the best practice of analytical philosophers. The first is always to anticipate objections and attend carefully to them and, when attacking an opponent's thesis, to formulate it in its strongest form. The second is a certain fundamental modesty in estimating the strengths and weaknesses of one's own position. We followed them in being suspicious of philosophical works which contain no paragraphs beginning 'It may be objected that …' or 'What I have claimed to show is …'. I remember with, I think, justifiable pride an occasion when I was about to give a lecture in a Dutch university and the professor of philosophy who introduced me said 'One thing we have learned when we have a lecturer from England is that it will at any rate be entirely clear what it is that he is saying.'

It remains to ask to what extent contemporary criticisms of analytical philosophy of religion are justified. It is ironical that what analytical philosophers are chiefly criticized for are what they take to be their virtues. It is complained that the very attempt to view the subject matter fairly and impartially and to do justice to their critics betrays a conviction on their part that they are able, in principle, to attain a viewpoint above the battle – what has been called a 'God's eye view'. Far from betokening modesty it indicates an ingrained pride and, at the same time, a sort of naïveté. From this perspective the very characteristics which Anglo-Saxon philosophers object to in the continentals, the exaggerated rhetoric, the disregard of objections, the unabashed attempt to persuade, are indications of a greater honesty, frank acknowledgment that every thinker is an existing individual intent upon communicating his or her personal vision, all the time admitting that inevitably he or she is self-interested and implicated in some group's lust for power.

This 'postmodern' critique is supplemented by a distinctively feminist one which sees analytical philosophy as the product of a typically masculine cast of mind. The preference for small-scale topics and precise argumentation exhibits the sort of tunnel vision with which the masculine mind concentrates on one thing at a time to the neglect of the broader context. The feminine mind, by contrast, is intuitive and consensual. In a review of Douglas Hedley's book on Coleridge, Stephen Holmes remarks on the aphoristic nature of Coleridge's thought: 'In contrast to any analytic tradition of philosophy which must proceed by a series of analytical steps, the essence of aphorisms is to be a series of brief arresting statements unconnected with each other, inviting the reader to pause, to think, to reflect. An aphorism is to be grasped intuitively rather than logically; it cannot be argued for, only experienced' (Holmes, 2001, pp.492–3).

Coleridge emerges from this assessment as a typically feminine thinker. However the intuitive and consensual aspects of feminine thinking, taken together, suggest, not that aphoristic insights cannot be argued for, but that the process of arguing for them must be such that they can be seen to cohere in a wider pattern in which nothing of consequence is left unattended to.

I have found it useful from time to time to draw a distinction between searchlight and epidiascopic thinkers. Searchlight thinkers explore each topic sequentially, taking care to illuminate each item to the fullest possible extent until the entire subject has been covered. The epidiascopic thinker, as in an old-fashioned epidiascope, pictures a whole area in a manner that is initially fuzzy and then labours to get the whole picture into clear focus. It may be the case that men are characteristically searchlight thinkers and women epidiascopic thinkers. Whether this is so is a matter for empirical research. In advance of such research one would expect to find that the distribution of these characteristics, like those of height and physical strength, is such that the masculine ones are found in a number of women and the feminine ones in a number of men. I remember a particular philosophical encounter between a male and a female philosopher in which the sharpness and aggressiveness were all on the woman's side while the man displayed unfailing gentleness and courtesy. It is noteworthy that the approach of the Metaphysicals as I have described it was collectively epidiascopic although the membership was always predominantly male.[2]

However this may be, both these critiques, the postmodernist and the feminist, are open to the charge that, unless carefully qualified, they undercut themselves. If analytical philosophers are to be successfully convicted of a failure to acknowledge non-rational causes of the arguments they advance, it is necessary to show in sufficient detail what these are and how they operate. This obligation could be avoided only if the critics are able to maintain that all philosophical theories are vitiated by unacknowledged biases such as an insidious lust for power. But in that case the critic's own arguments are similarly undercut.

In an admirably careful and impartial comparison between Anglo-Saxon and Continental philosophers of religion, Grace Jantzen (1996) outlines the latter's project of exploring the former's dependence upon an unacknowledged power base. This done, she deplores the tendency of Anglo-Saxon philosophers simply to ignore the work of Continental philosophers, together with the criticisms they advance of their own procedures. She calls for dialogue between them.

This plea seems eminently reasonable until one asks how the dialogue could be conducted, given the presuppositions of the 'Continentals' as she describes them. *Ex hypothesi* any reasons analytical philosophers advance to answer their critics

---

2   The exception for much of the time was Helen Oppenheimer.

will be dismissed as insidiously self-interested. The analysts, in their turn, cannot look for the hidden power base of their critics without implicitly accepting their case.

One explanation of the neglect that Jantzen complains of is that the Anglo-Saxons often do not recognize what the Continentals do as philosophy at all; it is rather a branch of psychology or sociology. It is, of course, a philosophical question to what extent an argument is invalidated by the discovery of a psychological or sociological explanation of its being propounded, and this could be the subject of dialogue, but it would not be a dialogue about the philosophy of religion; and it would be subject to an infinite regress if this philosophical inquiry itself were deemed to be similarly invalidated.

The postmodern critique is sometimes expressed in terms of philosophical viewpoints being 'culture-bound'. This thesis also is put forward with varying degrees of generality. It is often possible in retrospect to notice that thinkers of a particular historical period made certain assumptions which they never questioned and which can now be seen to be in need of justification, Collingwood's 'absolute presuppositions'. Once this is noticed we and our contemporaries are bound to wonder what assumptions we are making which we ourselves do not recognize. This possibility provides good grounds for caution, and is a sound reason for trying to establish and maintain conditions of enquiry and debate in which such assumptions can be detected and examined, but it offers no reason for holding that such examination cannot itself be reasonable or that the assumptions in question could not be justified.

Where this thesis is advanced in a form that is entirely general it is plainly invalid. It may well have been the case, for example, that the developments in logic and epistemology in fifth- and fourth-century Athens could not have occurred without the freedom of inquiry made possible by democratic politics. Spartan culture could not have engendered them. But this finding has no bearing on the validity of the advances made in these fields.

Nevertheless it cannot be denied that some cultural conditions may inhibit the recognition of certain truths and favour the acceptance of certain falsehoods; and that not only philosophers but academics in general are reluctant to consider these possibilities in their own case and that of their colleagues. It is indeed a familiar feature of academic life that, where a particular school of thought is dominant, it is promoted by a variety of non-rational methods. The reigning orthodoxy is maintained by control of appointments and syllabuses as well as by the more subtle means of gestures and tones of voice which I have already noted. In such ways a 'culture' in the journalistic sense of the word is perpetuated. It is well for individuals to be aware of this and ready to vindicate their independence of mind. The dangers of these practices can be mitigated by institutional arrangements such as diversity of appointing bodies, but, like political parties, these practices can have their own corresponding advantages. They favour the intensive development of a set of ideas among a group of thinkers who have certain basic assumptions in common, and they demand from critics a determination to seek an equivalent thoroughness in working out their own preferred alternatives.

Now that the issue of the role of feeling in thinking has been raised by feminists we may expect more attention to be paid to the question to what extent personal factors are, or should be, involved in philosophical reasoning. It should not be assumed, of course, that, where they are not explicitly avowed, they are not operative. Indeed it is part of the feminists' claim that they are bound to be operative, no matter how carefully they are concealed by the conventions of academic publications.

There are two poles involved in any kind of reflective activity, a creative and a critical one. The creative one is a matter of imagining how things might be understood or how they might be explained and this calls for lively imagination and a generous impulse of charity. But it is not enough to give entirely free rein to this impulse. Criticism is needed: is this putative insight capable of being expressed in a logically coherent form; is it consistent with what is otherwise known – with relevant empirical evidence or well supported theories? It may sometimes happen that, during the creative phase, the critical capacity needs to be temporarily suspended. A good teacher knows that there are times when it is best to withhold criticism, if a good idea is not to be throttled at birth. But eventually criticism is necessary. The analytical philosopher's 'but it may be objected that ...' is not ultimately dispensable, although feminists and others may on occasion legitimately claim that a particular philosopher has allowed his creative capacities to be inhibited by premature criticism.

No doubt there are instances in which personal involvement does threaten impartiality, but it need not do so, and does not do so in the case of the tenderer feelings which feminists chiefly value and seek to acknowledge and encourage, such as genuine love. This can be seen in the relation between teacher and taught, where both are committed to the discovery and dissemination of truth. The teacher needs to mingle encouragement and criticism. Without encouragement the pupil will not develop fully his or her creative capacities; without criticism the development will not advance towards truth. Insofar as the teacher is moved by a sort of disinterested love, this will enhance sympathy and understanding of the pupil, but will not inhibit impartial judgment which is equally essential to the pupil's intellectual growth.

The question remains what services analytical philosophers can render to theology. Theologians are engaged in the task of interpreting Christian doctrines in ways that are religiously illuminating and rationally defensible, and it is to the latter requirement that philosophy is relevant. One way in which it can assist theology is by detecting and criticizing philosophical assumptions embedded in the tradition as currently formulated; another is by criticizing assumptions involved in proposed new interpretations of doctrine. In such cases philosophers are not importing philosophy into theological realms hitherto untouched by it, but continuing a philosophical debate which is already under way.

Philosophical assumptions may enter theology by way of the different disciplines which theologians need to have mastered as an essential part of their education. The study of Scripture requires familiarity with the languages in which the various books are written and with others which the writers would have known, as well as with those of the classical period of the formation of Christian doctrine. The same is true of ancient history and literary criticism. A consequence of this is that theologians may be influenced excessively by passing fashions among the practitioners of these disciplines. Moreover they may be sensitive to the charge that they operate on the margins of these disciplines and have antecedent presuppositions of which their secular colleagues are free. Hence ancient historians sometimes complain that New Testament scholars are unduly sceptical in their handling of the evidence available to them; and they are, perhaps, tempted to defer excessively to current theories in literary criticism about the interpretation of texts. In this connection it is not unreasonable to suggest that philosophy in general and analytical philosophy in particular help to develop a 'nose for nonsense' which may serve as a prophylactic against these tendencies.

It does not follow, of course, that contemporary critics are always right and that the philosophical assumptions under attack cannot be rationally defended, but theology can be expected to benefit from the ensuing debate. An example would be the assumption that God is timeless, derived from Platonic and Neoplatonic sources, which has been called into question by, among others, J.R. Lucas (1973) and R.G. Swinburne (1977). It is noteworthy that both of these have been at pains to preserve the truth underlying this assumption by proposing an alternative concept of eternity which they claim is more congruent with biblical teaching about the activity of God.

More positively philosophers can open up for theologians a number of conceptual options for them to choose between. In a semi-serious fashion I did this in my essay, 'How to play theological ping-pong' (Mitchell, 1990b), where I claimed to discover in a number of mainly Protestant theologians a tendency to pose false alternatives.

A key example is provided by debates about the Resurrection. It is not uncommon for theologians to maintain that historical evidence cannot count for or against a theological judgment (relying here on 'Lessing's ditch' that historical facts, which are contingent, neither support nor undermine universal truths of reason). Given this assumption, liberal theologians may abandon the traditional interpretation of the doctrine altogether and claim instead that the Resurrection is to be understood, not as an event in the life of Jesus, but as a 'mythological' account of the response of the earliest disciples and the later church to his earthly life and death and its continuing impact upon them. Conservative theologians, sharing the same assumption, may insist that the doctrine in its traditional form is to be accepted on faith alone. The philosopher may question the assumption itself and draw attention to the difference made to the interpretation of historical evidence by belief in a Creator God who is able to intervene at this decisive moment in history.[3]

In this case, and in others, philosophers may help by enlarging the possibilities of

---

3   As did Richard Swinburne in *The Concept of Miracle* (1970) and elsewhere.

choice, as indeed Swinburne and Lucas did in their explorations of the meaning of eternity.

Another example is to be found in the controversy associated with *The Myth of God Incarnate* (Hick, 1977). It was often assumed that the choice lay between a fundamentalist insistence on literal fact and a mythological interpretation where 'myth' was taken to be a pictorial expression of a personal attitude. In consequence the possible uses of analogy which had preoccupied the Metaphysicals were simply overlooked.

Mention of analogy suggests another way in which philosophy can assist theology. Philosophers may be able to illuminate religious uses of language by comparison with accepted non-religious uses, as Janet Martin Soskice did in her book *Metaphor and Religious Language* (Soskice, 1985). To the extent that religious language is to be understood by analogy with everyday non-religious uses, the question arises as to how these themselves are to be properly understood. To take the most central analogy of all between God and the human person, the question is not only how the attributes of persons are to be ascribed to God but how human beings themselves are to be thought of. It was doubtless for this reason that Austin Farrer chose for his Gifford Lectures not an ostensibly theological subject but the freedom of the will. This is the most central, but far from being the only, instance in which Christian doctrine interacts with scientific investigation. So not only philosophy of mind and, as we have seen, philosophy of history but also philosophy of science become relevant to the interpretation of doctrine.

In this account of the relation between philosophy and theology, what is distinctive of analytical philosophy is that, in principle at least, its practitioners do not approach theology equipped with their own philosophically based worldview which theologians are challenged to take over or refute as, typically, do Continental philosophers. Theirs is confessedly an ancillary role.

But theologians may not be reassured. There are two worries. The first is that the modesty of philosophical claims may be deceptive. Analysis engenders criticism and criticism suggests revision; can theologians be content to surrender to philosophers the essential task of the development of doctrine? The second is that, at any given time in the hands of any particular thinker, philosophical analysis is likely to be influenced by some substantive metaphysic whose assumptions Christian thinkers may wish to reject in whole or in part. This is obviously the case when the philosopher is a confessed atheist, but may also happen with some whose intention is apologetic.

One solution to these problems would be for theologians to claim for Christian doctrine its own unchallengeable authority which is entirely beyond philosophical criticism. The whole burden of my argument has been that this is not the case.

Nevertheless, although theologians cannot have the sole word where doctrine is concerned, they must have the last word. It is for them in the last resort to estimate the weight of philosophical criticism in relation to all the varied considerations which they are bound to acknowledge in their endeavour to present a modern statement of Christian faith. This suggests that, ideally, the philosopher and the theologian should be the same individual, as is happily sometimes the case. Whether this is so or not, they need to be in respectful dialogue.

CHAPTER 2

The Value and Christian Roots of Analytical Philosophy of Religion

Richard Swinburne

Analytical philosophy of religion is important because it is very important in itself whether our beliefs about our origin, nature and destiny are true ones; and because true beliefs about these matters are needed if we are to have true beliefs about how it is good to live. Analytical philosophy of religion is one tool which can help many people to be good people and to live good lives.

I

There are on offer in today's world many different systems of religious belief, commending different kinds of conduct. We think it good to know who our ancestors are, what they did, how they made us what we are, why we behave as we do, what will happen to us and how we are related to other inhabitants of the world. This theoretical knowledge gives us a right perspective on things. It is even more important, then, to know whether God or unthinking chance made us and, if there is a God, whether he interacts with us and has plans for our future; or whether we go on living new lives, until we eventually attain Nirvana. Which religious or non-religious system is true makes a great difference as to what constitutes a good life. Certainly many actions are good, or bad, independently of which religious system is true. It is good to feed the starving and be kind to the sad; bad to rape and pillage – whether or not there is a God. But if there is a God who is the source of our being, he deserves our worship for his ultimacy and goodness, and our gratitude for making us. If we have used the lives he gives us wrongly, we ought to apologize and to seek his forgiveness. If we are ignorant of how to live, he may have told us, and we need to find out if he has. And if he wants us to be very good people and take us to be with him forever, we need to discover how to become such people. But if there is no God, it is objectively (even if we do not realize this) pointless to pray to him or to seek to be with him in Heaven. And if Islam rather than Christianity contains God's final revelation to humans, then the way to live a good life is by living life as the Qur'an teaches us rather than as the Christian Church teaches. Different consequences for which actions are duties and which actions are supererogatorily good follow from the more theoretical claims of different religions and different non-religious systems. So it is very

important to have a true belief about which religious or non-religious system is
true.

Within the limited time at our disposal, we need to assess the systems on offer and
discover whether one of them is certainly or probably true. For reasons of space, I
shall consider in this chapter only the process of assessing the truth of the Christian
religious system. The same considerations are relevant to assessing the truth of rival
religious and non-religious systems. And clearly, insofar as evidence suggests that
one system is true, it suggests that other systems are false in those respects in which
they disagree.

However, before I come to examine this process of assessing the truth of religious
systems, I need to mention that it may be good to follow a religious way even if on
our present evidence the religious system which provides the theoretical backing for
following that way is probably false. It may be that the thing of supreme value in life
far more valuable than anything else is to go to Heaven. In that case it would be good
to try to get there by the best route available, even if it is not probable that even the
best route will get there. Suppose our investigations show that the Christian religion
is more probably true than any other religion which offers a route to a Heaven
comparable to the Christian Heaven, but that even the Christian religion is probably
false. It will still be sensible to follow the Christian route, if we want Heaven above
everything else. In the stress he put on infinite 'passion', Kierkegaard may be telling
us that the Christian goals of serving God on Earth and seeking to serve him in
Heaven are so worthwhile that we should do those actions which alone will enable
us to serve God, even if probably there is no God.[1]

Up to a point, that may be right. The goals which the Christian (or some other)
religion offer are supremely worthwhile. But other actions which we could be doing
instead of worshipping God are also worthwhile, and so only if there is some
significant probability that there is a God would it be rational to worship. And
humans are not born saints; they need encouragement to become saints, and that will
be provided by a belief that the actions they are doing have some significant
probability of pleasing God and getting them and their fellows to Heaven. So we
need to investigate how probable it is that our religious system is true. For this
purpose we need first to set it out and see if it can be expounded in an intelligible
way without internal contradiction, and then find as much relevant evidence as we
can and consider how probable that evidence makes the system.

So how can analytical philosophy help in this task? 'Analytic philosophy' is the
somewhat misleading name given to the kind of philosophy practised today in most
of the universities of the Anglo-American world. This stream of philosophy started
off in the Oxford of the 1950s; it saw the task of philosophy as analysis, clarifying
the meaning of important words, and showing how they get that meaning; and this

---

1   For example, 'Faith is the objective uncertainty with the repulsion of the absurd, held fast
    in the passion of inwardness, which is the relation of inwardness intensified to its highest'
    (Kierkegaard, 1992, p.611).

was done by studying in what circumstances it was appropriate in ordinary language to use the words. The philosopher investigated when it was right to say that something 'caused' something else, or someone 'knows' something. Metaphysics was deemed a 'meaningless' activity. But the metaphysical urge which has dominated western philosophy quickly returned in the 1970s to Anglo-American philosophy departments, leading most philosophers in those departments to pursue once again the traditional task of seeking a true metaphysical account of the world. The Anglo-American tradition retained from its 'ordinary language' period a high valuation of clarity and coherence, and reacquired from the earlier British empiricist tradition of Locke, Berkeley and Hume awareness of the need to take serious account of the empirical discoveries of modern science (now especially, neuro-physiology, Quantum and Relativity theories). But the goal is now metaphysical: to give a correct account of what are the ultimate constituents of the world and how they interact. 'Analytic' is merely a title for this kind of philosophy inherited from its ancestry.

There were fairly few philosophers of religion in the Anglo-American universities of the 1950s, but those that there were were concerned with the meaning of religious utterances: whether they had any meaning, and, if so, how it differed from that of more ordinary utterances, without being too disreputably metaphysical. But religion, and above all the Christian religion, is centred on a metaphysical worldview; and the 'metaphysical turn' of the 1970s gave philosophy of religion the more obvious task of expounding religious claims, clearly and coherently certainly, but with their natural metaphysical sense, investigating whether they were true, and/or whether we are justified in believing them. Other branches of 'analytic' philosophy have developed useful tools to help in this activity. To start with, philosophy of language, no longer concerned solely with the meanings of particular utterances, has developed general theories of meaning: of when sentences have meaning and what determines what it is; and in particular theories of analogy and metaphor, showing how metaphysical expressions work and what determines what, if any, meaning they have. Since Christianity has always asserted that many of its sentences were to be taken in analogical or metaphorical senses, the utility of philosophy of language in helping to understand those sentences is obvious. Then there is moral philosophy, concerned with what makes actions good or obligatory. Christianity has an enormous amount to say about goodness and obligation – that God is good, and that we ought to obey him. Moral philosophy should be able to help us sort out what determines the truth of such assertions. Christianity is concerned with substances (God or the members of the Trinity, perhaps) and their properties (perhaps equivalent to their natures – divine or human). 'Metaphysics', as a sub-discipline of the now-metaphysical analytic philosophy, examines what a substance is and what properties are, and it examines the nature of identity, time and causation, crucial notions in Christian creeds. Epistemology examines what makes a belief 'justified' or 'rational' or 'warranted'. And it, with philosophy of science, examines what it is for evidence to render some claim probable. Philosophy of religion can use results from all these and other areas of philosophy, and could not do its work without them.

In few, if any, of these areas are there many generally agreed results; but there are in each area a number of competing plausible theories, and the philosopher of religion can assess which, if any, of these theories, is correct and utilize it. But the philosopher must be careful not to take any theory merely on authority, for non-religious philosophers working in some area may have missed possibilities to which those who have thought about religion (whether believers or not) may have become sensitive.

Armed with these tools, analytic philosophy of religion has examined theism (the claim that there is a God) and is now moving on to examine the doctrines of particular religions, especially, but not exclusively, Christianity. Philosophers have examined what it is for there to be a God of the traditional kind, and so what it is for a being to be omnipotent or omniscient; and so how (if at all) the claim that there is a God can be spelled out coherently – and similarly for such claims as that God in Christ provided atonement for the sins of the world. And they have examined whether anyone is 'justified' in believing these claims.

'Justification' and similar terms such as 'warrant' can be spelled out in different ways, and analytic philosophers have investigated whether religious claims are justified or warranted in different senses.[2] But there is a cluster of senses, concerned with probability on evidence, which my earlier arguments show to be all-important. In this cluster we must distinguish synchronic from diachronic justification, and objective from subjective justification.[3] A subject's belief is synchronically subjectively justified at some time if it seems to him that it is made probable (on objectively correct criteria) by his evidence. A subject's evidence consists of the content of his basic beliefs, that is, those beliefs which seem to the subject to be forced upon him by the world. My basic beliefs will include the immediate deliverances of sense and reason: that I am now hearing a loud noise or seeing a table, and that $2 + 2 = 4$. They also include what I seem to remember, what other people tell me, and general beliefs about what the world is like, which I believe that I have learnt from others (though I cannot recall who they were) and which I believe that everyone believes (what I take to be 'common knowledge'). I believe other things because I believe that they are rendered probable by these basic beliefs. I believe that footprints are caused by walkers because I believe that I have seen people walk on sand and thereby make footprints, and because I believe that I have never seen footprints made in any other way. We hold explanatory theories as true because we believe that they are supported by basic beliefs.

But we also believe that there are correct and incorrect ways to assess evidence,

---

2   See the very thorough and influential account of whether Christian belief is 'warranted' in a rather different sense from the sense in which I am understanding 'justified' in Plantinga (2000).
3   For a full account of these concepts, see Swinburne (2001).

and that not everyone sees the force of their evidence. We also believe that not all basic beliefs are rightly basic, ones which we are right to start from (because a priori they are probably true, or because they are probably true if we have them). And so we have a notion of a subject's belief being objectively justified in the sense of being rendered probable (by correct criteria) by his rightly basic beliefs. My view is that, in general, all basic beliefs are rightly basic, except any which are necessarily false (for example, 2 + 2 = 5). Plausibly they are all probably true (with a probability dependent on how strongly we hold them) merely in virtue of our having them. And a rightly basic belief that we have been told so-and-so makes it probable (other things being equal) that so-and-so is true. If we did not think all of this, then no other belief about the world would be probable, because all our beliefs derive any probability they have from these foundations. Beliefs are rendered probable by such beliefs in virtue of correct criteria of what is evidence for what are then synchronically objectively justified. However basic beliefs rightly basic on their own can be rendered improbable by other rightly basic beliefs and so no longer be credible. I have a rightly basic belief that I am seeing a table, but if I acquire other rightly basic beliefs that I put my hand through where the table seemed to be, and others told me that there was no table there, these new beliefs render the old belief no longer credible.

Beliefs are synchronically justified at some time insofar as we are right to hold them at that time. And most beliefs will be subjectively justified, for they will be probable on the subject's basic beliefs and his own criteria. But we need our beliefs on important matters to be as probably true as we can get them, and that means investigating the matters at stake further insofar as we have the time to investigate and insofar as our beliefs are not (by our own criteria) near to certainty to begin with. We seek beliefs (synchronically) objectively justified on as rightly basic beliefs as we can get. And this means checking our own standards (and whether our basic beliefs are rightly basic) and seeking more evidence. Insofar as we have investigated adequately by our own standards, our beliefs if synchronically justified will also be subjectively diachronically justified; and insofar as our standards are true ones, the diachronic justification will be an objective one. And if we really have no time to investigate a matter further (in the sense that our other duties do not allow us time), then any objectively synchronically justified belief will also be diachronically justified. The evangelist seeks to help us to acquire new beliefs, by trying to get us to assess our evidence in what he considers to be the right way and by presenting us with more evidence.

Some people have a basic belief that there is a God: they seem to have had a religious experience of God, or it may be taken for granted in their small community that there is a God; and, like any other belief about apparent experience or common knowledge, such a basic belief will be rightly basic, with a force proportional to its actual strength. Or some obviously wise and good person may tell us of his contact with God. Other things being equal, this other rightly basic belief will make it probable that there is a God. But when it is overwhelmingly strong, a basic belief that one is aware of the presence of God is only one piece of evidence which could yield to strong enough counterevidence suggesting that there is no God. And belief that there is a God deriving from the testimony of some others will, in almost all communities today, soon need to be weighed against the contrary testimony of yet others that there is no God.

Unless, as is unlikely, we find ourselves in a situation where it remains virtually certain that there is a God or that there is no God, in view of the importance of the issue we ought, depending on the time at our disposal, to investigate the matter further, in order to get, if we can, an objectively diachronically justified belief. And in most places in the world today that is going to involve doing natural theology: considering whether the existence of the world, the fact that it is governed by scientific laws, that these laws and the boundary conditions of the universe are such as to lead to the evolution of human organisms, that humans consist of body and soul, and so on, together make it probable that God exists; and considering whether the occurrence of suffering much diminishes that probability. One theoretical possibility is that there is a valid deductive a priori argument (for example, the traditional ontological argument) or that some of the phenomena just cited deductively entail the existence of God. These claims have never seemed to me very plausible, for if there is a deductively valid proof of the existence of God from a knowable necessary truth, then 'There is no God' would contain an inner contradiction. And if there was such a proof from a knowable contingent truth, such as the existence of the universe, then such a proposition as 'There is a universe, but no God' would contain an inner contradiction. These propositions would be like 'There is a round square'. But it is pretty obvious that 'There is no God', and 'There is a universe, but no God', although perhaps false and in some sense irrational to believe, are not incoherent; they do not contain an inner contradiction. There is also the slightly more plausible claim that the occurrence of suffering entails the non-existence of God. But if such claims fail to convince, we are left with probabilities other than 1 (that is, certainly true) and 0 (that is, certainly false). And the task of natural theology is to assess how probable the various evident phenomena make the existence of God. The answer will not, of course, be a precise number: one cannot give a precise number to the probability that James robbed the safe, or that Quantum Theory is true. But there are in my view fairly clear criteria whereby we can assess the probability of an explanatory hypothesis as high, or very high, or moderate, or low.

My account of these criteria, in very brief summary, is that a hypothesis is probable to the extent to which it is simple, and is such as to lead you to expect the evidence, which otherwise there is no reason to expect. I have argued that by these criteria the hypothesis of theism is made moderately probable by the evidence of natural theology.[4] But there is more to Christianity (as to Judaism and Islam) than the mere claim that there is a God. Christianity makes crucial claims about his nature

---

4   Swinburne (1991) and the more recent Swinburne (1996).

and what he has done, which affect the kind of life which it is good to live. There is, therefore, the philosophical task of investigating whether such doctrines (of God as a Trinity, of Jesus Christ as both God and human, and that Jesus provided atonement for the sins of the world) can be expressed coherently. And there is a philosophical task of investigating how great is the probability, given the existence of God, that he has the nature and has done the actions specified: the prior probability of these doctrines. But beyond that, with respect to most of these doctrines, there is also a historical task. Even if the philosopher of religion can settle whether one person can provide atonement for the sins of another, it needs to be shown that the life and death of Jesus of Nazareth were such as to provide that atonement, that life and death would need to have certain features not possessed by most lives and deaths; and only historical investigation can show whether it did. Although this means work for the New Testament scholar rather than the philosopher, the former needs to know the kind of evidence he is looking for, and how much of it he needs for his evidence to make it probable that Jesus atoned for our sins; and in this he needs the help of the philosopher.

The questions of meaning and justification which require solutions if someone is to be justified in following a religious way are very old questions. Modern analytic philosophy, I have been urging, has, however, forged tools and developed arguments with high levels of clarity and rigour which can help us to solve them. But why 'analytical philosophy'? Why not some other kind of modern philosophy? Limits of space allow only a very quick answer, but one that in my view is quite adequate. Clarity and rigour, among the distinguishing features of analytic philosophy, are features of good argument as such. Sensitivity to the developments of modern science is another distinguishing feature of analytic philosophy. We live in an age dominated by science as the paradigm of knowledge. (The overwhelming majority of westerners are moderns, not postmoderns.) No philosophy can hope to convince unless it takes seriously what we have learnt in recent years about neurophysiology or Quantum Theory. Other philosophies of the western world, many of which are often lumped together as 'continental philosophy', have in common an allegiance to Kant's claim that investigation of the nature of the world can discover only patterns in phenomena, not their unobservable causes, and hence 'ultimate questions' are beyond theoretical resolution. Kant lived before the establishment of the atomic theory of chemistry, the first scientific theory to purport to show in precise detail some of the unobservable causes of phenomena – the atoms whose combinations give rise to observable chemical phenomena. No one in the twenty-first century can seriously doubt that, what chemistry purported to show, it really did show, and that we now know a very great deal about the unobservable causes of things and the framework of the universe far beyond observation by the naked eye. The Kantian doctrine about the limits of human knowledge was a big mistake; and analytic philosophy, unlike Continental philosophy, has liberated itself from that doctrine.

Atheists have always recognized the need to face up to the fundamental questions of the meaning and justification of religious claims and to settle them by the best available secular criteria. But theologians of recent years have often suggested that this enterprise is alien to the Christian theological tradition. In the remainder of this chapter I wish to show that the Christian theological tradition is very familiar indeed with the use of the best available secular criteria to clarify and justify religious claims. Analytical philosophy of religion, having somewhat better tools than earlier theologians, can do the job a bit better.

II

That Christian theologians have devoted a great deal of ink to attempting to clarify Christian doctrine and show it coherent is hardly open to question. Jesus Christ was supposed to be in some sense both human and God. But was there not a contradiction here? Theologians of the fourth and fifth centuries tried to show what was involved in this claim and thereby to show its coherence, doing so using the technical terms of Greek philosophy translated into English as 'substance', 'individual', 'nature' and 'person'. And the medievals (with again much help from Greek philosophy) devoted an enormous amount of energy to spelling out the divine predicates ('omnipotent', 'omniscient' and so on) and trying to show how one being could have all of the properties designated thereby.

But did theologians of earlier centuries endeavour to show the probability of the Christian system? Indeed they did. Early in the third century AD the pagan critic Celsus complained that Christian evangelists said to their potential converts, 'Do not examine, but believe' and 'Your faith will save you.' In response, Origen acknowledged:

> If it were possible for all to leave the business of life, and devote themselves to philosophy, no other method ought to be adopted by any one, but this alone ['following reason and a rational guide']. For in the Christian system also it will be found that there is, not to speak at all arrogantly, at least as much of investigation into articles of belief … [as is the case with other systems] … We admit that we teach these men to believe without reasons, who are unable to abandon all other employments, and give themselves to an examination of arguments; and our opponents, although they do not acknowledge it, yet practically do the same. (Origen, 1869, pp.405–7)

And he goes on to claim that if, through hearing some Gospel, you find yourself believing it and have no time to inquire further, it is sensible to go on believing. I too claimed that we ought to believe what we are told in the absence of counter-evidence; and if one has no time to investigate further, one's belief will be objectively diachronically justified. Origen certainly thought that those who did have the time ought to consider arguments. In my terminology, that is necessary if their beliefs are to be diachronically justified. And in *Against Celsus* he provides arguments at considerable length in favour of and against objections to the particular propositions of Christianity. And many of the Fathers did the same, both for theism and for the details of the Christian creeds.

Gregory of Nyssa emphasized that arguments must take off from the things already believed by the audience:

> It is necessary to regard the opinions which the persons have taken up, and to frame your argument in accordance with the error into which each has fallen, by advancing in each discussion certain principles and reasonable propositions, that thus, through what is agreed upon on both sides, the truth may conclusively be brought to light. ... Should he say there is no God, then, from the consideration of the skilful and wise economy of the Universe he will be brought to acknowledge that there is a certain overmastering power manifested through these channels. If, on the other hand, he should have no doubt as to the existence of Deity, but should be inclined to entertain the presumption of a plurality of gods, then we will adopt other arguments. (Gregory of Nyssa, 1893 ch.1)

And if the audience is Jewish, then again different arguments are needed. Surely so. People can only change their beliefs if you give them new evidence or show them (on the basis of things they already accept) that they have assessed the old evidence in the wrong way.

That there were available good arguments from considerations of pure reason or from data recognized by both theist and atheist (of the existence of the universe, and evident general facts about its nature and constitution) for the existence of God, was stated or taken for granted by almost all Christians before Kant. The presentation of such arguments is natural theology. It is sometimes not immediately obvious that some biblical or patristic argument is a piece of natural theology, because it takes the existence of a 'god' of some sort for granted and argues for his goodness or his wisdom. But it is natural theology if it argues that the power in charge of the universe is not just any 'god', but God – omnipotent, omniscient and perfectly good. Given that, there are various short passages of the canonical (non-apocryphal) Old and New Testaments which are pieces of natural theology, as James Barr has argued recently (Barr, 1993).

The only biblical book which contains a sustained development of a natural theology is The *Wisdom of Solomon*. Barr points out that, since it belongs to the Old Testament Apocrypha, this book has canonical and so authoritative status only for Catholics and Orthodox, not for Protestants. Hence Protestants of the last two centuries, and above all Barth, could deny that there was much natural theology in the Bible. However it is there in the Jewish tradition, and so many of the Christian Fathers of the first millennium AD follow *Wisdom* with their brief few paragraphs of natural theology, arguing especially that the regular behaviour of the natural world points to an omnipotent and omniscient God as its creator. To cite but a few examples: Irenaeus, *Against Heresies* (Irenaeus, 1868, II, pp.1–9); Gregory of Nyssa, *On the Soul and the Resurrection* (Gregory of Nyssa, 1893 ch.1); Augustine, *On Free Choice of the Will* (Augustine, 1993, 2. 12.33); Maximus the Confessor,

Difficulties (Maximus the Confessor, 1985, 10.35) and St John of Damascus, *On the Orthodox Faith* (St John of Damascus, 1868, 1.3).

The brief paragraphs of the fathers of the first millennium became the long treatises of the medieval west; and Anselm, Bonaventure, Aquinas and Scotus developed natural theology at great length. The tradition continued with Leibniz and Clarke, Butler and Paley. Even Calvin affirmed that 'knowledge of God shines forth in the fashioning of the Universe and the continuing Government of it' (Calvin, 1960, 1.5); though he also claimed that we are too stupid and impious to recognize this clearly without the aid of Scripture. However, as a result of what I can only regard as rather bad arguments (the joint influence of Hume, Kant and Darwin), natural theology went out of favour for most of the nineteenth and twentieth centuries.

Not that any of the natural theologians thought that people had to believe as a result of considering arguments. The existence of God might be accepted on authority or as a result of religious experience. But, the claim was, the evidence for the existence of God is publicly available, and so atheists and pagans were not (objectively) justified in their disbelief. And natural thelogy could show that they were not justified.

But what about the more specifically Christian doctrines? How much was argument involved here? Patristic theology of the first five centuries was in large part argument in support of some view about the matters on which the Christian creed finally pronounced. Some of this argument tried to show the prior probability of these doctrines, that is, to show the probability that, if there was a God, he would be triune, become incarnate and provide atonement for the human race. To take but one famous example of this kind of argument, I cite Athanasius. He argued that it would have been wrong of God to leave Man whom he had created to perish through sin. But only God the Word 'was both able to recreate the Universe and be worthy to suffer for all and to be an advocate on behalf of all before the Father. For this reason the incorporeal and incorruptible and immaterial Word of God came to our realm' (Athanasius, 1971, pp.7–8).

But, as I wrote earlier, showing the prior probability of God doing something is not sufficient to show that he has done it on a particular occasion; the Fathers needed to show that all this happened through Jesus Christ. Much of their argument to show what God had done in Christ consisted of attempts to derive Christian doctrines from the New Testament texts. It depended therefore on an assumption that the New Testament gave a basically correct acount of the life, teaching, death and Resurrection of Jesus Christ. How far was that assumption to be defended by argument? The New Testament itself set the standard here, for it, and especially the first Christian sermons cited in *Acts of the Apostles*, contains a lot of 'we saw', 'we are witnesses', of the historical events on which the Christian creeds are based, above all the death and Resurrection of Jesus. St Luke tells us that, in writing his Gospel, he was one of many who were putting into writing what they had been told by those who, 'from the beginning were eyewitnesses and servants of the Word', and he was doing so in order that the recipient of his Gospel, Theophilus, 'may know the truth concerning the things about which you have been instructed' (Luke 1: 1–4). And the editor of the final chapter of St. John's Gospel tells us that the source of the Gospel is 'the disciple whom Jesus loved', who 'reclined next to Jesus at the Supper': 'This is the disciple who is testifying to these things and has written them, and we know that his testimony is true' (John 21: 20–24). My point here is not that we should believe what the New Testament says because of such claims within it (though I do in fact believe that), but rather, simply that the earliest Christian writings sought belief in the central Christian events on the grounds that their writers had seen these events or had learnt of them from those who had seen them. They also sought belief in certain things on the grounds that Jesus had taught them. For Jesus had a unique authority. This, the New Testament writers asssume or explicitly claim, is shown by his doing miracles and rising from the dead. He was 'declared to be the Son of God ... by resurrection from the dead' (Romans 1:4).

The earliest writings of the second century appealed to the New Testament, not as authoritative scripture, but as historical evidence. Clement tells us that the apostles' doubts were 'set at rest by the Resurrection of Our Lord Jesus Christ from the dead' (Clement, 1968, p.42). Ignatius (Ignatius, 1968, 3) and Justin (Justin Martyr, 1868, 9) (or the author of *On the Resurrection* attributed to him) both emphasize that the disciples touched the risen Christ; and Justin writes that they were by every kind of proof persuaded that it was He Himself. Irenaeus appeals for the truth of his teaching to its being taught in churches in which there was an apostolic succession of bishops from the apostles. As I read Irenaeus, the main point of this appeal is that it appeals to the best historical evidence: we should 'have recourse to the most ancient churches with which the apostles held constant intercourse' (Irenaeus, 1868, 3.41). He appeals to Polycarp, who was 'instructed by apostles, and conversed with many who had seen Christ' (ibid., 3.3.4).

With the third century different strains of apologetic (never completely absent) become far more prevalent. The very success of the Church (through the blood of the martyrs, and not force of arms), and the miracles of more obvious kinds associated therewith, help to authenticate it and the doctrine it teaches: see Origen's *On First Principles* (Origen, 1869b, 4.1.5). And the same kinds of argument appeared in the Middle Ages. The point was made that the main rival religion in the Mediterranean world after the seventh century, Islam, could cite virtually no miracles. Mohammed claimed to work no miracles, except the writing of the Qur'an and that was hardly a strong case for an event beyond the power of 'the whole realm of created nature' to bring about.

These arguments can be developed to include the argument that the fact that the Church had been given authority by Christ meant that we should believe the details of its teaching, not merely for the historical reason that testimony had been handed down from Christ, but that Christ had endowed it with a spiritual gift. Thus, already, Irenaeus: 'It is incumbent to obey the presbyters who are in the Church – those who, as I have shown, possess the succession from the apostles; those who, together with the succession of the episcopate, have received the certain gift [charisma] of truth, according to the good pleasure of the Father' (Irenaeus, 1868, 4.26.2). This kind of argument, crystallized later in the form that church councils or the Pope were infallible, of course only works if it can be shown that Christ can guarantee the reliability of the later Church because he has divine authority, and so needs to be backed up by arguments of the earlier kinds. Still it can lead to the authentication of particular doctrines when the historical evidence that Jesus taught them is thin.

The systematic listing of a catalogue of kinds of evidence in favour of the truth of Christian doctrine by Duns Scotus at the beginning of his sytematic theology, the *Ordinatio* (Duns Scotus, 1950, pp.100–119), may have been untypical of medieval thinkers, but all the kinds of evidence he mentions were known to and cited in an unsystematic way by other writers, and Scotus himself quotes other writers, normally Augustine, who cite these kinds of evidence. He lists ten separate reasons for the credibility of Holy Scripture, and thus of the doctrines which can be derived from it: (1) *Praenuntiatio prophetica* (the fulfilment of Old Testament prophecy in the New), (2) *Scriptuarum concordia* (Scriptures have a common message, and that includes the common witness of the New Testament writers to the teaching and deeds of Jesus), (3) *Auctoritas Scribentium* (the human authors' conviction that they spoke with God's authority), (4) *Diligentia recipientium* (the careful way in which the Church formed the canon of Scripture), (5) *Rationabilitas contentarum* (the prior probability of its doctrines), (6) *Irrationabilitas errorum* (the inadequacy of objections), (7) *Ecclesiae stabilitas* (the long and constant witness of the Church), (8) *Miraculorum limpiditas* (biblical and later miracles, including the great miracle of the conversion of the western world), (9) *Testimonia non fidelium* (alleged prophecies of pagan writers), (10) *Promissorum efficacia* (the sanctifying power of the Church's teaching in the lives of the faithful).

(1), (2), (3), (4) and (8) are all aspects of historical evidence for the miraculous foundation events of Christianty; (7), (8) and (10) involve the Church's fidelity to the teaching entrusted to it, confirmed by miracles, and its sanctifying efficacy; (5), (6) and (9) involve the prior probability of what was taught.

The post-Origen tradition sometimes simply emphasized the 'it seems evident' if you read Scripture that it is true; perhaps as an obvious truth of reason or a deliverance of religious experience (that God seems to be telling the believer that Scripture is true); and, as I claimed earlier, that is fine if it really does seem that way and there is no other evidence, or time to investigate it. And, in default of the availablity of detailed historical arguments and unwilling to appeal to the Church's history and authority, the Protestant tradition has often expressed the grounds for believing Scripture in this way. 'Scripture is ... self-authenticated' wrote Calvin, 'It is not right to subject it to proof and reasoning.' (Calvin, 1960, 1.7.5)

He did, nevertheless, go on to give a number of other reasons, similar to some of those of Scotus, which he regarded as 'useful aids' (ibid., 1.8.1) to back up the self-authentication.

The emphasis on the 'inward testimony of the spirit' and/or the Church's long unanimous tradition are understandable in ages and places where there were few well-worked out detailed objections to the truth of the Christian scheme. Yet, though understandable, the appeal by Calvin to all humans of sixteenth-century Europe to believe Scripture simply because it seems to you that it is true seems to me an irrational one. You would need a very strong religious experience indeed to make it obvious how to read Scripture, given the many different interpretations of it then prevalent and the many objections to the whole Christian scheme known to many, to make the resulting belief in Christian doctrines objectively justified. Even then there were arguments that could be given for the truth of Christian doctrines, and indeed were given by Calvin himself. I find very little of this appeal to the 'self-evidence' of Scripture before the fifth century. And strangely, in our day, when Christianity is subject to detailed challenge from every direction, we are in a better position than people far closer in time than we to the events of first-century Palestine, to discover what happened then. The ready availability of many documents, detailed historical techniques, communication between historians at the speed of light, make debating the historical case easier than it was even for Irenaeus.

But what this very brief survey of two millennia of Christian apologetic illustrates is that there is very often an appeal to natural theology to show the existence of God; and to detailed historical argument, supported by arguments of prior probability to show the truth of particular Christian doctrines. Without wishing to endorse all the detailed arguments which I have mentioned, let alone all those which have been offered, this rational approach is, I have argued, the right way to pursue these matters. And a modern philosophical tradition which can provide some sharp tools to help in the task is greatly to be welcomed.

CHAPTER 3

Transforming Metaphysics? Revisioning Christianity in the Light of Analytical Philosophy

Elizabeth Burns

This chapter will explore the role of analytical philosophy in the development of revisionist interpretations of the Christian tradition; that is, those which aim to preserve 'essential' elements of the tradition but do not require belief in God as a 'supernatural' being. It will consider the views of R.B. Braithwaite, the empiricist Cambridge philosopher influential for his revisionist readings of religious language. Braithwaite largely accepts and employs analytical philosophy. His work will be contrasted with the contemporary Edinburgh theologian Alastair Kee, and the twentieth-century novelist and philosopher Iris Murdoch, who adopt a more critical attitude towards the analytical method, thereby preserving a measure of ('non-supernatural') transcendence. It will be argued that Braithwaite professes to be a logical positivist but is actually an ineffective linguistic analyst, that Kee claims to be a linguistic analyst but is also ineffective, and that Murdoch, although she claims to reject linguistic analysis, is actually a more effective analyst than either Braithwaite or Kee. The conclusion will therefore maintain that some forms of analytical philosophy are compatible with, and indeed support, transcendent reinterpretations of the Christian tradition.

The Analytical Method

Since it is by no means clear what is meant by 'the analytical method', I will set out my understanding of this before I begin to consider its relationship with revisionist Christianity. Broadly speaking, 'analytical philosophy' could be said to encompass both logical positivism and logical analysis. The terms 'logical empiricism' and 'linguistic analysis' have also been used. John Macquarrie implies that the four descriptions are almost interchangeable labels for the same philosophical movement (1967, p.104), while John Passmore has suggested that, although there is a historical connection between logical positivism and 'analysis', they have different views of the positive role of philosophy and are therefore not identical (1957, pp.389–90). I shall take 'analytical philosophy' to refer to a single movement with two related parts: logical positivism (also called logical empiricism) and logical analysis (encompassing the analysis of both language and philosophical arguments).

Logical Positivism

According to A.J. Ayer, the origins of logical positivism may be found in the eighteenth century, in the final sentence from Hume's *Enquiry Concerning Human Understanding*:

> If we take in our hand any volume; of divinity or school metaphysics, for instance; let us ask, *Does it contain any abstract reasoning concerning quantity or number?* No. *Does it contain any experimental reasoning concerning matters of fact and existence?* No. Commit it then to the flames: for it can contain nothing but sophistry and illusion. (Quoted by Ayer, 1971, p.72)

Early in the twentieth century, a group of philosophers, mostly of mathematics and science, who became known as the Vienna Circle and later came to be called Logical Positivists,[1] developed the verification principle as a way of eliminating references to entities which cannot be observed. The verification principle was first explicitly stated by F. Waismann in 1930, in 'Logische Analyse des Wahrscheinlichkeitsbegriffs' (Passmore, 1957, p.371). The principle was that only two types of proposition are meaningful: analytic statements, particularly those of logic and mathematics, and those which can be verified by sense-experience.

The Vienna Circle thought that they had derived this principle from Wittgenstein's *Tractatus Logico-Philosophicus* (first published in 1921, and English translation 1922), in which he claims that '[a] proposition can be true or false only in virtue of being a picture of reality' (1972, 4.06) – the so-called 'picture theory of meaning'. This, in turn, may have been influenced by Bertrand Russell. According to Russell's doctrine of logical atomism, facts are comprised of logical atoms, the most basic elements of reality and, in a logically perfect language, 'the words in a proposition would correspond one by one with the components of the corresponding fact.'[2] Indeed Macquarrie claims that logical positivism 'owed very much to him [Russell] in its early stages' (1967, p.59). However, while Wittgenstein's *Tractatus* (his PhD thesis, supervised by Russell) was published after Russell's 1918 lectures and makes a number of references to Russell, Russell claimed that his own thoughts had been influenced by Wittgenstein's ideas (Copleston, 1967, p.205). Thus, Passmore suggests, 'Quite what [Wittgenstein] owed to, and quite what he contributed to, Russell's "philosophy of logical atomism" it is difficult to say' (1957, p.354).

---

1 In an article entitled 'Logical Positivism' published in 1931, by A.E. Blumberg and H. Feigl (Passmore, 1957, p.370).
2 *Logic and Knowledge*, quoted by Copleston (1967, p.206). *Logic and Knowledge* is a reprint of Russell's 1918 lectures on logical atomism, originally published in *The Monist* (1918–19).

The Vienna Circle were also influenced by Ernst Mach, who, in 1895, became professor of the philosophy of the inductive sciences at the University of Vienna, the chair later occupied by Moritz Schlick, the 'focal point' of the Vienna Circle. Mach argued that science must eliminate speculation about anything which cannot be experienced, such as absolute space, absolute time or even causality.[3] In England, Karl Pearson argued that science is concerned with every area of human knowledge and that neither metaphysics nor religion can contribute to this; we can attain truth only by the classification and rational analysis of facts.[4] Indeed Passmore suggests that the verification principle 'does little more than formalize the techniques of Mach and Pearson' (1957, p.371).

Unfortunately, early versions of the verification principle ruled out many statements which, although considered meaningful, could not be conclusively verified, including scientific laws (such as 'a body tends to expand when it is heated') and historical statements (Ayer, 1971, pp.50–51). The principle was therefore modified in various ways. For example, in *Language, Truth and Logic*,[5] Ayer argues that meaningful statements include not only analytic statements and those which can be 'practically' verified, but also those which can be verified 'in principle' – that is, those which could be verified by observation if we were in a position to observe (ibid., pp.48–50) – and those which experience renders probable (ibid., p.50). But, according to Ayer, even a modified version of the verification principle renders meaningless statements in the spheres of metaphysics, much of ethics, and theology (he posited the emotive theory of ethics, the view that the purpose of ethical propositions is simply to express emotions). For Ayer, 'there cannot be any transcendent truths of religion. For the sentences which the theist uses to express such "truths" are not literally significant' (ibid., p.155).

Logical Analysis

Even in its modified forms, the verification principle encountered difficulties which largely brought about its downfall. The principle itself apparently could not be verified. And, while 'strong' versions seemed to rule out many of the statements about science whose meaning they were concerned to preserve, 'weak' versions permitted many of the metaphysical statements which the principle was designed to exclude: almost any statement could be verified 'in principle',[6] and there is often much room for disagreement about whether a statement is probably true.

Although the verification principle itself was widely rejected, Ayer's claim that

---

3   *The Science of Mechanics*, 1883, English translation 1893 (Passmore, 1957, pp.322–4).
4   *The Grammar of Science*, 1892 (Passmore, 1957, pp.324–6).
5   First published in 1936 and revised in 1946: 'The classic statement of logical positivism', according to Macquarrie (1967, p.105).
6   For example, Keith Ward has suggested that, if he were God, he would be able to verify his own existence (1982, p.18).

the work of philosophy is not the formulation of speculative truths but clarification and analysis (1971, pp.68–9) continued to be influential. Wittgenstein later maintained that, in using his ideas as support for the verification principle, the Vienna Circle had misunderstood his verbal remarks; he had said that, in order to understand how a sentence is used, we need to ask how we would verify it, but, he objected, this was simply one way of clarifying the use of a word or sentence and not a theory of meaning (D.A.T. Gasking, and A.C. Jackson, cited in Passmore, 1957, p.371). For Wittgenstein, the main thrust of his view, even in the *Tractatus*, was that:

> Philosophy aims at the logical clarification of thoughts … A philosophical work consists essentially of elucidations. Philosophy does not result in 'philosophical propositions', but rather in the clarification of propositions. Without philosophy thoughts are, as it were, cloudy and indistinct: its task is to make them clear and to give them sharp boundaries. (1961, 4.112)

Part of this passage was chosen as the epigraph for *Philosophy and Analysis* (1954), a selection of articles from the journal *Analysis* (first published in 1933); thus the *Tractatus*, Passmore suggests, 'was read as a sort of analyst's handbook' (1957, p.365).

Nevertheless, it is G.E. Moore, a contemporary of Russell at Cambridge, who is usually regarded as the founder of analysis, even though he, himself, said that he was not concerned with the analysis of verbal expressions, and that he did not know clearly what he meant by 'analysis' (N. Malcolm, in Blanshard, 1962, p.311). In his *Principia Ethica* (1903), Moore claimed that a distinction can be made between the questions, 'What things are good?' and 'What does "good" mean?' Focusing on the second of these questions, Moore argued that, although goodness can be recognized, it cannot be defined in terms of any other property. According to Murdoch, this argument represented the point at which a definitive breach with metaphysical ethics occurred. From this time onwards, moral philosophers were no longer concerned with the nature of a transcendent goodness, but analysed the way in which the concept of goodness is used (1999a, pp.59–60). However, while Moore seems to have thought that analysis was concerned with the meaning of concepts, later analysts thought that it required us to describe how to use propositions (for example, Ayer, 1971, ch.2). This was much discussed, to the extent that Passmore remarks, 'analytic methods, it is fair to say, were more freely employed in the analysis of analysis than in the analysis of anything else' (1957, p.365).

Interpretations of Wittgenstein's later work also vary, particularly of the *Philosophical Investigations*, published posthumously in 1953. Colin Brown suggests that, for Wittgenstein, 'philosophy was a highly specialist discipline devoted to the analysis of language and thought' (1978, p.222). By contrast, Passmore argues that, on Wittgenstein's view, philosophy 'explains nothing, analyses nothing – it simply describes' (1957, p.433). There are no 'logically proper names' referring to ultimate constituents of the world which cannot be further analysed, 'from which it follows that the analytic theory of meaning, and with it the view that it is the special task of philosophy to offer ultimate analyses, must be wholly rejected' (ibid., p.437) However, while Wittgenstein's emphasis on the descriptive function of philosophy cannot be denied (see, for example, Wittgenstein, 1953b, paras 109 and 124), it may be that the difference of interpretation simply represents a difference of opinion about the nature of analysis. Although Wittgenstein is not, perhaps, concerned to identify unanalysable concepts in the manner of Moore, it could be argued that description is a form of analysis insofar as it attempts to elucidate the way in which words function within various language-games. Even Passmore appears to apply the word 'analysis' in this sense to Wittgenstein's view: 'an adequate analysis will have to concentrate its attention upon the ways in which we come to understand ... language' (Passmore, 1957, p.436). Indeed Macquarrie suggests that, for Wittgenstein, 'The business of analysis is to discover the various rules which hold in each particular game' (1988, p.302).

Thus it may be argued that, in its logical positivist form, analytical philosophy involved the analysis of statements in order to determine whether they can be classified as analytic, verifiable in some way by sense-experience, or meaningless. Previously it had been assumed that a statement such as 'God exists' is meaningful, and that the philosopher's task is to ascertain whether or not it is true. But now doubt was cast on the very meaning of the statement itself. In the form of logical analysis, analytical philosophy involved the analysis of concepts or statements in order to clarify their meaning, and this was often expressed in terms of descriptions of the way in which they are used.

However 'analytical philosophy' has also come to have a much broader meaning than either of those referred to above. Ayer argued that, although Hume did not put forward a view about the nature of philosophical propositions, 'those of his works which are commonly counted philosophical are ... works of analysis' (Ayer, 1971, p.72) and that, in fact, 'the majority of those who are commonly supposed to have been great philosophers were primarily not metaphysicians but analysts' (ibid., p.70). (Antony Flew makes a similar point in suggesting that all genuine philosophy may be described as 'linguistic': 1989, pp.484–90.)

Finally, in the preface to the second edition of *Language, Truth and Logic*, Ayer admits: 'I realize that for the effective elimination of metaphysics [the verification principle] needs to be supported by detailed analyses of particular metaphysical arguments' (1971, p.21). Thus philosophical analysis concerns itself not only with verifiability, clarity and description, but also with systematic and careful consideration of the effectiveness or otherwise of philosophical arguments.

Theological Responses

Broadly speaking, the responses of theologians who have been prepared to accept some form of the verification principle have been of three kinds. The first is acceptance of the verification principle as compatible with belief in a personal, active God. An example of this position might be John Hick's argument for 'eschatological verification', the view that, at the end of life, faith will be verified if the believer finds that there is life with God after death (1966, pp.177–8).

The second is acceptance of the verification principle, but not as the sole criterion of meaning, leaving 'space' for belief in a personal, active God. Other theologians have suggested that, while Wittgenstein's famous dictum 'What we cannot speak about we must pass over in silence' (1961, para. 7) could be interpreted to mean that statements about religious belief are meaningless, it may simply mean that religious belief is inexpressible. Since, as Wittgenstein later said, verification is only one method for clarifying the use of a word or sentence, even if it may be applied in some areas of human knowledge it does not necessarily rule out statements about religious belief.

Thus some scholars acknowledge that religious beliefs cannot be verified by sense-experience in the way that the verification principle seems to require (Macquarrie, 1967, p.107). Nevertheless, Macquarrie argues, each person 'tries to trace patterns of structures in the world that tend to support his point of view, and this is an empirical procedure, though presumably it is never conclusive'. For example, he suggests, in Genesis 45:4–8, Joseph pointed to the way in which past experiences had turned out well as evidence for God's providence (ibid., p.108). But this would not, strictly speaking, count as verification, since 'almost anything can be pressed into service as "verification" for a belief so wide in scope as ... the belief in divine providence.'

The third alternative is acceptance of some version of the verification principle as entailing that statements about religious belief must be interpreted in a revisionist sense. On this view, the various versions of the verification principle do rule out belief in a personal, active God, but permit reinterpretations of Christianity which do not require this belief. An example of this view can be found in Braithwaite's well-known lecture, 'An Empiricist's View of the Nature of Religious Belief' (reprinted, 1971).

Verification and Revisionist Religious Belief

Following the Logical Positivists, Braithwaite accepts that, before we can ask questions about the truth of a statement, we have to know what it means, but that the meaning of a statement depends upon whether, and how, its truth-value may be tested. However, although there are clear methods for testing the truth of statements about empirical facts, scientific hypotheses, and the logically necessary statements of logic and mathematics, none of these methods can be used for testing the truth of statements about religious belief. According to Braithwaite, statements about God cannot be tested by empirical observation, are not equivalent to scientific hypotheses because they cannot be refuted by experience, and are not logically necessary propositions because they are concerned with existence.

So religious statements are not verifiable in any standard way. But the same applies to moral statements, which are useful for guiding conduct and must therefore be meaningful in some sense. Thus, Braithwaite claims, the verification principle was modified either by glossing the term 'verification' or by changing it into 'the use principle: the meaning of any statement is given by the way in which it is used' (1971, p.77; Braithwaite here refers to Wittgenstein's *Philosophical Investigations*, paras 340, 353, 559, 560). Braithwaite argues that, on this interpretation of the verification principle, religious statements have meaning because they are useful, primarily as moral assertions. And moral assertions are used to express an attitude of the person making the assertion: they tell us what he thinks is right, what he considers to be his duty, or what he thinks is good. This attitude consists partly in a feeling of approval, but primarily in 'his intention to perform the action when the occasion for it arises' (1971, p.78); in other words, Braithwaite accepts a conative rather than an emotive theory of ethics. This means that, for Braithwaite, religious assertions do not simply express feelings, they express commitment to a way of life: 'the meaning of a religious assertion is given by its use in expressing the asserter's intention to follow a particular policy of behaviour' (ibid., p.80).

Nevertheless religious statements differ from moral assertions in at least three respects. First, the policy of behaviour recommended by religious assertions may be implied, not by assertions taken in isolation, but by the system of assertions as a whole. Secondly, religious assertions are often expressed in terms of concrete examples, rather than general principles. And, thirdly, religion is concerned not only with external behaviour, but also with internal behaviour: religion requires not only conversion of the will but conversion of the heart. Thus, while religious statements are not primarily expressions of feeling, they do express an intention to feel in a certain way. This is because 'Resolutions to feel, even if they are only partly fulfilled, are powerful reinforcements of resolutions to act' (ibid., p.83).

Braithwaite suggests that religions can be differentiated, even when they recommend the same policy of life, because 'the intentions to pursue the behaviour policies ... are associated with thinking of different *stories* (or sets of stories)' (ibid., p.84). It is not necessary to believe in the literal truth of the story, but it should be possible to interpret it in terms of empirical propositions; that is, it should have a meaning. Braithwaite argues that many people find it easier to carry through a difficult course of action if it is associated with stories, and suggests that this is recognized in the report of the official Commission on Doctrine in the Church of England (1938), which says that 'Statements affirming particular facts may be found to have value as pictorial expressions of spiritual truths, even though the supposed facts themselves did not actually happen ... It is not therefore of necessity illegitimate to accept and affirm particular clauses of the Creeds while understanding them in this symbolic sense' (ibid., p.87). Braithwaite also cites in support of his position the view of Matthew Arnold that the propositions of Christianity may be regarded as literature which feeds the imagination and thereby influences conduct (while rejecting Arnold's 'dogmatic' rather than 'fictional' interpretation of 'the Eternal not ourselves that makes for righteousness').

This means that a religious person can interpret the stories of their tradition in ways which are the most helpful to them, and which may not be consistent. But, Braithwaite suggests, one story is common to all the moral theistic religions, and is of great value in helping people to carry out their religious behaviour policies, the story that in doing this they are doing the will of God. However it is the decision to follow a way of life which is primary. The story just describes the decision in a new way.

Thus 'a religious belief is an intention to behave in a certain way (a moral belief) together with the entertainment of certain stories associated with the intention in the mind of the believer' (ibid., p.89). This does not mean that a person's religious beliefs are a purely private matter. Braithwaite suggests:

> we are all social animals ... What is profitable to one man in helping him to persevere in the way of life he has decided upon may well be profitable to another man who is trying to follow a similar way of life; and to pass on information that might prove useful would be approved by almost every morality. (Ibid., p.90)

And, although our way of life is a personal decision, this 'does not imply that beliefs as to what are the practical consequences of following such principles are not relevant to the decision'.

Responses to Braithwaite

Kee has raised a number of objections to Braithwaite's view. First, he claims that Braithwaite has allowed logical positivism to rule out religious assertions such as 'Jesus Christ died for my sins', but then allowed Wittgenstein to rule out logical positivism. And if logical positivism has been ruled out, there is no need to look for another way in which religious statements might be meaningful (1985, p.205). However, according to Braithwaite, Wittgenstein has not so much ruled out logical positivism as reinterpreted it. Initial versions of the verification principle failed because they ruled out statements about morality, but the principle was modified so that a meaningful statement came to be defined as one which is useful, thus permitting not only statements about morality but also statements about religious belief. Thus it may be unfair to suggest that Braithwaite's search for an alternative interpretation of religious statements is based on an outmoded positivism. He reinterprets it in the light of criticism, although, admittedly, he does so to such an extent that it becomes almost indistinguishable from some forms of linguistic analysis.[7]

Secondly, Kee objects to Braithwaite's contention that a moral assertion expresses a person's 'intention to perform the action when the occasion for it arises', saying that, instead, a moral assertion expresses the view that an action is right, 'whether or not he himself fails to perform it' (ibid., p.207). However the asserter's failure or otherwise to perform the action in question is not the issue; Braithwaite is concerned with what a person would consider the right course of action in given circumstances, even if they never encounter those circumstances, and even if they do encounter those circumstances and fail to carry out their intention. Kee also objects that, for Braithwaite, the analysis of moral statements in terms of intentions implies that there is no difference between 'It is wrong to kill' and 'It is wrong to buy a black car in a hot climate' (ibid., p.208). But, while Braithwaite does say, 'the reason why I do the action is simply that I intend to do it, if possible' (1971, p.79), as we saw above, he also claims that his view 'does not imply that beliefs as to what are the practical consequences of following such principles are not relevant to the decision'. Thus the problem seems to be not so much a theoretical shortcoming as a literary inconsistency on Braithwaite's part.

Thirdly, Kee objects that, although nineteenth-century liberalism reduced Jesus to a great moral example, 'Jesus is Lord' means more than this; 'the teaching of Jesus is fundamentally eschatological, and cannot always be made the basis of a moral way of life' (1985, p.211). For example, the parables of the Buried Treasure and the Unjust Steward (Matthew 13:44; Luke 16:1–8 and 9–13) use an immoral action to illustrate 'the singleness of mind appropriate to the time of judgement'. Space does not permit a detailed exegesis of the passages in question, but it would, at least, seem reasonable to acknowledge that Christianity is not only an aid to moral behaviour; it also offers a sense of purpose and hope for the future, and these aspects of it are not considered in Braithwaite's lecture. It should be noted that, in subsequent discussion, Braithwaite said: 'I have never for a moment thought that the positive account I gave in the lecture is the whole truth about religious belief' (1966, p.88).

Finally Kee objects to Braithwaite's claim that, although religious stories may help us to carry out our intended behaviour, they need not be believed. Kee argues that this may apply to some religious stories (he cites the account of Jesus at the marriage of Cana, or the Transfiguration) but that 'should we come to doubt whether a man existed about whom such stories could appropriately be told, then this would have a corresponding effect on the content of Christian belief' (1985, p.213). However, in response to a similar – and earlier – criticism from D.M. Mackinnon (1966, pp.79–81), Braithwaite differentiates between four types of religious story.

---

7   Similarly, Paul van Buren has argued that 'the heart of the method of linguistic analysis lies in the use of the verification principle – that the meaning of a word is its use in its context. The meaning of a statement is to be found in, and is identical with, the function of that statement' (1963, p.104). Van Buren does, in fact, describe Braithwaite's view as linguistic analysis (ibid., pp.92–6).

Some of these stories contain at least some historical element, but others contain at least some non-empirical or meta-historical element and it is elements such as these which Braithwaite understands in a pictorial way because, he says, '*ich kan nicht anders*' – 'I can do no other' (1966, p.91).

Perhaps one of the most significant criticisms of Braithwaite's view is that, as E.L. Mascall suggests, he seems to have no place for a God who is, in any sense, transcendent (1957, pp.55–62). 'Doing the will of God' is simply a story which describes the decision to carry out a particular behaviour policy. Braithwaite has, as Paul van Buren recommends, translated 'God-statements' into 'man-statements' (van Buren, 1963, p.103). But if, as Kee argues (1985, p.223), the 'use principle' requires us to examine the way in which statements about religious belief are used, perhaps Braithwaite should acknowledge that statements about God are, in many instances at least, used to refer to a transcendent reality. Braithwaite has reinterpreted the verification principle in such a way that the resulting philosophical method may be more appropriately termed 'linguistic analysis', but, instead of analysing the way in which the word 'God' is used, he has used an earlier version of the verification principle in effect to rule out its use. Thus Kee might, after all, be right to identify dependency upon an outmoded version of the verification principle in Braithwaite, even if that dependency does not take quite the form which he describes. Kee does, however, raise this objection in connection with the views of van Buren (ibid., p.217).

Analysis and Transcendence

Transcendence without God

Like Braithwaite, Kee rejects supernatural interpretations of religious belief, but, unlike Braithwaite, he does attempt to analyse the way in which statements about God have been used. Although, he claims, many people are now unable to believe in God (1985, p.226), he thinks it likely that Christianity 'has been on to something real, though its description is now seen to be inaccurate, crude or misleading' (ibid., p.228). And it is the nature of this 'something real' which Kee attempts to determine. This project is, he thinks, of vital importance, because '*The future of Christianity is not viable unless we can find a way of presenting it which includes the old doctrine of God, but does not demand belief in God as a condition of becoming a Christian*' (Kee's italics). Thus, for Kee, the problem with Braithwaite is not so much that he has largely got rid of the word 'God', but that he has got rid of what it tried to describe.

So what is the 'something real' which Kee identifies? He suggests, 'For Israel, God represented a reality presenting an insurmountable obstacle to man in so far as he pursued his own ends, but equally, a never-failing source of power to pursue quite different ends.' This, Kee thinks, is 'basically what theology is on to, and our task involves the reconceiving and redescribing of this understanding of reality' (ibid., p.240). For us, '"God" is what we mean by taking as our ultimate concern that which came to expression in Jesus Christ' (ibid., p.235). Kee acknowledges the influence of Paul Tillich in making this point (ibid., pp.231–4). This 'God-reality' cannot be described in terms of the supernatural, which implies a split between two realms of reality, or as metaphysical, which is now taken to refer to issues with no empirical content. Kee therefore recommends the terminology of transcendence (ibid., p.242).

Kee does not deny that the Israelites believed that Yahweh was a god, but suggests that they also believed in other things we now find problematic, such as the imminent end of the world. This seems to imply that, since Jesus was also wrong about the imminent end of the world, he was similarly wrong about the nature of God. However Kee argues that, in some sense, Jesus was right about both: 'If we commit ourselves without reserve to the way of transcendence, then indeed our little world, the world which we construct to suit our own (immanent) purposes, does come to an end' (ibid., p.249). With regard to God, we can say that Jesus shows us what 'God' is like: 'Jesus is the very incarnation of the way of transcendence' (ibid., p.251). And Jesus is Saviour to those who see that, in him, the history of the revelation of transcendence came to fulfilment (ibid., p.254).

Kee suggests that people can be divided into those who are committed to transcendence and those who are committed to immanence (ibid., p.256) and that, for those committed to the way of transcendence, nothing significant is lost if they do not also believe in God, as traditionally understood: there is no evidence to suggest that those who believe in God are more sensitive to what they must do, or that their belief strengthens their motivation to pursue the way of transcendence (ibid., pp.257–8). Kee argues that concern for the way of transcendence can be seen in the growth of secular 'caring' organizations, left-wing politics, interest in religions, and the 'spirit' phenomenon (ibid., pp.259–2). Thus, he claims, in many of our world's activities, the line is drawn, not between those who believe in God and those who do not, but between 'two ways of understanding life and living it' (ibid., p.262). Kee argues that Christians are inhibited from participation in the debate by their desire for belief in God to be 'established as a presupposition'. But, he suggests, 'if our ultimate concern is the way of transcendence, as revealed supremely in Jesus Christ, we are surely ready to enter this dispute about reality, for they are playing our tune, discussing our very theme, perhaps even struggling in the darkness that could be enlightened by our gospel' (ibid., p.263).

Thus it is not only Christians who are committed to transcendence, but Christianity is distinctive because Christians claim that Jesus Christ is the embodiment and final revelation of the way of transcendence. The choice of the way of transcendence is based on a value judgment – it is not in accordance with our natural inclinations. However, 'In choosing the way of transcendence we make an act of faith. We test out our suspicion that the "real" nature of man is ... embodied in Jesus Christ, and not a Nazi Fuhrer' (ibid., p. 269). Faith does not require us to accept that God exists; rather, it requires the risk of commitment to a decision, and is confirmed if that decision is confirmed by subsequent experience (ibid., pp.269–71).

We have seen that, unlike Braithwaite, who fails to analyse the way in which the word 'God' is used, instead employing an earlier version of the verification principle in effect to rule out its use, Kee does attempt to analyse and preserve the function of the word, if not the word itself. However, although he claims that his position is 'not a positivist one' (ibid., p.264), it could be argued that Kee himself makes tacit use of a version of logical positivism to rule out traditional belief. He criticizes van Buren for using positivist assumptions arbitrarily to cut off certain dimensions of theology (ibid., p.218), but later agrees that 'Van Buren is right to point out that the old supernaturalism is incompatible with our secular culture, and that we cannot continue with this view of God' (ibid., p.224). He also appeals, ultimately, to faith, and says that this is confirmed by experience.

Even if Kee does appeal to a version of positivism to rule out that which he cannot believe, it could be argued that his analysis of the function of belief enables him to preserve more of it than Braithwaite; specifically, the function, if not the 'person', of a transcendent God. And this function, it might be argued, is of vital importance. However the nature of this function and the reason for its importance are unclear. He argues that what used to be described as 'God' is expressed in Jesus Christ, and that this is the Christian's ultimate concern. But, I would suggest, it is Murdoch, in her concept of the Good, who gives this function a 'focus' and provides us with a more effective analysis of its significance.

A Transcendent God: the Concept Revised

We have seen that Kee claims to reject logical positivism but seems to adopt a form of logical analysis. Murdoch appears to reject both forms of philosophical analysis. This is because she thinks that, in the field of moral philosophy, the task of analysis has been too narrowly conceived (1999a, p.73). It has been too concerned to analyse the word 'good' in terms of what the individual should choose and can attain by an act of the will, to the detriment of other interpretations, such as that supplied by 'the vanishing images of Christian theology which represented goodness as almost impossibly difficult, and sin as almost insuperable and certainly as a universal condition' (1970b, pp.50–51). In opposition to analytic moral philosophers, she argues, 'The problem is to accommodate inside moral philosophy, and suggest methods of dealing with the fact that so much of human conduct is moved by mechanical energy of an egocentric kind' (ibid., p.52).

Murdoch suggests that the methods of religion are familiar to us. Prayer, she claims, 'is properly not petition, but simply attention to God which is a form of love. With it goes the idea of grace, of a supernatural assistance to human endeavour which overcomes empirical limitations of personality'. And God 'was (or is) a *single perfect transcendent non-representable and necessarily real object of attention*' (ibid., p.55, Murdoch's italics). But, even in a world without God, as traditionally understood, something analogous to prayer, grace and God can be retained. Murdoch recommends attention to the Good, a transcendent reality which, when contemplated, helps us to see the world as it really is. Attention to the Good 'is not just the planning of particular good actions but an attempt to look right away from self towards a distant transcendent perfection ... This attempt ... may be the thing that helps most when difficulties seem insoluble ... This is the true mysticism which is morality, a kind of undogmatic prayer' (ibid., p.101).[8] Thus, while Braithwaite simply 'resolves' to feel loving towards his neighbour, Murdoch suggests a process by means of which a change of heart might be achieved. For Murdoch, the pursuit of unselfish goodness also entails acceptance of 'real death and real chance and real transience ... only against the background of this acceptance, which is psychologically so difficult, can we understand the full extent of what virtue is like' (ibid., p.103).

Thus Murdoch, unlike the analytical philosophers whose views she rejects, preserves a God-like concept which is transcendent in a non-metaphysical sense: the Good lies beyond our own selfish concerns, and even beyond the world in which we live; it is an ideal which is never exemplified (ibid., p.93). But the Good is not amenable to philosophical proof; she suggests that a kind of faith is required: 'All one can do is appeal to certain areas of experience, pointing out certain features, and using suitable metaphors and inventing suitable concepts where necessary to make these features visible.' However, Murdoch admits, 'No more, and no less, than this is done by the most empirically minded of linguistic philosophers' (ibid., pp.74–5). More specifically, she refers to 'arguments from experience concerned with the realism which we perceive to be connected with goodness, and with the love and detachment which is exhibited in great art' (ibid., p.75). We cannot recognize or explain goodness, or great art, Murdoch thinks, without the notion of a transcendent standard of goodness to which they point. Thus the good functions 'transcendentally, as the fundamental and necessary condition for human knowing' (Antonaccio, 2000, p.56).[9]

Although Murdoch seems to reject analysis, she claims that her criticisms of its often inadequate account of the 'background' to moral choice and its liberal bias against transcendent realities (1999a, pp.68–71, 1999b, pp.93, 95–7) also come from the empirical tradition (1999a, p.59). And we saw above that, like that of Kee, her own view ultimately relies on the support of experience. Further she does think that words must be taken seriously, suggesting that 'the concept of truth, for instance, contains tangles and paradoxes the unravelling of which would show us really interesting features of the modern world' (ibid., p.73).

But, for Murdoch, analysis, even when practised with integrity, has limitations.

---

8   See Burns (1997), for a discussion of what Murdoch means by attention to the Good.

9   Cf. the suggestion of R.M. Burns that the God of natural theology is 'a hypothetical transcendental deduction of the conditions of the possibility of an intelligible universe', and that while we cannot be sure that it is true, experience suggests that 'either this or something like it (*Phaedo*, 114d) must be true' (Burns, 1989, p.293).

She suggests that 'It is very well to say that one should always attempt a full understanding and precise description, but to say that one can always be confident that one has understood seems plainly unrealistic. There are even moments when understanding *ought* to be withheld' (Murdoch, 1999b, p.90).[10] 'There are,' she says, 'moments when situations are unclear and what is needed is not a renewed attempt to specify the facts, but a fresh vision which may be derived from a "story" or from some sustaining concept which is able to deal with what is obstinately obscure, and represents a "mode of understanding" of an alternative type' (ibid., p.91). Analysis may sometimes help us move towards clearer descriptions of the way in which we use some of our most significant words and propositions, but sometimes we are 'struggling in darkness'[11] we can only hope to illuminate by means of parables and stories which may be ambiguous, paradoxical and open to continual reinterpretation (ibid., pp.90–91). In the midst of their complexity, we may find new ways of looking at our world which shed new light on difficult problems. For Murdoch, stories are not, in the manner of Braithwaite, just loosely associated with our moral choices; they are a fundamental means by which we explore the nature of reality, while accepting that our understanding may yet be far from adequate.

Conclusion

In this chapter we have seen that, broadly speaking, philosophical analysis has taken two forms, logical positivism and logical analysis. In its positivist forms, philosophical analysis seems, at least, to have shown that religious truth-claims (for example, 'There is a God') are different in kind from the truth-claims typical of the natural sciences (for example, 'A body tends to expand when it is heated') and that they must be supported to some extent by experience of some kind. The views of all three scholars we have considered are compatible with, and perhaps supported by, positivism to this limited degree.

However, if logical analysis requires us to describe statements about religious belief in terms of their function, I would suggest that Murdoch's view is the most successful of the revisionary accounts we have considered. Her reservations about analysis are partly concerned with the way in which it has, in fact, been practised, and partly concerned with its focus on description of the ways in which language is used, rather than exploration of the ways in which it could be used more effectively. But, even if the analytic tool has sometimes been misused in the past, this need not prevent its more appropriate use in the future. And it may be possible for analysis to encompass both descriptive and explorative tasks. It is, I think, important to distinguish between analysis of how language is, in fact, used, and analysis of the ways in which it is reasonable for us to use it. If description does not, as Wittgenstein

---

10   A similar point is made by H.D. Lewis (1963, p.40).
11   Note that Kee also uses this phrase (1985, p.263).

and some of his followers have suggested, require us to 'leave everything as it is' (1953, para. 124; cf.1965, p.1), but can include description of what words and propositions *could* reasonably be taken to mean (perhaps inspired by stories, based on experience and, employing 'analysis' in its broader sense, supported by careful consideration of philosophical arguments), then analysis may, indeed, be a useful tool for developing our understanding of religious belief. Since this broader interpretation of analysis permits exploration, as well as description of the status quo, it is, in this sense, revisionary. But this is not necessarily to imply change in the nature of the reality we struggle to describe; it may be that it is our *understanding* of this reality which has developed through many centuries, and continues to grow.

Thus, *contra* Kee, and, to a lesser extent, Murdoch, I would suggest that it is important for revisionists to retain the word 'God', provided that their interpretation of it can be seen as related to ways in which the word has previously been understood, which itself may be disputed (see Byrne, 1998, pp.105–18), and as part of a developing history of attempts to comprehend that which is described by this difficult but significant word. On this view, 'God' is the transcendent guarantee of disinterested goodness, a standard without which we cannot adequately explain why we should be concerned for others when this is not in our individual or collective self-interest. And this standard is manifested, although perhaps not exclusively so, in Jesus of Nazareth and in the stories told by and about him. In meeting as communities to recite, hear, contemplate and discuss the Christian stories, we explore and subject to critical analysis the language which has been handed down to us, work out as best we can what it implies for Christian life today, and submit ourselves to a process of transformation so that we may be better equipped to undertake the task.

CHAPTER 4

The Wittgensteinian Revolution

Cyril Barrett

Wittgenstein is generally regarded as a logician, and he undoubtedly made a considerable contribution to philosophical logic; but that was not where his heart lay. It lay in what he called 'the problem of life' and all that was connected with it: aesthetics, ethics and religious belief or, in a word, value. He speaks mysteriously about it when he says: 'The solution of the problem of life is seen in the vanishing of the problem.' And he points out that anyone to whom the sense of life became clear was 'unable to say what constituted that sense' (Wittgenstein, 1961, 6.521).

In his early work, *Tractatus Logico-Philosophicus*, published in 1921, the only book to be published in his lifetime, Wittgenstein laid a foundation for his later investigation of religious belief. At the time when the book appeared very few people, if any, understood it. Bertrand Russell, who wrote the preface, and described the book as 'one which no serious philosopher can afford to neglect', admitted that he did not accept the conclusion, 'the part upon which he [Wittgenstein] himself would wish to lay most stress' (in Wittgenstein, 1961, xxii). Frege, his other mentor, claimed that he did not understand even the logical concepts *Tatsache*, *Sachverhalt* and *Sachlage* (fact, state of affairs and situation). Wittgenstein was so depressed that he spent the next ten years as a gardener in a monastery, a teacher and in building a house for his sister. It would seem that only his friend Paul Engelmann, an architect, understood him. They corresponded from December 1916 until 1937.

No one paid much attention to the book until the middle 1920s. By then it was gradually being 'realized', that is, accepted fairly universally, that *Tractatus* was perhaps the most extreme expression of Logical Positivism yet written. Certainly this is how the more extreme Logical Positivist movement, the so-called 'Vienna Circle' (Schlick, Carnap, Waismann Feigel and others) viewed it. And it is not hard to see why they did so. The book begins with the statement, 'The world is the totality of facts' (Wittgenstein, 1961, 1.1) and ends with the statement, 'What we cannot speak about we must pass over in silence' (ibid., 7). In other words, not only is there nothing to know but empirical facts, but we cannot even *talk* about anything but empirical facts. To try to talk otherwise is to talk nonsense. Thus it is a fact that people admire or adversely criticize works of art, that they approve of or disapprove of certain ways of behaving and that they believe or do not believe certain articles of faith – these are empirical facts. But that these works of art or these ways of behaving are good or bad, or that the religious beliefs are true or false, these are not empirical facts: they are subjective beliefs or judgments that cannot be empirically justified, much less verified. Therefore we cannot make true or false statements about them and so the only reasonable and logical thing to do is to pass over them in silence and not pretend that we are making statements of fact.

The basic empiricist and, particularly the Logical Positivist, position could not be put more succinctly or more eloquently. In Engelmann's words: the difference between the Positivists and Wittgenstein is that 'they have nothing to be silent about' and he had a great deal. Engelmann continues: 'Positivism holds – and this is its essence – that what we can speak about is all that matters in life. *Whereas Wittgenstein passionately believes that all that really matters in human life is precisely what, in his view, we must be silent about*' (Engelmann, 1967, p.97, original emphasis). Wittgenstein himself makes this clear in a letter he wrote to the publisher, Ludwig von Ficker, in 1919:

> I once meant to include in the preface a sentence which is not in fact there now but which ... will perhaps be a key to the work for you. What I meant to write, then, was this: My work consists of two parts: The one presented here plus all that I have *not* written ... In short, I believe that where *many* others today are just *gassing* (*schwefeln*), I have managed in my book to put everything firmly into place by being silent about it. (Quoted in German and English in von Wright, 1982, pp.82–3)

This explains why section 7 has only the one sentence exhorting silence. The rest of the section is 'visual silence', symbolizing what cannot be spoken about.

Not suspecting that this was the true meaning of *Tractatus*, the Vienna Circle were keen to meet Wittgenstein. But Wittgenstein, knowing that they were poles apart, was not keen to meet them; not, I should imagine, because he feared a confrontation, but rather because they had very little in common. Eventually a meeting with Schlick was arranged at Wittgenstein's sister's house in 1926. It was not a great success. Each thought the other mad, but eventually they and other members of the Circle met in Schlick's house to discuss matters logical. Friedrich Waismann published an account of these meetings in *Ludwig Wittgenstein and the Vienna Circle* (Waismann, 1979). Ironically this encounter with a philosophical position diametrically opposed to his own reawakened in Wittgenstein an interest in returning to philosophy. Meanwhile he had found a mate in, of all people, Heidegger. In a discussion in Schlick's house he said, 'I can imagine what Heidegger means by Being and Anxiety. Man feels the urge to run up against the limits of language' (ibid., p.68).

Wittgenstein returned to this notion of running up against the boundaries of language in a lecture on ethics which he gave to 'The Heretics' three years later, in 1929, when he had returned to Cambridge. He concludes the lecture with the words: 'My whole tendency and I believe the tendency of all men who have ever tried to write or talk Ethics or Religion was to run against the boundaries of language' (first published as Wittgenstein, 1965, p.12). Why, you may ask, should talking about religion – and even more so, about ethical and aesthetical matters – be attempting to go beyond the boundaries of language? The simple answer is that they are not statements about empirical facts. Beauty is not a quality of an exquisite Chinese vase similar to the shade of blue of the vase, though it may be that shade of blue that makes it so beautiful. 'Beautiful' is a judgment word. Similarly, 'morally bad' is not a quality of an action but a judgment on it. You may stab a man and kill him to prevent him committing a serious crime, and that may be described as 'good'. You may also perform the same action on an innocent person in order to take his money and that may be described as 'bad'. But these 'descriptions' do not add anything to our knowledge of the action. We know what stabbing is. So what does 'good' or 'bad' add as a description of it? Nothing. It is a judgment on the moral nature of the action. As such it reaches beyond the limits of descriptive prose. Likewise, to say of a religious belief that one accepts that it is true may be a fact, but the belief is not an empirical proposition. It is just, and no more than, a statement that you believe it to be true. You cannot prove that it is empirically true for the simple reason that it transcends any empirical criteria of truth and falsity. Whereas it may not be immediately obvious that, in talking about ugly or superbly beautiful buildings, or good works and hideous crimes, as going beyond the boundaries of language, hardly anyone can question the contention that the boundaries of language are strained when religious people say of their dead relatives that they are alive, living in heaven, and that they will see them again.

Wittgenstein's lasting message is first, the inexpressibility of religious belief, ethical principles and aesthetic judgments in empirical terms and hence, second, the absurdity of attempting to give an empirical account of them. And one might add that Wittgenstein did not make the egregious mistake of saying that they are meaningless because they cannot be empirically verified.

In one sense there was nothing new in all this as far as religious belief is concerned, though it was certainly a new and dramatic way of expressing an ancient idea. The idea dates back to the sixth century, when the notion of the *via negationis* or *negativa* was introduced by the pseudo-Dionysius. It received its classical expression in Nicholas of Cusa's *Docta Ignorantia* (Learned Ignorance). It is the view that all we can know about God is negative; for instance, that God is immaterial and, therefore, incorruptible; extratemporal and so on. What this means is that a seemingly positive attribute, 'almighty', is also negative since we do not know all that an almighty being can do: all we know is that there is nothing he cannot do short of doing something that is self-contradictory, such as squaring a circle.

What is new and revolutionary in what Wittgenstein writes is his insistence on silence or, rather, the voice of silence. For, as Wittgenstein saw things, or rather heard them, the silence of ethics, aesthetics and religious belief was eloquent but not in ordinary speech. But that is not how most people treat words about God, including the word 'god' itself. To put it another way, they use ordinary words in an extraordinary way when they apply them to God and to the supernatural, but they treat them as though they were using them in the ordinary way. One of Wittgenstein's major contributions to the philosophy of religion was to try to curb this practice in a dramatic manner by telling people that, when they speak about matters religious, they are dashing themselves against the boundaries of language in thinking that they can say what remains unsayable. In a way Wittgenstein is doing no more than the Hebrew prophets were doing when they refused to give God a name.

Putting matters like this, Wittgenstein is articulating something not very different from what Hume and Kant had said before him, except that he draws the opposite conclusion from that which Hume drew and takes some of the mystery out of Kant (while adding some of his own).

Hume did not do anything as radical as the Ockhamites, Nicholas of Autrecourt and John of Miracourt,[1] when he pointed out that moralists, aestheticians, metaphysicians and theological philosophers cannot give meaning to the signs they use since they do not refer to anything known by experience, and therefore they talk nonsense. Kant accepts Hume's analysis but attempts to redeem metaphysical statements and expressions of value, somewhat, by his notion of the 'transcendental', which is the product of pure reason. The 'transcendental' is that which transcends the empirical as a necessary condition for our understanding it, and which makes intelligible the constructions we put on our perceptions and other experiences. Wittgenstein does not take this Kantian road. He returns to Hume and turns him on his head. He agrees that expressions of value and metaphysics are not empirically meaningful and, given the language we speak, they are nonsensical (*Unsinn*). But 'their nonsensicality was their very essence'. They are an attempt to say the unsayable in order to make sense of the sayable. A good act is not good *for* anything; a good performance of a piece of music is not good *for* anything, not even for giving pleasure, since it is because it is good in the first place that it gives pleasure. Cynics may say that prayer, worship, faith (with or without good works) are good *for* getting a good place in heaven. Anyone who thinks that may be in *for* a rude awakening.

In some ways Wittgenstein was his worst enemy where intelligibility is concerned, unless he was hell-bent on being misunderstood. In the preface of *Tractatus* he says, 'what we cannot talk about (*reden*) we must pass over in silence' (Wittgenstein, 1961, 2–3). In the famous last entry, section 7, he says, 'What we cannot speak about (*sprechen*) we must pass over in silence.' Neither the word *reden*, which really means to chat or gossip about something, nor *sprechen*, which means to speak about or talk about, have the technical significance of *sagen* which means 'to say, state, affirm as true in an empirical sense, utter a proposition and so on'. We spend our lives talking and speaking about matters ethical, aesthetical and religious. One thing is certain: no-one, least of all Wittgenstein, has passed over these matters in silence. And yet they are not 'saying' anything in his technical use of 'say'.

Perhaps it would be clearer, as I have already suggested, if we used the word

---

1   John of Miracourt and Nicholas of Autrecourt were logical sceptics who rejected notions such as causality, not because we cannot experience causality, but because the notion of cause cannot be derived from an event, so it does not follow that every event ('effect') must have a cause.

'describe' instead of 'say'. We can describe a sunset but we cannot describe the beauty of a sunset. We can describe the sexual act of a rape but we cannot describe the evil of rape. We can describe the lives of holy people, but we cannot describe their holiness as such. This is a matter of judgment about the facts described but is not in itself a fact or a description of a fact. Nevertheless we can describe a sunset as beautiful or a sexual act as evil or a certain person as holy. A person spoken to in these terms might not agree with these descriptions, but would accept the description of the facts: that it was a sunset, that sexual intercourse had taken place or that the 'holy' person had lived the life narrated. I was once in a boat on the Grand Canal in the midlands of Ireland and a spectacular sunset began to fill the western sky. After the flood of ecstatic exclamations from all the passengers had died down, the boatman was heard to mutter, 'What's all this fuss about? All I can see is a bleedin' sunset', which, of course, was empirically and philosophically true.

From 1929 onwards, Wittgenstein revised some fairly fundamental ideas in *Tractatus*, but not as radically as most commentators would have us believe. Three new ideas are (a) language games, which means that words are understood by the way they are used in a particular context and the rules that govern their use, (b) philosophical grammar or the form of life in which the word is relevant, and (c) the essentially public (social) nature of language, or the impossibility of a private language. As far as religious belief, ethics and aesthetics are concerned these ideas are no different from what Wittgenstein had said in the *Notebooks 1914–1916*, *Tractatus* or '*Lecture on Ethics*'.

As regards religious belief, this is made apparent in the three 'Lectures on Religious Belief' that Wittgenstein delivered *circa* 1939. The way I read these lectures is as a further development of the brief and cryptic remarks in the earlier writings just cited. What Wittgenstein is saying is that expressions of religious belief are still nonsensical in the sense of nonsense (*Unsinn*) as used in *Tractatus*. He illustrates this with three words commonly used in religious discourse: 'God', 'believe' and 'life after death'.

On 'God', Wittgenstein is rather amusing. The word as he says is one of the first learnt (he was brought up a Roman Catholic) but, though he did not know what it meant, he learned how to use it correctly when asked questions. To him the remarkable features of the word were that (a) pictures of God were not like pictures of aunts: they did not tell him what God looked like; (b) God was supposed to see, reward and so on, but he had no eyes, was nowhere around and was not supposed to be at all like his picture; and (c) though there was normally nothing wrong in not believing in something, it was considered bad not to believe in God. 'Believe', too, is not used in the same way when talking about religious belief as in talking about other beliefs. It is not an opinion about what might be the case about which one is not certain. Religious belief or faith is unshakeable acceptance of teachings for which there is flimsy evidence.

'Life after death' is surely an oxymoron. To use the word 'alive' of someone who in any ordinary sense is dead, is, to say the least, odd. And yet there are religious people who believe that those who have without doubt died in the ordinary sense are alive. By 'alive' one normally means that they are not dead. Clearly this is not the case. So what does saying they are 'alive' mean? We simply do not know. We use such phrases as 'they have not ceased to exist' and 'they are disembodied spirits', but what this means in reality we do not have the foggiest idea. In one sense it is nonsense, just as it is to talk about a 'cheeky little wine' or say that 'lichees taste as roses smell'. But in another sense this nonsensical talk is quite intelligible. Aquinas speaks of it as analogical discourse. That is, something between simile and metaphor, on the one hand, and empirical discourse, on the other. To say 'my Redeemer liveth' is not a metaphor, as you might say that Bach lives on in his music. No, it is literal. It means 'lives', but how a dead man lives is beyond our capacity to say. This is where belief comes in. We believe that our Redeemer liveth even though we do not know what that means in real terms.

Wittgenstein draws a conclusion from this that may not be immediately obvious, namely that religious controversy is impossible and that a believer cannot contradict an unbeliever and vice versa. But, you will say, they seem to do that all the time. Protestants contradict Catholics about the Eucharist; Jews and Muslims contradict Christians about the Trinity; and so on. They may give the impression of contradicting each other, and they may treat what they are talking about as facts (the Real Presence, the Three Persons in one God, and so on) but they are not facts, they are beliefs. All that believers and unbelievers can say is that they do not believe what the other believes. They may say that it is false, but that still only means that they do not believe it. It is not like saying that sulphuric acid is bad for you.

The crunch of the matter is that there cannot be any empirical evidence for a religious belief, since religious belief transcends what can be shown empirically (Wittgenstein, 1966, pp.57–9). Yet there are religious people who will insist that the existence of God can be known from the nature of the universe, organic life and human intelligence. The British Jesuit mathematician, Fr O'Hara, declared that the events described in scripture would stand up to the severest scientific criticism (O'Hara, 1931, p.112).[2] Richard Swinburne believes he can establish that the existence of God is more probable than God's non-existence, thus exposing his head to the lions of scientific atheism (Swinburne, 1979). Wittgenstein would have none of this. He says, 'We don't talk about hypotheses, or about high probability. Nor about knowing. In a religious discourse we use such expressions as: "I believe that so and so will happen," and use them differently to the way we use them in science' (Wittgenstein, 1966, p.57).

But, you may object, if religious belief is not based on evidence, then it is irrational. There is what we call evidence of a kind but it would be better to say that

---

2 A note from the editors: the Rev. Fr C.W. O'Hara, S.J. contributed to a symposium on religion and science broadcast in 1930 and published in *Science and Religion: A Symposium*, London, 1931. The page numbers to O'Hara's contribution are pp.107–16, but we have not been able to find further bibliographical information.

believers have reasons for believing, though these reasons are not conclusive or compelling. Christians are not irrational for believing in the Trinity. They base their belief on the teaching of the New Testament and of the Councils and the doctors of the Church. Jews are not irrational for not accepting Jesus as the Christ, the Messiah. Nor, to be fair all round, are agnostics and non-believers irrational for not believing in any religious faith. But that does not make them more rational than believers. Belief in reason alone or rationalism is just as much a belief and article of faith as religious belief.

The type of religious reasoning that Wittgenstein favours is very similar to that of John Henry Cardinal Newman in *The Grammar of Assent*. Wittgenstein refers to Newman's 'curious remark' in the first entry in his book, *On Certainty*: 'any proposition can be derived from other propositions. But they may be no more certain than it is itself. (On this a curious remark by H. Newman.)' (Wittgenstein, 1969, 2e.1). In the *Lectures* he says, 'As it were, the belief as formulated on the evidence can only be the last result – in which a number of ways of thinking and acting crystallize and come together' (Wittgenstein, 1966, p.56). As a description of Newman's account of either how we come to accept a faith or how those born into one persevere in it, I cannot think of a more succinct and accurate description of that great book. This is precisely what happens. Whether one is converted to a faith or overcomes one's doubts about one's beliefs, or indeed returns to one's faith having abandoned it, the process is the same. Bits fall into place. There is no great irrefutable argument.

The final contribution to the philosophy of religion that I wish to mention is Wittgenstein's notion of a picture to live by. He first mentions this in the context of firm and unshakeable belief. He says:

> Suppose somebody made this his guidance for life: believing in the Last Judgment. Whenever he does anything, this is before his mind. In a way, how are we to know whether to say he believes this will happen or not?
>
> Asking him is not enough. He will probably say he has proof. But he has what you might call unshakeable belief. It will show, not by reasoning or by ordinary grounds for belief, but rather by regulating for all in his life. (Ibid., pp.53, 54)

This notion of living by a picture or pictures is essential to Wittgenstein's idea of how what cannot be said can be shown. By pictures to live by he means examples or exemplars, parables, models or anything that can *show* what is of value, or how a thing should be done, or how to behave. In matters of religious belief, a prediction such as the Last Judgment or the story of Job or the parable of the Good Samaritan might be pictures to live by.

So what are we to make of Wittgenstein as a philosopher of religion? My Dominican friend, the recently deceased, Fr Herbert MacCabe, once said in a discussion following a public lecture on the Catholic contribution to the philosophy of religion in the twentieth century: 'Philosophy of religion ended with Descartes and did not begin again until Wittgenstein.' Strong words, but not a jot too strong.

In the seventeenth century, the century of Galileo and Newton, and the beginning of the modern scientific era, Descartes introduced into philosophy of religion the notion of proof and certainty on the model of mathematics, and persuaded others to follow suit. Hence the rationalist approach to religious belief and the search for rational certitude. However, by the eighteenth century, with the advancement of science, this approach was challenged by the British Empiricists and, culminating in Hume, this led to religious scepticism. The nineteenth century saw great advancement in science, in, particularly, the Darwinian revolution, which further undermined religious belief and led to the positivism, of, say, Comte and the beginnings of 'scientific atheism'. So far the most that had been claimed against religious belief was that (a) it cannot be established empirically and (b) it is not necessary for understanding the origin of life or of the universe.

However, with the coming of Logical Positivism and Analytical Philosophy, a new blow was struck against the possibility of proof for religious beliefs. This was only the logical conclusion of Hume's and Kant's arguments that, if concepts cannot be given any empirical meaning, then they are empty; that is, in talking about God we do know what we are talking about. Even though Kant postulated the 'transcendental idea' of God in order to make the world and the responsible self, the basis of morality, intelligible, this transcendental idea could have no basis in experience. This meant that there could be no rational proof for the existence of God, since the term 'god' did not refer to anything that could be experienced. Instead God had to be postulated, which is different from arriving at God's existence as the conclusion of a rational argument. That was bad enough, but, when the Logical Positivists enunciated their theory of verification, matters got decidedly worse. Not only was the concept of God outside experience but it was meaningless because it could not be verified empirically, even in principle (cf. Ayer, 1936). So, if not atheism, at least agnosticism, stood supreme.

But not quite.

This is where Wittgenstein comes in. He does not accept this conclusion. Far from it. He turns it on its head and says, 'I see that these nonsensical expressions were not nonsensical because I had not found the correct expressions, but their nonsensicality was their very essence ... [that] the tendency of all men who have ever tried to write or talk about Ethics or Religion was to run up against the boundaries of language' (Wittgenstein, 1965, p.12).

You may say that Kant coped with the Empiricists by developing his transcendental reasoning. In a sense he did, but to little purpose. Transcendentality in itself is not enough, if it is anything. We have to go all the way and admit that we are trying to say what cannot be said in ordinary language nor proved by ordinary methods of proof. This Wittgenstein did. He restored faith in Faith and took rationality down a peg.

What does that make him? He was certainly not a metaphysician in the Aristotelian or Thomistic sense. And he was certainly not a Logical Positivist. That he was a Linguistic Analyst in some sense is beyond question, though to what extent he was the progenitor of that philosophical method would be difficult to say, since in some form it was in existence before *Philosophical Investigations* was published (1953) or even before *The Blue and Brown Books* were in circulation in typescript.

He claimed to be a phenomenologist (cf. Gier, 1975). This would seem to be what he was. Although he has been accused of neglecting the phenomena in pursuit of concepts, this is precisely what a phenomenologist, as distinct from a phenomenalist, does. He was concerned not just with our usage of words but with the context in which we use them and the form of life that this implies which will lead to a better understanding of the concepts that are contained in the words. This, at least, is what he is doing in the lectures on religious belief. He is studying how people act in relation to what they profess to believe. What better way to understand religious belief? To this extent he might be called a Linguistic Phenomenologist.

It is claimed that Wittgenstein was a Fideist, or at least that his followers presented him as such.[3] This he clearly was not, if by 'fideism' one means that he considered that religious belief has no basis in reason. As we have seen, he does not consider believers to be unreasonable. He even endorses the kind of reasoning described by Newman which is based on an accumulation of pieces of evidence that are not sufficient to support a convincing argument, but which supports beliefs that are 'too big to be blunders' (cf. Wittgenstein, 1966, p.62).

What leads philosophers critical of Wittgenstein's philosophy of religion to think of him as a Fideist is his insistence on the vital importance of understanding the language game of religious discourse as if that made it immune from criticism and somehow self-justifying. Anyone is free to reject a specific religious belief on the ground that it is inhumane (if it involves human sacrifice, for instance); or to reject all religious beliefs on the ground that they are the cause of wars or are incompatible with the pain and suffering in the world; or to reject a specific belief such as the doctrine of transubstantiation, for instance, on the grounds that it is inherently contradictory. These are legitimate criticisms within the language game of religious belief. But they are not proofs that the beliefs are false or wrong in a logical or empirical sense. They are merely reasons for not believing them. But they are reasons. That is how the language game of religious belief is played. Religious belief does not depend on empirical proofs, which anyway could not be forthcoming since religion deals with the transcendent. Rush Rhees, who was greatly influenced by Wittgenstein, makes that quite clear:

> you might think that I meant that the language about God was just a sort of beautiful pretence; or perhaps it was just part of the formality of a ceremony, like after dinner speeches. I do not mean anything of the sort, of course, and if I wanted to avoid *that* the language about God certainly does not refer to something. But then I should want to say something about what it is to 'talk

---

3   There are good discussions of Wittgensteinian Fideism to be found in Nielsen (1982, pp.65–139), Geivett and Sweetman (1992, pp.81–127), D.Z. Phillips (1986) and Arrington and Addis (2001).

about God', and how different this is from talking about the moon or talking about our new house. (Rhees, 1969, pp.128–9)

Though Wittgenstein did not regard religious belief as irrational, he certainly did not regard it as rational either. He was no rationalist in the modern sense as, say, Richard Swinburne is. Swinburne holds that the existence of God can be shown to be probable by rational argument. Moreover he holds that this must be the case, otherwise there is no objectivity in religious belief. His argument is that it is more probable that God exists than that he does not (Swinburne, 1979). Such an approach to belief in the existence of God and other religious beliefs Wittgenstein totally rejects. He would have no dealings with this kind of talk. In his view, which he shares with Karl Barth, the god that can be proved by rational argument is not the God to whom believers pray and whom they worship. He is just part of our universe, a finite being like the rest of us, even if greater than all of us.

It has been suggested that Wittgenstein might be described as a 'soft rationalist', a term devised by William J. Abraham (1985). Personally, I would not use it. Rationalism, as traditionally understood, implies strict logical argument, whether a priori or a posteriori. Swinburne's method of argument fits into the a posteriori category of rational argument. He speaks in terms of probabilities, which belong to scientific reasoning. The cumulative reasoning advocated by Newman and Wittgenstein (and here we can probably include Basil Mitchell (1973) who inspired William Abraham's 'soft rationalist' position) is not what I would recognize as rationalism, hard or soft. But it is, as Wittgenstein says, *reasonable*; that is, it is based on an accumulation of good reasons for belief, such as you might appeal to for allowing a nanny to take a young child for a walk in the park. We are dealing here with what Aristotle called 'practical reason', which concerns such practical matters as ethics, politics and religious belief. So it is not just its rationality, that is, logical argument, but the amount you are prepared to accept and risk in your life for your belief and for what reason you are prepared to do so that makes your belief either reasonable or foolish.

This, then, is Wittgenstein's revolution in philosophy of religion. He turned both traditional and twentieth-century philosophy of religion on their heads. The traditional, post-Cartesian, rational approach he rejected by saying that belief based on rational argument was not genuine religious belief because it reduced God to the level of creatures and he rejected twentieth-century developments because he would not accept that religious belief was meaningless by not being empirically verifiable.

Can people see, let alone accept, this revolution in the philosophy of religion? I think not. People see what they want to see and do not see what they do not want to see. And, worse than that, they cannot see what is before their eye: 'they have eyes and see not'. Wittgenstein describes this phenomenon at some length in chapter xi of Part II of *Investigations* where he speaks of 'seeing an aspect'. This consists of looking at something which can be seen in two (or more) ways, now one way, now another. Wittgenstein cites the classical example of psychology textbooks, the so-called 'duck–rabbit', which can be seen as a duck or a rabbit according to whether you interpret part of the picture as ears or an open beak.

But what he calls 'aspect blindness' is more relevant to what I want to say here. Aspect blindness is the inability to see an aspect, whether a duck or rabbit, or the look of menace in a face or the ugliness in a building. If someone has this inability, there is little that can be done, least of all by argument, to get them to see ugliness, menace or any other physiognomical feature of a face or a building. One may try various techniques to help them, but logical and empirical argument is not one of them.

So I am afraid that Wittgenstein's brilliant attempt to turn on its head the Logical Positivist notion that religious beliefs, along with ethical and aesthetical judgments, are empirically nonsensical by showing that their empirical nonsensicality is their very essence is not very likely to succeed. The successors to the Logical Positivists, the physicalists and other scientifically obsessed philosophers, will not take to heart Wittgenstein's recommendation at the end of *Tractatus*:

> My propositions serve as elucidations in the following way: anyone who understands me eventually recognizes them as nonsensical, when he has used them – as steps – to climb up beyond them …
> He must transcend these propositions, and then *he will see the world aright*.
> (Wittgenstein, 1961, 6.54, italics added)

But if you see the world in a Positivist light, then there is no prospect of seeing it as Wittgenstein saw it and wanted others to see it. Above all, in Wittgenstein's view, there can be no rational argument about it, as there can be about scientific, economic, legal, political and even historical matters. On the surface, the world will look the same whether it is dependent on a transcendent being or not, since, according to Wittgenstein, 'God does not reveal himself *in* the world' (ibid., 6.432, original emphasis), much less leave his DNA, so to speak, in the world. There are atheist philosophers and believers alike who think that the purpose of the philosophy of religion is to prove the existence of God by rational means. Wittgenstein would have none of that for the reasons given here.

So what prospect does the Wittgensteinian revolution have? Not good, as far as I can see. I cannot see that many people in this generation or in the next (or perhaps in any future one) will see the world as Wittgenstein saw it and wanted others to see it. They are too preoccupied with science and scientific evidence, and those who should know better still cling to the idea that we can give a rational account of faith.

Postscript: Brian R. Clack

Cyril Barrett died on 30 December 2003. Those concerned with Wittgenstein's thinking on religious matters will forever be in debt to Cyril for two things: his editing and publication of the *Lectures and Conversations on Aesthetics, Psychology and Religious Belief* (Wittgenstein, 1966) and his own monumental study, *Wittgenstein on Ethics and Religious Belief* (Barrett, 1991). Reviewing this brilliant book as a research student back in 1992, I praised it as the definitive study of Wittgenstein's thinking on religion, but nonetheless expressed misgivings about its thoroughgoing attempt to locate Wittgenstein within mainstream Christian thought. Cyril's final thoughts on Wittgenstein, as they appear in this volume, compound these misgivings.

The really valuable contribution that Cyril Barrett has made to Wittgenstein studies lies in his understanding of the early Wittgenstein, helpfully summarized in his chapter here. The difference between the author of the *Tractatus* and the Logical Positivists lies in their respective attitudes to that which goes beyond the intelligible limits of language. Wittgenstein's silence is a consequence of his conviction that 'There are, indeed, things that cannot be put into words' (Wittgenstein, 1961, 6.522). This suggestion that language is simply inadequate to speak of 'what is higher' (ibid., 1961, 6.432) and that, in attempting to describe the ineffable, one may in fact debase its value, places Wittgenstein, as Barrett makes clear, in a tradition running back at least as far as the Hebrew scriptures (compare Ecclesiastes 5:2: 'Be not rash with your mouth, nor let your heart be hasty to utter a word before God, for God is in heaven and you upon earth; therefore let your words be few'). No such concerns were present in the minds of the members of the Vienna Circle, whose reasons for banishing talk of religious matters were perfectly summarized by Otto Neurath: 'One must indeed be silent, but not *about* anything' (Neurath, in Ayer, 1986, p.32).

Throughout Barrett's work on Wittgenstein, his sympathies have clearly been with Wittgenstein's early philosophy, so much so that he has a desire to read the 'Lectures on Religious Belief' as 'a further development of ... the earlier writings', so that 'expressions of religious belief are still nonsensical in the sense of nonsense' (*Unsinn*) as used in *Tractatus*' (Barrett, p.000). The problem with such a reading is, first, that its plausibility depends upon radically underplaying the differences between Wittgenstein's early and later views of language; and, second, that there is really no textual evidence within the 'Lectures' themselves to support it. To deal (briefly) with the first point, the Tractarian view set up a monolithic structure of language (one broadly modelled on the discourse characteristic of the natural sciences) in which the sole function of language was to depict possible or actual factual situations in the world. Any form of discourse which transgressed these pictorial bounds (for example, the language of ethics, of metaphysics, of theology) was deemed nonsensical. In the latter work (expressed most perfectly in the *Philosophical Investigations*), however, these boundaries are rejected as arbitrary and artificial: language is not one thing, not merely concerned with the articulation of empirical facts, but is, rather, a motley and endlessly extendable collection of linguistic practices each with their own criteria of truth and falsity, sense and nonsense. As such, one cannot say of any one sphere of discourse that it is in itself 'nonsensical'. One must instead *wait* on the practice and try to grasp (through attention to what speakers say and do, how their words relate to their behaviour and actions) the meaning of their words: what Wittgenstein would call the *grammar* of this particular sphere of discourse. And this is precisely what Wittgenstein attempts to do in the 'Lectures on Religious Belief' by attention to the theistic belief in a Last Judgment: we have here a puzzling belief and a puzzling way of speaking, and our puzzlement is to be ameliorated by paying attention to the role (or use) of such a belief in the lives of the religious.

Wittgenstein wants to suggest that there is no contradiction between the believer and the unbeliever over religious questions (God, Last Judgment and so on): a perplexing suggestion perhaps, but only if religious belief is viewed in the standard manner, namely as the belief in superempirical entities and occurrences. He says, contrariwise:

> Suppose someone were a believer and said: 'I believe in a Last Judgement,' and I said: 'Well, I'm not so sure. Possibly.' You would say that there is an enormous gulf between us. If he said 'There is a German aeroplane overhead,' and I said 'Possibly. I'm not so sure,' you'd say we were fairly near.
>
> It isn't a question of my being anywhere near him, but on an entirely different plane, which you could express by saying: 'You mean something altogether different, Wittgenstein.' (Wittgenstein, 1966, p.53)

So there is something 'altogether different' about the character of religious language. It is not that religious language is 'nonsensical'; rather it has a distinctive grammar. Wittgenstein's task is to discern what this is. By attention to the employment of the idea of the Last Judgment in the life of the believer, he reaches the conclusion that a religious belief is a 'picture', something constantly before the believer's mind, entering the believer's deliberations whenever wrongdoing tempts. 'Whenever he does anything, this is before his mind' (ibid.). If religious belief is described in this manner the issue of contradiction disappears:

> Suppose someone is ill and he says: 'This is a punishment,' and I say: 'If I'm ill, I don't think of punishment at all.' If you say: 'Do you believe the opposite?' – you can call it believing the opposite, but it is entirely different from what we would normally call believing the opposite.
>
> I think differently, in a different way. I say different things to myself. I have different pictures.
>
> It is this way: if someone said: 'Wittgenstein, you don't take illness as punishment, so what do you believe?' – I'd say: 'I don't have any thoughts of punishment.' (Ibid., p.55)

These thoughts seem somewhat different from Barrett's gloss on Wittgenstein's view: 'All that believers and unbelievers can say is that they do not believe what the other believes. They may say that it is false, but that still only means that they do not believe it' (Barrett, p.66). That sounds a little too like the familiar conclusion of a fruitless after-dinner argument ('We'll have to agree to disagree', where one might be discussing abortion, US foreign policy or some other pressing issue), and what it ignores is the 'entirely different plane' occupied by the believer and – crucially – the dynamic nature of the religious belief, the way that belief is fused with a way of *living*.

That religious belief, for Wittgenstein, is fundamentally connected with action and behaviour can be seen in the following reflection on how belief in God is sometimes seen as something morally requisite:

> If the question arises as to the existence of a god or God, it plays an entirely different role to that of the existence of any person or objective I ever heard of. One said, had to say, that one *believed* in the existence, and if one did not believe, this was regarded as something bad. Normally if I did not believe in the existence of something no one would think there was anything wrong in this. (Wittgenstein, 1966, p.59)

Here a number of crucial elements coalesce. A difference is discerned in the attitude taken to believing in God and believing in other odd entities (phantoms, fairies and so on). With the latter, no condemnation of the unbeliever occurs, whereas this often occurs in religious matters, where the unbeliever may be seen, not as mistaken, but as depraved. This should suggest to us, then, that a religious belief is not a speculative belief; indeed, that it is not – if we run this to its logical conclusion – a belief in the *existence* of anything at all. In *Culture and Value*, Wittgenstein writes of religious belief that 'although it's *belief*, it's really a way of living, or a way of assessing life' (Wittgenstein, 1980, p.64). So the contention seems to be that religion is only apparently a set of quasi-theoretical statements (concerning God, the destiny of the individual, and so on) and is, in reality, an aid to conduct, a collection of regulating pictures.

Barrett's interpretation sidesteps all of this; so much so, indeed, that we almost lose sight of Wittgenstein altogether. Wittgenstein says that in matters of religious belief there can be no appeal to *evidence*; and that *reasons* are also absent here: 'Not only...is it not reasonable, but it doesn't pretend to be' (Wittgenstein, 1966, p.58). Barrett, on the other hand, contends that Wittgenstein thinks that religious belief *is* reasonable (cf. Barrett, p.70), and that, though we don't have 'conclusive and compelling' evidence, 'there is what we call evidence of a kind' (p.66). Even where Barrett highlights the difficulties of looking for evidence, he holds that the lack of evidence for religious belief is due to the fact that 'religious belief transcends what can be shown empirically' (p.66). This conclusion is a result of reading the 'Lectures' in Tractarian perspective, and it misses the point. It suggests that God is just tantalizingly out of reach, whereas Wittgenstein is asking us to think about God in a very different way, as not something either within our reach or beyond it, not a thing at all, a *no-thing*.

'What prospect does the Wittgensteinian revolution have?', asks Barrett. Given how he defines this revolution – a reining-in of rationalism and a rejection of verificationism – I do not share his pessimism about its fate (particularly since verificationism has had its day anyway). But if Wittgenstein's revolution is more radical than this – if, that is, religious belief is to be interpreted as a set of life-regulating pictures; as a way of living rather than a set of beliefs concerning transcendent realities; as a practice not dependent on the existence of any superempirical being – then its prospects are not so good. While it is feasible that the non-religious might embrace Wittgenstein's view as a plausible account of the nature of religion, it is doubtful that religious believers could accept it. Do not believers have to think that there is a God, that there will be a Last Judgment, and that these are not simply admonishing pictures? As John Searle has remarked, 'You have to be a very *recherché* sort of religious intellectual to keep praying if you don't think there is any real God outside the language who is listening to your prayers' (Searle, in Magee, 1987, p.345). In a time such as ours, in which philosophers of religion tend not to be objective observers of religious practice, but rather staunch defenders of (a somewhat conservative kind of) theistic belief, it seems unlikely that Wittgenstein's views will be widely accepted. To this extent, then, the Wittgensteinian revolution is likely to be an abortive one.

CHAPTER 5

The God's Eye Point of View:
A Divine Ethic

Charles Taliaferro

You and I are having an argument about the morality or ethic of some act or institution. Our concern is normative: what ought to be or what ought not to be. The concepts and vocabulary may be quite various: we may talk of what is right, wrong, permissible, impermissible, required, prohibited, good, evil, better or worse. And our topics may be various, from abortion to US foreign policy, from the economic and social hegemony of a gender or class to the settlement of refugees and the War Crime Tribunal in the Hague. In arguing with one another, I suggest there are in play at least three elements: an appeal to the relevant facts which ground our moral judgment, impartiality and taking into account the affective points of view of the involved parties. These three features, under ideal conditions, constitute what may be called *A God's Eye Point of View*.[1]

I seek to articulate a moral theory which sees a God's Eye Point of View as a desirable ideal. This theory will then require defence against a series of objections which are often launched against theories such as the one I defend which give centre stage to impartiality and objectivity. Some philosophers and theologians hold that appeals to impartiality are fruitless or based on spurious assumptions. The very idea that ethics can be objective has been under assault from Ancient Greece onward. My hope is to offer a version of an impartialist ethic which avoids many of the classic and current objections.

The Logic of Moral Reflection

I shall highlight the three components which I believe partly constitute moral reflection, West and East, North and South. I will work from a modern setting and extrapolate from there.

Imagine you and I are arguing over any action (X) you like in which I think X is permissible and you think X is impermissible. At a minimum I believe we will each seek to bring into focus different facts. If our argument is over the use of nuclear power as a source of energy, I may argue that you resist it because you are employing

---

1 I have defended an Ideal Observer theory in several places (see Taliaferro, 1988a, 1988b, 1998, 1999).

a faulty physics, a mistaken probability calculus and an exaggerated and unrealistic view of risk taking, and so on. You may reverse the charges on each of these fronts and bring in facts I have neglected. Imagine, for example, I have failed to see that in modern nuclear energy policy there is more risk placed on the economically disadvantaged than on the privileged. I may also be working with the implicit assumption that energy policy involving risks are voluntarily imposed in a democracy. You point out that this imposition will, in practice, always be imperfect and in some cases essentially flawed (for example, children and the severely impaired cannot function as independent parties voluntarily assuming risks).

Early on in a moral dispute much of the work will, I believe, go into identifying different facts, either challenging what one or both of us presume to be factual or bringing to bear new, not commonly recognized facts. But a disputation of facts is often tied in with an appeal to impartiality.[2]

Even if you and I agree about what I am calling the facts involving nuclear energy, disagreement may still occur owing to partiality. Imagine I come from a country which benefits chiefly from nuclear energy. My country places other people at risk who do not benefit from this energy practice. You may tell me that I have failed to carry out an essential element in the thinking behind the Golden Rule of putting myself in another person's shoes. Would I *still* favour the use of nuclear power if, say, the roles were reversed and I was receiving the burden without the benefit?

An appeal to impartiality and facts do not cover all the elemental stages of moral reflection. There is also an affective dimension to inquiry, an appeal to *what it is like* to be an agent or victim or bystander. In approving of nuclear energy policy, am I taking seriously (affectively incorporating) what it would feel like (or be like) to suffer from radiation sickness, to give birth to a child suffering from radiation poisoning or to be that child? Presumably it is because of the perceived need to take this affective dimension seriously that those of us in wealthy countries sometimes fast in order to remind ourselves (albeit in a fragmented and highly artificial way) of the needs of those who starve. In the city where I live, there are programmes which you may enter in which you are placed in economically destitute settings for short periods in order for you to get some hint of what it might feel like to be homeless. In my schooling as a child we were sometimes asked to go through the day in a wheelchair or wear a blindfold in order to get some feeling for what it might feel like to be physically impaired. Such practices may seem like pathetic examples of merely simulating an aspect of moral reflection, but I can report that such educative practices shaped my own and other students' perspectives.

In classical theism God is understood to be necessarily existing, omnipotent, eternal, the free, gracious Creator and sustainer of the cosmos, worthy of worship

---

2   Of course to prevent the IOT from being circular, the facts here may be referred to as 'non-moral facts', facts which do not explicitly involve moral properties like being wrong. Otherwise there is this problem of circularity: an IO is a being which knows all moral facts. True, but unhelpful.

and the object of our supplications. These features do not (as yet) enter the above portrait of moral reflection. But in theism God is also pictured as all-knowing or omniscient where this may be understood to include not just the facts but the acquaintance with the affective life of all involved parties. In Christianity as well as Judaism and Islam, God is also understood to be impartial.[3]

If we look just to the features of omniscience of facts, impartiality and affective incorporation, moral reflection can (I suggest) be understood as our seeking a God's eye point of view. This view of moral reasoning is customarily called The Ideal Observer Theory (IOT). Versions of it may be found in the work of David Hume, Adam Smith, Henry Sidgwick, R.M. Hare, Roderick Firth, Peter Singer, Tom Regan, Tom Carson and even Immanuel Kant and J.S. Mill. I will not try to distinguish the different ways in which each philosopher developed the theory, though I will comment later on the significance of the theory being employed to such different ends.

As for supporting documentation for the IOT in terms of seeking facts, impartiality and affective incorporation, I appeal to the documentation in the Blackwell *Companion to Ethics* (ed. Singer, 1991). From Mary Midgley's treatment of early ethics to the entries on African, Asian and early American ethics, there are repeated recourses to seeking impartiality, facts and affective incorporation. Obviously the material is too rich and complex to review here – even superficially – but I take note of the natural (or intuitive) appeal of the IO theory when one takes into account the documented, essentially social nature of humanity and the occasions when companionship and cooperation need to be negotiated. Historical moral disputes have been marred by a failure to secure a common background philosophy of the relevant facts (you and I have, say, different views of the individual's relation to family, state, empire or religion), we may have uneven powers of putting ourselves in the others' shoes, and impartiality can be flawed by either excessive attachment to or detachment from local customs, but I see in the history of ethics a pattern in which ideal knowledge, affective identification and impartiality are proper goals to achieve, or at least to simulate.[4]

The IOT faces a series of objections which I will try to meet. This will also serve to lay the groundwork for a final section of this chapter in which I offer a Cusanian version of the IOT (after Nicholas of Cusa, 15th century).

---

3   This claim may seem completely at odds with traditional teaching about the 'chosen people', and God's specific provident action. However, in the Hebrew Bible and Christian New Testament, God's specific acts are commonly cast as ultimately leading to the good of all (see Taliaferro, 1992).

4   The early entries (Singer, 1991) on the origins of ethics support the IOT portrait as moral reflection began to take shape historically. The history of ethics which unfolds in the *Companion* contains, of course, a wide diversity of positions which give different weight to the features I have identified. Compare, for example, Mo Tzu and Confucius on impartiality. I still read the *Companion* as documenting a broad general concern for impartiality, scope of knowledge and affective identification.

Objections and Replies

Objection A   There are no 'facts', as you suppose; there are only points of view from the standpoint of different communities, traditions, genders, classes, individuals.

Reply   I subscribe to the counterargument that the denial of facts is self-refuting. If there are no facts, then it is a fact that there are no facts. If there are 'only' points of view and no facts, then there is this problem: to assert that there are points of view is implicitly to assert that it is a fact that there are points of view. The denial of any 'facts' not tied to human points of view also gives rise to several worries. What about communities based upon what appear to be racist and sexist horrors? Aren't these societies functioning on a false understanding of race and gender? What about non-human sources of value as with non-human animals? Isn't it possible that living, sentient beings deserve our respect even if there is nothing within our 'points of view' which welcome such respect? Even if you still deny community-independent facts, an IOT may still have use as many communities applaud impartiality, facts and affective incorporation.[5]

Objection B   The IOT is an ahistorical impersonal point of view. The theory is a view from nowhere.

Reply   The IOT sketched here is not a view from nowhere but, if you will, a comprehensive view from everywhere. Some worry about the idea of a God's eye point of view because it may obscure or falsify the way things look from the ground, just as you may have little idea of what a village is like when viewed from your plane at 35000 feet. The IO theory here is also *not* a matter of impersonal calculation, but personal appraisal, a taking into account of personal, specific circumstances.

In the mid-twentieth century there was a dominant portrait of philosophical inquiry as something impersonal. A classic version of this may be found at the end of Bertrand Russell's *A History of Western Philosophy*, where he celebrates an impersonal 'scientific truthfulness'.

> In the welter of conflicting fanaticisms, one of the few unifying forces is scientific truthfulness, by which I mean the habit of basing our beliefs upon observations and inferences as impersonal, and as much divested of local and temperamental bias, as is possible for human beings. (Russell, 1945, p.836)

The IOT defended here is explicitly anchored against bias, but there is also the explicit claim that moral reflection involves an affective component which takes seriously local temperaments and personal observations.

---

5   Alan Ryan claims that the movement to dispense with an objective view of facts undermines the historic claims of politically oppressed minorities: 'The minority view was always that power could be undermined by truth ... Once you ... [say] that truth is simply an effect of power, you've had it' (see Ryan, 1992, p.21). For a more general assessment of anti-realism, I commend the work of Roger Trigg (Trigg, 1989).

Objection C   But the theory upholds detachment and disinterest as ideals which surely falsify a key component of moral judgment which involves passion and desire.

Reply   'Impartiality' is not the same as being dispassionate, disinterested or apathetic. When I condemn child molestation with fierce passion I am not *ipso facto* partial. I believe that an *impartial* assessment of the harms involved ought to give rise to *passionate*, *determined* disapproval. An impartial assessment of friendship ought to give rise to an approval with pleasure.[6]

Objection D   But impartiality is an unattainable ideal. Even if there could be an IO (or if God is one), why should I care?

Reply   I submit that impartiality is easily achieved in a wide range of cases (who would claim that it is merely bias to think that skinning and salting babies is wrong?) and that, in the hard cases, impartiality remains an ideal we may approach, even if we cannot fully achieve it.

As for the person who does not care, I take the (somewhat controversial) position that not to care at all about how your acts affect others, or how they would be viewed from an impartial point of view, is to court an amoral life. I do not doubt there are sociopaths or egoistic individuals or societies which reflect egoism on a massive scale. I just doubt whether one can do this and still claim to be ethical or reflect ethically.

Objection E   But the IO theory still promotes a fundamentally false idea, the ideal that one can or should shed one's own point of view.

Reply   I suggest that taking into account positions other than one's own is a basic capacity which is evident in much recorded historical moral debate. In fact finding one's *own* moral point of view (that is, one which you recognize as authentically yours) may be latent and subsequent to grasping the points of view of others. Søren Kierkegaard has taught us that many of us can go through life in an unreflective, routinized fashion merely accepting the status quo or having alien, destructive points of view forced upon us which then perversely tend to cripple us and those we love. Finding one's own stance can involve an essential comparison of alternative moral positions.

---

6   I have drawn on this affective element in defending an ideal observer theory about beauty and ugliness (see Taliaferro, 1990). Two worries: is the ideal point of view atemporal, transcending time; second: does the IO theory privilege seeing? Doesn't it put the emphasis on remote spectating rather than action? In reply to the first question, the value of some acts can depend upon future consequences. Insofar as they do, an ideal vantage point would include knowledge of the future. But the relevant ideal which we seek in moral disagreement is rarely to gaze at things *sub specie aeternitatis*; we simply try to get the most reasonable estimation we can of the future. In reply to the second query, I employ Nicholas of Cusa's language later in the chapter, which emphasizes vision; the IO theory is about *observation*, not literal seeing. One may observe people and things with all the senses, and certainly blind people can observe (perceive, notice) states of affairs. My father is legally blind and yet a keen observer of human behaviour and passion. And he is no mere spectator, but uses his observations in his loving, sensitive action.

I should also add this caveat: it is in keeping with the IOT developed here that there may be times when the pursuit of objective impartiality may be impossible or dangerous. Imagine I am in a culture where the ostensible objective biology as taught in schools is profoundly racist. The IOT allows us to say that such so-called 'objectivity' is spurious, and that the pursuit of such learning would be noxious. The IO theory can allow that, while ideally impartiality is the goal of moral reflection, there are times when a person cannot (and should not be expected to) pursue that goal.

At the end of the day, I suggest that the IOT articulated here does more to promote the virtue of humility than the vice of arrogance. Many of those who have struggled to place narrow self-interest to one side (Iris Murdoch, Virginia Wolf, Martin Luther King Jr, Gandhi) testify to the arduous strain in truly recognizing and responding to the values in and around us, without acting on only our own desires come what may. In closing I consider two further powerful objections, one stemming from a philosophical source and the second religious and existentialist. I will use the latter to suggest a Cusanian version of the IOT.

Objection F   Philosophers often object that the IOT is insufficient. Could not IOs disagree? After all, if Kant and Mill both looked to an IO, do we not have all the evidence we need to reject the theory as unhelpful? Or does the IO theory support both Kant's duty-based ethic and utilitarianism?

Reply   Let me approach these questions indirectly. Imagine I am a utilitarian and you are a duty-based ethicist. As we argue over nuclear policy, I suggest we will probably give different weight to different facts. I may highlight who will and will not suffer or be happy; you may do this as well as draw attention to what may be called the phenomenology of duty – the felt rightness or wrongness of an act or the felt supreme goodness of the intention to be just. Many IO theorists have been utilitarian. On this point, though, I follow my teacher, the late Roderick Firth, in thinking that utilitarianism overlooks the felt demand quality of certain acts. Firth combined his version of the Ideal Observer theory with an appreciation of the phenomenology of values. He did not think (as I do not) that there is a sharp distinction between facts and values. In keeping with my early construal of the IOT as a theory from everywhere as opposed to nowhere, I suggest that the disagreement between us will have to come out in the details of arguing back and forth, of my looking for the vindication of your moral phenomenology, of my questioning the layers of training which may have affected (rightly or wrongly) your point of view. Here I do not envisage an abstract theoretical exchange, but debate on specific moral problems, in particular historical settings.

Pamela Anderson raises the objection that the IO conditions are insufficient as cases arise in which parties may be matched with equal abilities in terms of knowledge, impartiality and affective identification, and yet they remain in painful disagreement.[7] If she is correct, the IO theory is not thereby shown to be dispensable;

---

7   These are developed in Chapter 6 of this volume.

the IO theory may be seen as identifying the necessary but not sufficient conditions. Anderson employs two cases in her objection, one involving adultery. A woman is having an extramarital affair. She and her husband are in anguished disagreement over the permissibility of this affair, notwithstanding equal awareness of the non-moral facts, etceteras. Three replies are possible. First, they are both correct. The affair is both good and bad, right and wrong in different respects and the IO theory accurately captures the reasoning of both parties. Second, in a case where it is reasonable to believe that IOs would disagree, the affair is morally neutral. Perhaps the affair is not good, but not morally prohibited. Third, in the thought experiment we can readily imagine that either one or both parties' judgments are clouded by self-interest, jealousy and powerful erotic desires.

A Cusanian Ideal Observer Theory

For a final objection here, I consider the charge that the IOT creates a spectre of sorts, a point of view which threatens our subjectivity. Jean-Paul Sartre is perhaps the most prominent philosopher to vilify a God's eye point of view as something which diminishes or kills our subjectivity. Famously Sartre claimed that the judging apprehension of another person threatens one's freedom and identity.

> The Other is the indispensable mediator between myself and me. I am ashamed of myself *as I appear* to the Other. By the mere appearance of the Other, I am put in the position of passing judgment on myself as an object, for it is as an object that I appear to the Other. (Sartre, 1956, p.222)

This critique of external observation may also be found in the work of Simone de Beauvoir, whom some scholars credit with influencing Sartre's position. Pamela Anderson has also suggested to me that the observation which is in play in the IO theory is in tension with the subjectivity of our embodied, personal experience.

In *The Vision of God*, Nicholas of Cusa offers a sustained meditation on God as the all-seeing, 'omnivoyant', Creator. The gaze of God is a centrepiece to God's being: 'For God, who is the very summit of all perfection, and greater than can be conceived, is called *theos* from this very fact that He beholdeth all things' (Cusa, 1928, p.7).[8] As Nicholas of Cusa develops this account, God's gaze is all-encompassing and yet it does not obscure or overshadow the gaze of others. God's 'absolute sight' is said to embrace and include limited sight.

> For without Absolute Sight there can be no limited sight; it embraces in itself all modes of seeing all and each alike, and abideth entirely freed from all variation.

---

8   This volume includes a good introduction by Evelyn Underhill. Nicholas of Cusa's picture of God's gaze accords with Tom Carson's most recent work on theistic ethics (see Carson, 2000).

> All limited modes of seeing exist without limitation in Absolute Sight. For every limitation existeth in the Absolute, because Absolute Sight is the limiting of limitations, limiting not being limitable. (Ibid., p.10)

The IOT has been articulated independently of theism, though some proponents are explicitly indebted to theism; for example, Roderick Firth developed his IOT with one eye on the attributes of God. But for those of us who are theists, one may understand the IOT as not delimiting an ideal which may or may not exist, but as demarcating elements in the actual loving Creator God. In this schema, God's omniscience has been articulated by Nicholas of Cusa as loving ('Thy glance is love'). Moreover the interplay or unitive life of creature and the Omnivoyant Creator may be seem as comprising an ideal integration of an individual creature.

I have argued elsewhere (Taliaferro, 1994, final chapter) that an individual person may be remote from themselves when they have radically false beliefs about themselves (I believe I am the greatest rock climber when the fact is I am among the worst and a hazard to anyone who trusts me). I may be remote from myself when my memories are all bent by self-delusion and I have 'lost touch' with what I did in the past (perhaps I was a prison guard in a death camp and, not being able to face this, I have repressed or distorted the memories). Many parts of ourselves seem remote from our sensory or cognitive awareness (the unconscious, dreams, the future). If there is an IO or, rather, if God is this IO who lovingly apprehends our lives, then there is a sense in which a relation with this God would involve our coming to terms with this broader, more comprehensive and exacting perspective. This, in any case, is how Nicholas of Cusa understands our relation to God. *Contra* Sartre, the gaze of the divine Other opens up our freedom, and calls us to integrity.

> But I know that Thy glance is that supreme Goodness which cannot fail to communicate itself to all able to receive it. Thou, therefore, canst never let me go so long as I am able to receive Thee. Wherefore it behoveth me to make myself, in so far as I can, ever more able to receive Thee. But I know that the capacity which maketh union possible is naught else save likeness. And incapacity springeth from lack of likeness. If, therefore, I have rendered myself by all possible means like unto Thy goodness, then, according to the degree of that likeness, I shall be capable of truth. (Cusa, 1928, p.16)

Because of God's ideal point of view of ourselves, not a view from above only but a view from below, around, within and above, this loving God calls one into a life of feeling and agency in the world as it is and not merely as we fantasize about it.

Of course all of the above involves substantial claims which (like most interesting claims in philosophy) are controversial: the coherence and truth of theism, realism with respect to facts, and so on. I make two observations in closing. First, I wager that most objections to the IOT will reflect one or more of the conditions I have sought to highlight, such as the following. Is the IOT itself truly impartial? Is the IOT compatible with certain affective dimensions of the moral life? Does the IOT privilege arbitrarily some fact to the neglect of others? Objections to the IOT may reflect the very conditions which the IOT identifies and safeguards. Second, the IOT with its Cusanian component, presents a picture of personal exchange, of shared disclosure in a moral life which is mutually enriching.

> For every intellectual spirit perceiveth in Thee, my God, somewhat which must be revealed unto others in order that they may attain unto Thee, their God, in the best possible fashion. Wherefore these spirits, full of love, reveal one unto another their secrets, and thereby the knowledge of the Beloved is increased, and yearning toward Him is aflame, and sweetness of joy. (Ibid., p.128)[9]

---

9   Ibid., p.128. I have previously offered a somewhat lighthearted defence of the compatibility of God's knowledge and our understanding of individual privacy (see Taliaferro, 1989). I am very grateful to Pamela Sue Anderson for her critical observations (in this volume and elsewhere) and a continuing exchange in this and other areas of philosophy of religion. Her constructive feminist standpoint will be the focus of another essay as I study further her important contribution. A version of this chapter was presented at the Sino-American Philosophical Forum, Tsinghua University, Beijing China, 2002. I am grateful to my commentator Professor Zhenming Zhai (Zongshan University). In conversation the IO theory was 'tested' by considering it as a framework for Jewish, Christian and Islamic dialogue post-9/11. It was also considered as a framework by which to identify and articulate strands of Chinese ethics.

CHAPTER 6

What's Wrong with the God's Eye Point of View: a Constructive Feminist Critique of the Ideal Observer Theory

Pamela Sue Anderson

Introduction: the Ideal Observer Theory

Feminist philosophers of religion seek to transform those core concepts and patterns of reasoning in western philosophy which have been oppressive to women, especially as employed by contemporary philosophers of religion. My critical attention has been drawn to the concepts and reasoning which shape the Ideal Observer theory of knowledge and action.[1] The ideal agent has played a significant role in modern ethics, and the ideal observer as subject of knowledge and belief has dominated western epistemology. This subject who knows and acts is assumed to observe an empirical reality 'out there', that is, independent of the observer. The subject as observer is, then, opposed to empirical objects in the sense of that which is observed, known and acted upon. Objectivity as agreement about what is out there, or what actually occurs, independent of the subject's point of view grounds knowledge and the search for truth, as well as judgment of right action. The subject's judgments of true and false states of affairs are made about a world independent of that very same subject. A definite, spatial–temporal framework determines this account.

Following the philosophical tradition deriving from Hume and Kant, the subject observes in time; and the subject's observations of empirical objects are made up of discrete perceptions or intuitions, which change in time. This observer's spatial–temporal framework shapes the perspective(s), or points of view, from which the subject observes the world.[2] The crucial significance of the adjective, *ideal*, is

---

1   For variations on conceptions of an ideal agent, see Smith's judicious spectator, Brandt's ideally rational agent, Hare's archangel, Rawls's competent judge, Nagel's impartial spectator whose view is from nowhere (Smith, 1976; Brandt, 1979; Hare, 1981; Nagel, 1986; Rawls, 1971).

2   I appropriate Moore's definition that 'a point of view' is 'a location in the broadest possible sense [including] points in space, points in time … different roles in personal relationships … and the sensory apparatus of different species' (Moore, 1997, pp.1–6, 282). Moore's question is whether there can be thought about the world that is not from any point of view.

here that the ideal observer is not limited by a spatial–temporal point of view. Instead of being restricted by space and time, the ideal observer transcends the limitations which create disagreements between subjects in the domains of both ethics and epistemology. This transcendent ideal has been called 'the God's eye point of view', since it exists beyond the spatial–temporal limits that normally inhibit human knowledge of what is true or right.

This brief account of the ideal observer is rough and basic, yet the features I have just sketched will be significant for my reconstructive feminist critique. The theory of the ideal observer can be both attractive and dangerous. I aim to expose both extremes in Charles Taliaferro's refined conception of this theory. My critique begins by recognizing a problem built into the ideal observer theory, that is, a problematic gap between fact and value. The ideal agent imagines herself or himself overcoming this gap, but in fact begs the question.

A Modern Refinement of the Ideal Observer Theory

Taliaferro is a modern philosopher of religion who has defended the ideal observer theory more energetically than possibly any other.[3] He has also revised and adapted the dominant account of the ideal observer. His theory sheds light both on human ethical reflection and on a divine ethic. He derives the features of the ideal observer and agent from a conception of the theistic God as omniscient, omnibenevolent and omnipotent. Taliaferro also seems to assume passibilism; that is, God feels our pain, sorrow, pleasure and joy. He argues that there are three crucial elements characterizing his ideal observer theory: an *appeal to all relevant facts*, *impartiality* and *taking account of the affective dimensions of the lives of the persons involved*.[4] Taliaferro derives these elements from a theistic ideal, implying that we seek a God's eye point of view in our ethical reflection.

I have two objections, which I intend to develop in this chapter, to Taliaferro's use of the God's eye point of view in resolving ethical disagreements. First, I question the overall *coherence* of his conception of the Ideal Observer theory. It is not obvious how the terms he employs to characterize his ideal ethical agent are compatible with each other. Do 'all relevant facts' include 'the affective dimensions' of people's lives? If so, then we must also assume that those facts about affections are compatible with Taliaferro's concept of 'impartiality'. In other words, Taliaferro

---

3   For a modern philosopher who has energetically and persuasively argued against such a conception of moral reflection, acknowledging domains where such an impartial conception is impossible even to imagine, see Williams (1985, pp.132–55). Williams distinguishes knowledge (or science) from ethics precisely on the grounds that our perspectives are always partial in the ethical domain; so ethical disagreements are not resolvable. For his more recent account of perspectivalism, see Williams (2000, pp.482–5).

4   See Taliaferro's own account in his chapter in the present collection.

himself has tried to refine the ideal observer theory so that 'the relevant facts', although 'impartial', can be connected with human 'affections'. Yet can we accept that non-natural, personal or social 'facts' are in some sense impartial? We will return to address this question. For now, Taliaferro makes it clear that his use of impartiality does not require impersonal observation. Instead impartiality requires comprehensiveness and personal–critical agreement which, then, includes taking account of the affective dimensions of other persons' lives: 'feeling what it is like to be [or suffer as] an agent or victim or bystander' (see Chapter 5). Despite this refinement of terms, it would, I suggest, be difficult for either a Humean or a Kantian philosopher to accept that the three elements of Taliaferro's ideal observation avoid fundamental contradictions. After I explore this difficulty, I will question the adequacy of his ethical reasoning.

First, the objection concerning contradictions in terms is made more precise if we think of the debates in moral philosophy since Hume and Kant, especially those concerning the gap between fact and value. Does Taliaferro overcome the fact/value dichotomy? Hume demonstrated that any move from a fact of nature to a value is invalid. This was later named the naturalistic fallacy: non-moral facts of nature could not provide the ground for moral judgments. Does Taliaferro's resolution of ethical disputes depend on the existence of moral facts?[5] In the twentieth century, J.L. Mackie famously describes any supposed moral fact as 'queer', since unobservable (Mackie 1977, pp.38–42). Mackie's post-Humean account would render impossible the reading of all relevant facts as inclusive of moral facts. If holding the latter, Taliaferro's position falls under Mackie's criticism of treating facts as queer.

So what about finding support for Taliaferro's theory in Kantian moral philosophy? Kant did claim that the moral law was a 'strange' sort of 'fact of reason', experienced as a source of demands whose force is independent of natural inclinations (Kant 1997, pp.28–9, 41–2). And, crucially, this strange 'fact' of reason is for Kantians the ground of a moral feeling of respect for that law which remains impartial. Morality and impartiality, then, come together in Kant's *Critique of Practical Reason*. Subsequently impartiality serves as the condition for objective knowledge of reality, including events which take place in an empirical world independent of us as noumenal subjects or ideal agents. Impartiality is treated by Kantian ethicists as the ground for the moral law, resolving ethical disputes about what we ought to do. Yet this ground separates that which is rational (and so moral) from natural inclinations; typically the latter is understood to include 'affections'.

The question is, then, whether Taliaferro can hold on to his concept of impartiality, while allowing 'facts' to cover things which might render them, in Mackie's terms, queer and, possibly, strange or contradictory for Kantian moral

---

5   Generally in this chapter I employ 'ethical' to cover both ethical and moral. However, I employ 'moral' for moral philosopher and to follow the philosophical traditions of Kant or Mackie when their distinctive conceptions are at issue, as with 'moral law' or 'moral fact'.

philosophers. Kant thought impartiality possible and necessary for morality. But for him impartial clearly meant 'disinterested', that is, not determined by the concerns of a particular (or Taliaferro's 'personal') point of view. The moral law, according to Kant, is in this sense disinterested and, ultimately, universal. A truly impartial, ethical argument would compel universal agreement, not on the basis of self-interest, but on grounds of reason.

Admittedly contemporary ethics, including post-Kantian ethics, do not find impartiality quite so straightforward as a ground for ethical reasoning or agreement. Major challenges to ethical theory have radically changed contemporary discussions. Notably the prominent twentieth-century moral philosopher Bernard Williams persuasively demonstrated the sense in which impartiality is neither the necessary nor the sufficient condition for the resolution of ethical disagreement (Williams 1985, pp.65–9, 133–6). I hope to develop Williams's view further below. However here it should be made clear that Williams demonstrates that we might agree about a particular action being ethical (strictly) on the grounds of *partiality*. For example, we might agree that the most ethical thing to do is support the life of a child in one's own village rather than save the life of a child in a far-off third world country. If so, impartiality is not necessary here. In fact, if we aimed to be suitably impartial in this case, we might well find that impartiality is not sufficient for us to choose between the lives of the two children.

Now let us focus on Taliaferro's move away from the ethical reasoning of either Humean or Kantian ethicists, and see if Williams's account might support him. Clearly Taliaferro wants to resist any crude fact/value distinction. He insists that impartiality does not mean disinterestedness, or detachment from the world of particulars. Instead impartiality, modelled on his conception of God as omniscient and passible, achieves personal–critical agreement on ethical disputes. Yet here Taliaferro is also unlike Williams, who insists upon the partiality of our reasons for acting ethically. Neither impartiality nor God comes into Williams's conception of ethical action. Thus the terms of Taliaferro's ethical theory are unlike those of major moral philosophers, including Hume, Kant, Mackie and Williams, precisely in his appeal to (non-moral) facts, impartiality and omnipercipience.[6] Taliaferro brings in the latter concept to ensure that we *do not* remain disinterested in, and detached from, *how it feels* to be a victim, to suffer, to fail to know and do the right thing, or to see the world differently from another person's perspective. But again, is this coherent? Wanting to know all facts, to remain impartial and to feel whatever the other party feels is not only ambitious but, arguably, impossible for human agents. Thus we are brought face to face with the theistic grounding of Taliaferro's Ideal Observer theory. It is precisely his use of three theistic attributes which not only constrain Taliaferro's position, but beg questions about the actual capacities of human agents, while threatening contradiction. His concepts of (moral) facts and

---

6   The use of omnipercipience as the third element of his ideal observer theory appears in
     the earlier account; see Taliaferro (1997, pp.207–11).

impartiality remain strange, if not queer: each is in direct tension (if not contradiction) with taking account of the affective dimensions of other people's lives. Moving on, at this point, I turn to my second objection, that Taliaferro's theory also remains inadequate for resolving ethical disputes.

Two examples illustrate the inadequacy of Taliaferro's refinement of the ideal observer theory. Failure of ethical reflection to reach ethical agreement exposes the serious nature of the inadequacy. First, imagine a (perhaps unusual) husband who knows all the relevant facts about his wife's adulterous affair; he also clearly understands why his wife needs and wants a relationship with another man. The wife may equally understand her husband's feelings of jealousy, abandonment and deep disappointment in both knowing the relevant facts and understanding why and how the affair came about. The couple may have an intimate and sympathetic knowledge of each other's feelings, values and attitudes, and yet disagree about whether adultery, in this case or any other, is wrong. In this light, the individual persons involved are rational.[7] They are also well-informed in making their ethical judgments, and yet they end up with different conclusions about what is the right thing to do. Both wife and husband can become well acquainted with the ethical issue, know all the relevant facts, understand the feelings of the other person(s) involved, even seek to be impartial in assessing their knowledge of the facts and their understanding of the situation, but ethical disagreement still persists.

Second, consider an example concerning abortion. The individuals are less personally well-known to each other than in the previous example, yet they know well the differences between each other's ethical and religious beliefs. The moral judgment that abortion is wrong is made by a person who is thoroughly acquainted with the nature of abortion and the points of view of those women who abort unwanted foetuses. The opponents, who support abortion, may want to claim that this anti-abortionist lacks a genuine understanding of the feelings of those women whose lives have been made (unspeakably) difficult by unwanted pregnancies.[8] The counterargument is that the pro-abortionists are only projecting this lack of understanding onto their opponents because they think the anti-abortionist is wrong. But in this case, the anti-abortionist does not lack evidence, knowledge or compassion regarding the other position, yet she does hold certain religious beliefs about the sanctity of life. The two sides to this debate about abortion might (also) have a more fundamental disagreement over what constitutes *genuine understanding* or a belief that the other *does not truly understand*.[9]

---

7 Here 'rational' means that the agents have at least reasons for their actions and attempt to follow rules of consistency, coherence and so on.

8 There is a genuine case to be made concerning the anti-abortionist who does not understand the woman's choice for an abortion. On the struggle to gain the rights of women to choose for or against abortion, where lack of understanding is a major issue, see Le Doeuff (1991, pp.131–3, 268–78).

9 I thank Harriet A. Harris for this point and other helpful comments made on a draft of this chapter.

Whatever the degree of understanding, Taliaferro's theory is not adequate for resolving the ethical disputes, as evident in my examples (above). To reach agreement more is needed than knowledge of all relevant facts, impartiality and feeling what it is like to be the person(s) involved. The degree and manner of discourse have an impact on the degree to which the other person is understood. We have already recognized the related lack of coherence between the elements of his theory. I turn to focus more closely on one of these elements in the next section.

Impartiality and Reasons for Action

At this stage it becomes useful to scrutinize Taliaferro's concept of impartiality. Scrutiny of the tension between trying to make sense of impartiality as personal–critical agreement or a comprehensive point of view and intending impartiality as disinterested and detached judgment remains necessary. In the latter sense, impartiality would be incompatible with feeling as if one were another person (for example, a victim)[10] while compatible with gaining knowledge of all of the facts of the matter. It is difficult to understand how Taliaferro's equation of impartiality with 'personal appraisal' and 'passionate disapproval' is anything other than a confusion of terms. A person may feel passionately about the personal appraisal of an action. She may also find that a higher level of impartial assessment supports the disapproval of the same action. However the justification for such disapproval insofar as it is impartial could not depend upon either the passionate feeling or the personal appraisal. Otherwise it is not impartial.

Think again about the example of abortion. If what prevents ethical agreement is differences of deeply held religious beliefs, then an impartial assessment might conclude about the rightness or wrongness of having an abortion, but this would not resolve the disagreement between a pro-abortionist and an anti-abortionist. As long as the assessment is restricted by impartiality, it remains unable to address the differences of the deeply held religious beliefs about abortion. Alternatively we could modify Taliaferro's theory by introducing a new level of reasoning at which ethical reasons can be understood in terms of a regulating ideal. Impartiality accepted as a regulative ideal would not force a complete rejection of Taliaferro's use of impartiality. But impartiality would have to be treated as an ethical, however unachievable, ideal (or *telos*), limiting what is achievable by women and men. The positive outcome of this modification is rendering it unnecessary to force a choice between either strictly secular justification (which is thought to be impartial) or religious dogma (thought to be partial) to support religious belief as a legitimate reason for an action: for example, against abortion (cf. Nagel, 1987, pp.227–37).

---

10   Kant could be read as maintaining both impartiality as disinterestedness in ethics and autonomous thought as compatible with taking the standpoint of everyone else; cf. Kant (1997; 2000, paras 40–41).

It is important for parties in an ethical dispute to be able to give reasons, including religious beliefs, which guide action and expect them *to be understood* to some degree by persons who do not accept the belief.[11] The issue is, then, what to do about the ethical disagreement over these reasons (Moore, 2003b, pp.2–3, 15–17, 174–5). Here the introduction of a distinction between an individual level of ethical reflection and a collective level of ethical reasoning offers a limited sort of solution to irresolvable differences. It allows the parties in the ethical dispute both to maintain the *partiality* of points of view of an individual agent and to advocate reasoning at a collective stage of corporate decision making. Accepting the role of the latter as 'dialogical equilibrium' enables discussion of the conflicting reasons for action which generate the disputes over abortion.

Suppose two young women, Alison and Carol, disagree on the morality of abortion. Alison thinks that there is no reason to treat the foetus as morally viable. The foetus does not have enough of the properties which moral beings possess. Carol thinks that a human life has value in itself and so the foetus as a life, or a potential life, has moral worth at whatever stage it is in its development. So each of Alison and Carol has, from her own point of view, reason to think that her position on abortion is right. This means that not only has each woman reflected upon her beliefs, worked out her position clearly and found reason for her action or inaction, but she can equally understand the cogency of the other's position.

Each agent has a cogent, but partial position. Although each agent has reason to think that her position is right, she is equally aware of her own limitations. Each of the women knows that she could be wrong. Nevertheless their carefully thought-out positions are rational and potentially insightful. To incorporate the ethical insights and valuable aspects of each position would be to attempt a constructive discourse that generates new knowledge and points of possible agreement. Yet notice that this is not to advocate Taliaferro's ideal observer view: it is not an impartial or omniscient perspective on ethical action. It is not even a comprehensive view from everywhere. Yet the goal of collective discourse is rational in the sense of being open to new insight and able to adapt one's personal position. Such discourse aims to achieve an equilibrium with others, and so an acceptable ethical conclusion, insofar as ethical, collective discourse accepts the possibility of relevant insights from each person involved in the discussion, or decision making. Now it is my contention that here partiality feeds into a higher level of collective discourse which, nevertheless, aims at the best possible degree of impartiality.

On this level of collective discourse, aimed at (partial) impartiality, Alison and

---

11 We can recognize certain action-guiding concepts that enable us to give reason(s) for what we do. It is also possible to keep open a discussion about which concepts should guide action. To confront ethical disagreements we can attempt to give reasons for an action; these are reasons understood by others, including the religious beliefs which shape a person's ethical view, such as the sanctity of life. Moore describes the reasons, which support those action-guiding concepts, as *normative*, *general*, and they may be *defeasible* (Moore, 2003b, pp.xv, 5–6, 43–57).

Carol would seek to reach a conclusion which both would agree incorporates better than any other outcome what each regards as ethically significant. So Alison would hold on to her idea of the moral worth of a human life, and accept that, at a certain point in its development, the new life is recognized by its potential for moral responsibility and its compelling need for protection and care-knowing.[12] Carol is content that the value of human life is preserved, even though she is forced to concede that, at an early stage in the development of human life, the 'life' is not yet morally viable.

Consider what has been achieved in this initial sketch of collective ethical discourse, in seeking agreement, which is not to be confused with ethical compromise. Call the aim, 'reflective equilibrium' and then this version of the abortion example can be fleshed out more fully. If we allow Carol her background beliefs, including her religious belief in the sanctity of human life, then we can allow Alison also her own background beliefs as well. Alison's beliefs, unlike Carol's, are secular and feminist, and yet these latter are no less compelling and insightful for the development of their collective ethical discourse. The aim is not to create a complete picture of the positions of Alison and Carol. Instead it is to suggest a process of dialogue between ethical agents whose views are necessarily partial, but no less rational or morally significant. This level of discourse is significant, enabling collective ethical discussion from which we construct a *more impartial* (or less partial) form of reasoning.

The debate about adultery can be developed in a similar manner to that of abortion, with a focus on action-guiding concepts (say, a religious concept such as chastity which, in Bernard Williams, could be a 'thick ethical concept'[13]). The overriding factor in this example for a feminist is the power relation(s) between the husband and the wife. The husband traditionally has the greater power in the marital relationship, yet the man and the woman must each work out a cogent case for their view of adultery. The man believes adultery is simply wrong; no matter how well its causes and nature are understood, it is breaking a covenant with God, and between husband and wife. At the same time, it is understandable that the wife finds the very institution of marriage problematic. The traditional conception of marriage is based upon a relationship in which one party is always treated as superior since more powerful, informed or articulated when it comes to success in the world beyond the home. The wife does not have the power, or rational authority, of the husband. Her cogent case for adultery (in this case) enables her to break with an oppressive situation in which she lacked rational authority. This action has value as a step towards 'principled autonomy', which is expressed in action whose maxims or laws could be adopted by all others (O'Neill, 2000, pp.150–56; 2002, pp.83–95).

---

12   On the cognitive value of caring, and care-knowing as an intellectual virtue, see Anderson (2004a, pp. 87–8, 92–4).

13   Bernard Williams's 'thick ethical concepts' will be defined and critically discussed in a later section of this chapter; see note 18, below.

Admittedly adultery breaks a legal (and religious) commitment, which cannot be legally or ethically right. Nevertheless this wrong act still tells us something about the immorality of a marital life which is oppressive and undermining of a woman's autonomous use of reason in public life.

By contrast to my proposal to distinguish between personal reflection and collective reasoning, God as the model or the omni-natured exemplar for the ideal observer runs us into the danger of false idealization. This danger is decisive for me as a feminist and moral philosopher. I object to the centrality given by Taliaferro to an ideal agent who acts as the exemplar for individual human agents. This inevitably leads to a false idealization of human agency.[14] Insofar as no human agent can either achieve ideal agency or be an ideal observer, it is dangerous to give the ideal subject unwarranted authority on ethical matters. Further dangers rest in both assuming that he or she determines and achieves the ideal and failing to distinguish between the necessary partiality of an individual perspective and the possible impartiality of a collective discourse constructed by rational agents. Moral and political philosophers have strongly objected to the exclusion of difference, which inevitably results from advocating judgment as, or from the point of view of, an ideal person (ibid., pp.144–67; cf. Benhabib, 1992; Young, 1997). This ideal is necessarily exclusive (and dangerously so) insofar as it gives certain individuals authority (on the basis of contingent differences) over others which can be both pernicious and oppressive.

The God's Eye Point of View: Towards an Alternative

In this section I intend to focus critically upon the objections which Taliaferro himself raises concerning the God's eye point of view, and his responses. The constructive side of my feminist critique here aims to demonstrate the way(s) in which Taliaferro is a feminist-friendly philosopher.[15]

The first objection is that there are no facts, but only points of view. Essentially Taliaferro's reply is to claim that the denial of facts is self-refuting. Undoubtedly the denial of all empirical facts about the world is self-defeating. However both this first objection and this reply should be more precise. From the outset of this chapter, it has not been possible to work out clearly what Taliaferro intends to cover by his use

---

14 For more discussion of the dangers of (false) idealizations, see O'Neill (2000, pp.68–80). O'Neill not only defends Kant's own work against the charge of false idealizations, but she looks at the development of John Rawls's work, tracing how he attempts to purge his own thinking of false idealizations – both in his response to critics and in his anticipation of criticisms concerning his own use of ideal persons or agents. O'Neill also looks at the ways in which idealizations in theories of justice have excluded women, especially poor women from poor countries, whom she identifies as 'impoverished providers' (Ibid., pp.144–67).

15 Taliaferro himself aspires to be a feminist philosopher; elsewhere I have suggested the possibility that men can become feminist insofar as they take up a 'feminist standpoint' (Anderson, 2001).

of facts. A precise answer to this question would help to clarify not only the earlier queries about moral facts, non-natural, social or personal facts, but a decisive question for the Ideal Observer theory: can an ideal observer represent the world from no point of view?[16] The facts important for Taliaferro's ethical reflection are less stable than empirical facts in the sense that they need to be read in the context of varying epistemic practices. These practices include the recognition of ethical knowledge (that is, knowledge grounded in the use of 'thick ethical concepts', which will be introduced under discussion of the fourth objection below) and the social or personal knowledge gained from taking account of the affective dimension of other people's lives.[17] As already seen, reading the facts of a matter in an ethical debate about abortion or adultery involves learning to recognize when a particular interpretation of an action is simply different from one's own experience and when it is perverse (that is, incompatible with norms of goodness). The assessment of hermeneutic practices opens up a range of feminist concerns about epistemic injustice (Fricker, 2002, pp.84–93). Whose interpretation or testimony do we trust? Whose is perverse? And who has the rational authority to give trustworthy interpretations?

The second objection claims that the ideal observer is occupying a view from nowhere, and is ahistorical and impersonal. Taliaferro's reply is categorical. His Ideal Observer theory is not about a view from nowhere, but 'a comprehensive view from everywhere'. Yet achieving the latter is doubtful and it may become an attempt to achieve the former. Bernard Williams's perspectival view of ethical disagreement and the necessary role of partiality in ethics would enable ethics, especially feminist ethics, better than the comprehensive view from everywhere, even if the latter claims to account for 'personal, specific circumstances'. When Taliaferro advocates ethical reflection involving an affective component, taking seriously local temperaments and personal observations, he moves closer to Williams and other feminist friendly philosophers. However, once again, Taliaferro seems unaware that his emphasis on local and personal needs has to be reconciled with his insistence on impartiality. To avoid contradiction between the impartial and the partial, I have proposed a distinction between the discourses of reason-seeking impartiality and of partial ethical reflection; the latter, of course, is also meant to involve reason in shaping a cogent case. Without such a distinction, Taliaferro's reply to this second objection is incomplete.

The third objection is to the detachment and disinterestedness which typically characterize the ideal agent. Taliaferro's reply is to insist upon having both impartiality and passionate approval, not detachment or disinterestedness. His reply here is feminist-friendly insofar as he acknowledges partiality. Yet, as discussed in the

---

16   For a thorough discussion of this question, see Moore (1997).
17   For further reflection upon this claim, it is helpful to gain some background; see Williams (1985, pp.132–55) and Fricker (2002, pp.86–9). But, for the larger picture on this, see Moore (1997; 2003a, pp.337–54).

previous sections, how can Taliaferro have it both ways? My proposed modification of Taliaferro's position concerning (im)partiality aims to offer a cogent alternative.

The fourth objection is that impartiality cannot be attained. Taliaferro remains completely confident that impartiality is easily achievable in a wide range of ethical cases, and he gives various examples. Yet I maintain that he mistakes local agreement for impartiality. His examples of abortion, war crime tribunals and refugee settlement each suggest that ethical agreement is achievable within a highly specific location and with certain ethical cases. Williams's account of a 'hypertraditional society' is helpful here. This is a society where right and wrong behaviour, including the proper use of such 'thick' ethical concepts such as brave, coward or lie is fairly uncontentious (Williams, 1985, pp.128–30, 142–5). Thick describes those ethical concepts which supply both prescriptive and descriptive reasons for action. Williams calls thick concepts 'world-guided', meaning that their descriptive component is rooted in the agent's 'world' or social location. These concepts are so embedded that right behaviour could seem to be impartial to the degree that everyone in society agrees on the sort of action that is, say, cowardly. In other words, Williams coined the phrase 'thick ethical concepts', for those terms with a rich and determinate empirical content.[18] Claims which employ thick ethical concepts have fairly straightforward truth conditions and can be the object of ethical knowledge (Williams, 2002, pp.305–6, n.21). However the problem is that different societies (or different individuals) do not have the same thick ethical concepts, and so would not agree on their employment of them. Yet, for us, a relevant implication of Williams's thick ethical concepts is undermining a sharp fact/value distinction; when it comes to ethical agreement, societies and individuals with the same thick ethical concepts can agree, and even agree on value-laden facts, for example 'social' facts.

The right behaviour in the hypertraditional society would be bound up with thick ethical concepts, ethical agreement and the ethical knowledge built upon these concepts and this agreement. Ethical behaviour in such a context *could seem to be* impartial to the degree that everyone agrees on the sort of action which is, say, cowardly. Similarly we might find ethical agreement in a particular suburban, white, middle-class community where everyone agrees that abortion under the right conditions is acceptable. Yet this agreement would hold mainly for women in a certain location, such as in a highly specific context where women are secular, affluent, autonomous and so on. In fact, this context-relative quality renders thick ethical concepts such as sanctity of life highly perspectival. So thick ethical concepts allow us to talk confidently about right and wrong ways of acting, which are deeply rooted in particular locations of ethical discourse.

In contrast, thin ethical concepts transcend social location but render a substantive agreement on the meaning of the concept impossible (Williams, 1985, pp.128–9, 133, 136–45; cf. Moore, 2003a). The thin ethical concept lacks the 'world-

---

18   On thick ethical concepts, see Williams (1985, ch. 8; 2002, p.305n21) and Moore (2003a, pp.338ff).

guidedness' characteristic of thick ethical concepts, making it difficult to say when the former are employed correctly. Thick ethical concepts, on the one hand, make ethical agreement possible, but note that this is not because they are impartial or universal; Williams himself describes them as both world-guided and action-guiding. On the other hand, thin ethical concepts do not have enough determinate empirical content to be action-guiding, world-guided or constitutive of ethical knowledge; it would be impossible to work out ethical agreement between individuals or societies if the ethical concepts are thin and so lacking truth conditions. When it comes to Taliaferro, it is likely that he only sees thick ethical concepts, in that his ethical concepts are both world-guided and action-guiding. Yet, if this is so, his ethical discourse is not only strictly local, but he is unaware of the locatedness of his world (which, I have suggested, may be similar to what Williams calls hypertraditional society).

The fifth objection rejects the idea that we can or should shed one's point of view. Taliaferro's reply, in defence of shedding one's point of view, appeals to the history of philosophy, or the ethical theory shaping this history. Yet this appeal would not be persuasive to the feminist philosopher who rejects this very history as biased. Western philosophers have generally failed to be aware, let alone take the point of view, of another who is distinctively different from those agents represented by their own tradition. Moreover the very idea of shedding one's point of view has been a highly contentious issue for feminist debate. Feminist and other political philosophers have written, published and republished their responses to the question whether it is possible to take the standpoint of another without excluding differences (Arendt, 1968; 2001; Lugones and Spelman, 1983; Benhabib, 1992; Seller, 1994; Young, 1997). As regards a feminist philosophy of religion, I contend that we need to listen more carefully when seeking to think from the standpoint of another. However this is not a simple or straightforward task; for a feminist, at least, it would necessarily involve struggle[19] – and, I suggest, a reflexive critical openness (Anderson, 2001, 2004a; Fricker, 2002). Taliaferro is obviously feminist friendly in raising this objection and seeking a reply which encourages thinking from the point of view of someone different. Nevertheless he still needs to push his account much further, in order to take on board the difficulties raised by the multiple differences of agents according to race, class, gender, sexual orientation, ethnicity and material and social conditions.

The final objection raised and addressed by Taliaferro is the insufficiencies of the Ideal Observer theory. His reply admits that the insufficiencies are in the criteria for distinguishing and choosing between two different ethical positions, for example between Kant and Mill. But we have already seen the inadequacies of Taliaferro's Ideal Observer as an ideal agent. His Ideal Observer theory is inadequate for reaching agreement between any human agent on all ethical issues. Taliaferro's own

---

19   For an insightful discussion of women's struggle for truth, to which I am gratefully indebted, see Harris (2001).

reply is indirect, appealing to concrete examples to defend his theory against this final objection. His reply focuses on the debate upon specific ethical problems in particular historical settings. Unfortunately his examples do not demonstrate that the three elements of appeal to relevant facts, impartiality and feeling what it is like to be a victim, to suffer or to be a bystander, manage to reach ethical agreement. The insufficiencies of the Ideal Observer are not overcome by appeal to the concrete, the specific or particular in a hypothetical case. The problem is not abstraction, but inadequate ethical reasoning about lived experiences. This ethical reasoning excludes the significant role of partiality, on the one hand, and the role of collective discourse in ethical discussion of one's (partial) perspectives, on the other hand. Hypothetical cases, imagining the ideal observer point of view, are simply not sufficient for feminist philosophers who seek to change, not merely the imagined or the ideal, but the lived experiences of real women and men.

In the end, Taliaferro does not have an adequate defence of his Ideal Observer theory for either modern moral philosophy or feminist philosophy of religion. His most recent account of the Ideal Observer remains more or less the same as that given in his *Contemporary Philosophy of Religion* (1997). However the objections which he raises and to which he responds suggest that what he advocates under the heading of 'Ideal Observer' theory might become attractive to feminist philosophers of religion (at least in part) under a different heading and with further qualifications. Yet this attractiveness would depend upon giving up the ideal observer–agent as a false idealization.

Taliaferro appropriates Nicholas of Cusa's 'loving glance' as the sensible embrace enabling a shared and enriching exchange. This appropriation implies that Taliaferro seeks (new) ethical insight for both religious and non-religious philosophers. It could also offer an alternative to the God's eye point of view, yet I propose a slight alteration; that is, 'all loving, *yet discerning* embrace'. This alternative proposal replaces the ideal observer–agent as the guiding idea for ethical discourse. If introduced into Taliaferro's theory, this alternative image has the potential to guide the reshaping of its central elements without giving them up completely. Admittedly this would still assume an ideal in the sense of an 'ideal' discourse situation aimed at discernment of one's and another's action-guiding concepts. However this ideal is regulative, blocking any individual from being objectified as the ideal observer–agent. Once again, 'regulative' is understood as limiting the claims made by, in this context, any individual's 'loving glance'. The aim of the ideal discourse situation would be less limited knowledge created by our discussion with other agents in the best possible context. The ideal discourse situation limits the individual's claims by uniting agents in reasoning together about ethical decisions. And this is the union imagined as a loving embrace.

Taliaferro himself does not advocate replacing the Ideal Observer with the loving embrace, yet this reconstruction is a reasonable response to criticisms of the Ideal Observer theory and of the God's eye view. Feminist philosophers have criticized the theory for relying on an 'ideal' knower or agent, its idealization and projection

(Soskice, 1992; Anderson, 2004a), on an 'observer' implying sight and partial points of view, thus, separation and domination excluding other (non-spatial) senses or sources of knowledge (Keller and Grontkowski, 1983, pp.215–19) and on the visual and spatial imagery of a God's eye point of view (La Caze, 2002, pp.119–45). These criticisms suggest that the theory objectifies and fixes its object as a virtually atemporal position, since seen from an ahistorical point of view. Taliaferro himself recognizes these dangers and so tries to dissociate his theory from positions such as Jean-Paul Sartre's view of the other as objectifying, or from Thomas Nagel's view from nowhere (Nagel, 1986). As has been demonstrated in this chapter, the central elements of Taliaferro's theory – facts, impartiality and 'putting oneself into another person's shoes' or taking the standpoint of every other person involved – raise objections to which Taliaferro responds.

I maintain that his response is attractive insofar as it gives content to his divine ethic in terms of love and attention (Taliaferro, 1997, p.208; cf. Soskice, 1992), giving an affective dimension and a certain value to the other. Yet, in a more general sense, feminist philosophers would object to a male-neutral appeal to facts, to impartiality and to feeling as if the male-neutral agent or observer can genuinely understand the other person. 'Male-neutral' describes a philosophical concept or account which is male, but remains under the pretence of sex/gender neutrality (Anderson, 1998, pp.13, 148).

Clearly my own position would not want to do away with marriage or advocate adultery, yet I recognize the need to assess critically the nature of the marital relationship as it has begun to evolve for women and men. At least a less oppressive, less patriarchal institution is morally significant as a goal. This includes subverting the idea that male power in marriage should be greater than female power. The parties in a collective discussion of this example might accept the feminist insight that the (im)morality of marriage is a critical issue. In other words, ethical discourse needs to address gender relations. Admittedly not every woman, or even every feminist philosopher, will agree upon the precise moral status of adultery. The obvious dangers in undermining a (legally) binding commitment, but also the very notion of marriage, are not made light of. Yet at the level of collective ethical discourse the parties to the discussion seek, not the point of view of the Ideal Observer, but an equilibrium, giving in at points where each party can accommodate the ethical insight of the other(s). Masculinists, as well as feminists, require such accommodation in order to get on. The definite challenge is distinguishing between something which is different and something which is morally perverse.

Conclusion: a Constructive Feminist Standpoint[20]

Instead of placing the emphasis upon an Ideal Observer as the model for individual

---

20 For a more technical discussion of a feminist standpoint, see Anderson (2001).

agency, I have advocated a conception of rationality that binds individuals together in constructive ethical decision making. This conception is not incompatible with certain aspects of Taliaferro's own divine ethic. I have endeavoured to stress the role of reason in our collective discourse in ethics. Although ethical disagreements are inevitable, the possibility that they can be overcome depends upon accepting a non-ideal agent as the starting point for meta-level discussions between individuals, about their own limited perspectives and their partial judgments. This stage of discourse can be guided by the rational and cogent positions already achieved by each party to the discussion; this assumes that each party has worked out a view, which is as cogent as possible for each, about her or his particular ethical position or action.

Recall the disagreement between the two women on the issue of abortion. Both women are able to develop a cogent view, which they attempt to work out rationally; that is, consistently, coherently and reliably. Each can understand the other's position as rational. However the two women continue to disagree on whether abortion is right. So ethical disagreement does not end once each party knows all the relevant facts, or when each party has attempted to be impartial in their understanding of the other's position, at least as far as this is possible. Ethical disagreement persists even when each party has attempted to grasp the affective dimension of the other's life. But this need not be the end of the story. Instead I see this as the beginning of a constructivist ethical discourse which builds upon the twofold fact that cogent views of ethical positions can be achieved by each person and that these views can be gradually understood through a continuing dialogue or discourse with another person, whether the persons are intimately related or not. On this basis, an equilibrium between different agents, whether intimately known to each other or not, can be rationally constructed.[21]

The attraction of this position for a feminist philosopher is the condition of collective discourse, enabling women as well as men to collaborate in listening and working out the most acceptable outcome for all parties at the stage of collective ethical discourse. Implicit here is the fundamental value of the integrity of each party to the ethical discourse. Moreover, principled autonomy is necessary to ensure that the ethical conclusion is one that all *could* accept and follow (O'Neill, 2002, pp.83–95). I admit that much more work needs to be done to defend this picture of collective ethical discourse. However, here, I can only end by incorporating Taliaferro's insight with my own collective ideal: the divine image of persons corporately and honestly united in a loving and discerning embrace.

---

21   For the intellectual virtues enhancing a feminist collaborative project, see Anderson (2004a).

Does Analytical Philosophy Clip our Wings? Reformed Epistemology as a Test Case

Harriet A. Harris

Where is our Philosophical Ambition?

In teaching philosophy of religion, I am interested in how far students' expectations of the subject are met. In interviewing students about this, I have learned that many choose to study philosophy of religion because they are interested in 'spiritual' matters, in a nebulous sense, which they articulate in such ways as 'I thought it would be about people' and 'the wider picture', or 'about things that matter' (Harris, 2002). I interpret this as a legitimate, if often rather unformed, expectation that philosophy of religion would speak to our deepest questions about life in ways that might help us to integrate our experiences, attitudes and beliefs and so grow in wisdom and understanding. One might hope that philosophy of religion would advance wisdom for living, and yet many of its practitioners would regard this aim as too lofty and beyond their remit. Philosophers of religion more typically aim at clarifying which beliefs it is rational to hold (though linguistic philosophers have more humble aims: to describe how language functions), which then leads to a focus on criteria for justification and on the desirability or otherwise of operating with a justification-based philosophy. Testing the rationality of beliefs (most commonly, beliefs involved in arguing for or against the existence of God and the coherence of theism) involves breaking arguments down into propositions, clarifying the use of terms within each proposition, and examining the logical steps from one proposition to another. Belief claims are analysed quite separately from the context and shapes of our lives, and the patterns, disciplines, rituals and experiences of faith. Philosophers of religion disagree over whether this separation is a help or a hindrance to effective execution of their work.

Linda Zagzebski, a pioneer in the burgeoning field of virtue epistemology, holds that contemporary philosophy neglects the kind of integrating work that fosters understanding and wisdom. She attributes this neglect to a number of factors including the predominant practice of isolating single beliefs for analysis, and lack of attention to the social aspects of cognitive activity (Zagzebski, 1996, pp.43–51). Writing from a different stable, but sharing some of the same frustrations as Zagzebski, Robert Solomon makes some observations about contemporary university philosophy departments. He is writing principally about the United States, but his observations would apply in other parts of the English-speaking world. Solomon aims to fashion philosophy as a passionate way of life and as a discipline concerned with emotions (for example, Solomon, 1977, 1995, 1999, 2004; Solomon and Higgins, 1997), but he notes that undergraduate prospectuses no longer describe philosophy 'as "thinking about life" or "self-examination", much less the joy of ideas' (Solomon, 1999, p.7). Rather philosophy has been narrowed down to a set of conceptual skills and an 'all but exclusive preference for argument and logical analysis', with a corresponding resistance to talking about experience and especially about feelings and the concrete details of life' (ibid., pp.3, 9). Kimura and Insole in their contributions to this volume express similar concerns, while trying to avoid caricature, that philosophy of religion can tend to become narrow, disengaged and overly technical, irresponsibly theoretical and even petty. These qualms are in large part about the effect of types of philosophical analysis upon philosophy.

I would like to suggest that the narrow focus and rigour promoted by analytical philosophy reduces the ambition of philosophers of religion. It clips our wings by restricting itself to what Basil Mitchell in this volume calls 'minute philosophy', philosophy that stays with those topics that can be treated with exemplary clarity and rigour. Arguably we come to greater understanding not only by developing and practising analytical skills but by cultivating a wide range of virtues, including attentiveness, perseverance, integrity, humility and patience. While such virtues are pertinent to the careful work of analysis, they also take us far beyond it: to careful and patient attentiveness to persons and situations; to integrity and humility in seeking to reflect the complexity and depths of suffering when considering the problem of pain, for example. It is worth looking for ways to articulate this in an academic context. Virtue epistemologists are exploring how the development of intellectual, moral and spiritual virtues (these categories blend into each other) bears on the development of understanding (Sosa, 1991; Zagzebski, 1996; Wood, 1998; Fairweather and Zagzebski, 2001). Would it not be appropriate for philosophers of religion to seek to develop a religious epistemology along these lines, as a few are already trying to do (Soskice, 1992; Wood, 1998; McGhee, 2000; Wynn, 2002, 2003; Anderson, 2004a, 2004b; Harris, 2001, 2004; Hollywood, 2004, cf. Charry, 1997, who comes at the same matter more theologically)? Could there even be room within mainstream philosophy of religion to acknowledge that spiritual disciplines such as forms of contemplation can be significant in developing one's understanding of matters at the heart of philosophy of religion's concerns (cf. Coakley, 1992, 2002; McGhee, 1992, 2000; Wood, 1998, pp.190–93)? One philosopher whom I discuss later on in the chapter does suggest that contemplatives have a particular quality to their perception, but he does not develop this thought in terms of what we might learn from contemplatives in order to become more effective in our perception and understanding. Philosophy of religion is a relatively modern discipline (see Ann Loades's contribution to this volume). Its relation to the classical 'faith seeking understanding' tradition of Christian thinkers has been complicated by a felt need to make it a respectable discipline in the philosophical climate of the mid-twentieth century. As a result, little space is made for the suggestion that the development of virtues or spiritual disciplines might privilege an agent.

Modern western thought and culture is thought to be very confident about autonomous rationality,[1] which lends an irony to the seeming lack of ambition in analytical philosophy. In a recent introductory textbook in philosophy, Robert Solomon describes the central demand of modern western philosophy as 'the autonomy of the individual person'; a demand, he says, which 'means that each of us must be credited with the ability to ascertain what is true and what is right, through our own thinking and experience, without just depending upon outside authority' (Solomon, 1997, p.15). A frequent feature of this model of philosophy is the notion that we each have a duty as individuals to check the rationality of our beliefs, particularly in such important matters as religion where one might be vulnerable to peer pressure, the weight of tradition or charismatic figures leading one astray. In Solomon's words, when it comes to matters of religion, 'whether you believe in God must be decided by you, by appeal to your own reason and arguments that you can formulate and examine by yourself' (ibid.). This is part of the legacy of Locke, who insisted that all *doxa* or opinion must be regulated to eradicate falsehood, and that to believe on the basis of tradition marks a failure to conduct our understanding aright (Wolterstorff, 1996a, pp.225–6). Locke argued: 'We should not judge of things by men's opinions, but of opinions by things' (1901, sect. 24); evidence must be collected for a proposition, and the proposition should be believed with only that firmness proportioned to what reason tells us is the probability of the proposition on that evidence. He applied this principle to religious faith as to other forms of believing: '*Faith* is nothing but a firm Assent of the Mind: which if it be regulated, as is our Duty, cannot be afforded to any thing, but upon good Reason' (Locke, 1975, IV, xvii, 24).

Anglo-American philosophers of religion have for the most part conformed to the model of philosophy that Solomon describes and Locke helped to establish (Wiles, 1987; Wolterstorff, 1996a; cf. Plantinga, 2000, ch.3; Anderson, 1998, pp.33–5). Editors of a representative collection of essays on religious epistemology propose that 'it is our *duty* as rational human beings to confront the God question', by which they mean the question of 'whether or not it is rational to believe in the existence of God', because the answer to this question carries 'enormous implications ... for human existence' (Geivett and Sweetman, 1992, p.3). How can dutiful investigation of such an important matter, conducted without the option of falling back on tradition, nonetheless seem lacking in ambition?

The lack of ambition relates to the narrowness and technicality of approach. Philosophers of religion have focused overwhelmingly on the rationality of belief in God, attending painstakingly to the logical construction of our arguments for God's

---

1   Often based on a misreading of Kant's notion of autonomy. See O'Neill (2002), Anderson (2003, pp.149–64; 2004a, pp.97–102).

existence or non-existence, and the way that language functions within such arguments. They have even come to regard the rationality of belief in God as, in Geivett and Sweetman's own words, 'one of the most important of all human concerns' (ibid.), even though most people do not come to believe in God on the basis of arguments or evidence. The contentious feminist philosopher of religion Grace Jantzen mocks Geivett and Sweetman for their sense of human priorities, pointing out that the majority of people have to contend with far more pressing matters than how rational philosophers' arguments are for the existence of God (Jantzen, 1998, p.79). Preoccupation with justifying beliefs, she holds, not only distorts the activity of religious believing, but fails to comprehend that practical and moral struggles necessarily take precedence for most people. She maintains that religion has gone adrift when people put epistemology and ontology before ethics (ibid., p.257, for example). This extreme contrast of approach between Jantzen and Geivett and Sweetman arises perhaps because philosophers of religion for much of the twentieth century were not aiming to represent the concerns of most people so much as to legitimate their discipline to other philosophers (Anderson, 1998, pp.13–18).

Whether or not one agrees with Jantzen, her critique reflects the problems alluded to at the start of this chapter: the perception that philosophy has become detached from our lived concerns. Jantzen is attempting to address the problem by focusing on the practical, but in doing so she is reinforcing the dichotomy that has opened up between theory and practice. She criticizes philosophers who think that we need to get our beliefs right before we decide how to act. Geivett and Sweetman are typical of philosophers of religion who assume that having right belief must come before embarking on religious practice or following certain moral paths (Geivett and Sweetman, 1992, p.3; cf. Swinburne in this volume). This masks the extent to which our beliefs are shaped by our practices. But Jantzen's solution is to recover our practical concerns, rather than to develop a philosophy that recognizes the constant interplay between how we live and how we think. We may not agree with Jantzen that philosophy of religion should prioritize the practical over its interest in truth and justified belief. Instead we might hope that religions, in the various ways in which they promote discipleship, make our transformation their priority, and at the same time that philosophy serves religions by attending to their truth-claims and beliefs (Harris, 2000b; Anderson, 2001, pp.193, 211, n.50). Then we might look to develop the epistemological task in ways that take moral and spiritual development into account (Harris, 2001, 2004). Nevertheless Jantzen's critique has emerged out of a context in which philosophy of religion has seemingly become alienated from the matter of how we live and how we gain wisdom in such a way that a philosopher as able as Jantzen has lost the will even to try to engage with and reintegrate it in its dominant forms.

So there is a cluster of concerns emanating from diverse quarters, about modern western philosophy and analytical philosophy in particular. One set of frustrations is with a process of isolating beliefs and breaking them down for analysis in such a way that we lose sight of how the beliefs we form relate to our practices, values, concerns and experiences; in short, how they are integrated with the rest of our lives. Another is with an assumption that it is our epistemic duty to scrutinize all beliefs that come our way, combined with a failure to reflect within epistemology the ways that beliefs are affected by the lives we lead, and that religious beliefs are shaped by religious practices. It has become difficult to bring our beliefs, practices, attitudes and experiences back together, or to see their integration as part of our philosophical concern. This has led to dissatisfaction with the narrow agenda that analytical philosophers have set themselves, and to disaffection with the philosophy of religion amongst students who had hoped to be engaged in a discipline that would help them to grow in understanding or gain wisdom for living.

Introducing Reformed Epistemology

However, there is a prominent school within Anglo-American philosophy of religion that is critical of many aspects of the legacy of analytical philosophy while nonetheless remaining within that tradition. I am thinking of Reformed epistemology, which is strong in America and also influential in Britain.

The leading Reformed epistemologists are Alvin Plantinga and Nicholas Wolterstorff. They challenge what they regard as dominant assumptions about epistemic duty deriving from the philosophy of Locke (Wolterstorff, 1996a; Plantinga, 2000, ch.3). From the 1980s onwards they have become increasingly interested in the processes of belief formation, the situatedness of our believing and the role of communities in moulding rational agents. They show varying degrees of interest in the social and psychological factors affecting knowers. Hence they go some way towards attending to what Insole calls the 'lived dimension of faith'.

Much philosophy of religion focuses on the question of whether there is evidence for or against belief in God. Plantinga and Wolterstorff develop a religious epistemology that is not (or not strongly) evidentialist. They hold that most theists do not base their faith on evidence, or at least do not arrive at faith by assessing evidence. Instead, says Plantinga, the route to faith is something like this: 'We read Scripture, or something presenting scriptural teaching, or hear the gospel preached, or are told of it by parents, or encounter a scriptural teaching as the conclusion of an argument (or conceivably even as an object of ridicule), or in some other way encounter a proclamation of the Word. What is said simply seems right; it seems compelling' (Plantinga, 2000, p.250). Plantinga betrays his Protestant bias by conceiving this as happening only in relation to hearing the Word (which he in turn conceives primarily in terms of receiving words) or being taught certain beliefs within a religious community. He has not considered the development of faith in relation to habitual religious practice. His interest in the role that communities play in shaping the beliefs of their members extends only to testimony, and not to practices that instil belief. Nevertheless his contention that in 'the typical case ...

Christian belief is *immediate*' and 'doesn't proceed by way of an argument' (ibid., p.259) would seem to be right (however important argument may subsequently become for many people in the ways that they examine or develop their faith). Therefore he and his fellow Reformed epistemologists reject the notion that theists are duty-bound to check whether they have sufficient evidence to be rationally justified in believing in God.

Defending the Epistemic Rights of Theists

Plantinga and Wolterstorff have a specific agenda: to uphold the right of theists to believe in God even when they do not know how to defend the rationality of that belief. It is tempting to view their work, especially Plantinga's, as falling into two phases: an early phase defending belief in God as properly basic, and a later phase developing the notion of warrant. But Plantinga sees it as a unified project governed by the question 'whether Christian belief can get warrant, not by argument but by virtue of (broadly construed) religious experience' (Plantinga 2000, p.136). He has been developing a line of argument, since his early publication of *God and Other Minds* (1967), that belief in God resembles some other beliefs that we commonly form, such as that minds other than my own exist, or that I have indeed just done what my memory tells me I have just done, in that it can be warranted without our needing to understand how. An initial objection might be that belief in other minds and in the trustworthiness of one's senses are beliefs that almost everyone forms, whereas belief in God is not. He holds that belief in God is in fact the product of a natural belief-forming mechanism, albeit one that is not universally acknowledged (Plantinga, 2000, p.245). His and Wolterstorff's view, which they attribute to Calvin, is that belief in God is warranted because produced by a natural disposition, the *sensus divinitatis*, endowed by our creator.[2] This disposition functions improperly wherever belief in God is resisted. They also draw on Calvin's theology to explain why the disposition is resisted, that is, because of the noetic effects of sin. They hold that a disposition to believe in God can be nurtured, which is why they become interested in the role of communities in shaping people's beliefs, and in the situated nature of rationality.

To see how they come to defend the theist's epistemic rights we need to look at their rejection of certain kinds of foundationalism and their theory of warrant.

Challenges to Classical Foundationalism

Plantinga has famously attacked what he calls 'classical foundationalism' (Plantinga, 1983). Classical foundationalism is a particular model for the way we

---

2   Stated most fully in Plantinga (2000, Pt III), but found in most of their writings. Calvin scholars have questioned their reading of Calvin. Calvin advances a stronger argument that the sparks sown in us by God are smothered, corrupted or extinguished, which would suggest that they cannot be likened to other belief dispositions as able to yield immediate belief (Beversluis, 1995).

should organize our beliefs in order to ensure the maximum possible level of justification. It proposes that we build our system of beliefs upon foundations that are, to use Plantinga's phrase, 'properly basic'. Plantinga identifies classical foundationalism amongst ancient, medieval and modern philosophers. Broadly speaking, he says, ancient and medieval foundationalists held that

> a proposition is properly basic for a person only if it is either self-evident [for example 2+2=4] or evident to the senses [for example, 'I see a desk']; and modern foundationalists, such as Descartes and Locke, hold that 'a proposition is properly basic for S only if either self-evident or incorrigible [for example, 'I seem to see a desk'] for S'. (Ibid., pp.58–9)

He and Wolterstorff argue that this account of proper basicality is too narrow, and omits certain types of belief that we accept immediately, such as beliefs furnished by our memory.

In developing their epistemology, Plantinga and Wolterstorff draw on the Common Sense philosophy of Thomas Reid, the Scottish enlightenment philosopher who, in response to David Hume's scepticism, defended a range of beliefs as immediate and irresistible. Reid held that within our constitution there are principles of common sense that are discovered by self-reflection and which yield immediate, irresistible and unanalysable conviction, such as that the objects of our perception are real, and that events we remember were real in the past. All human beings form beliefs immediately on the basis of their senses, memory, consciousness and the testimony of others. Most of these beliefs cannot be justified by reason, but Reid and the Reformed epistemologists agree that we do not therefore have to be sceptical about them. 'No man seeks a reason for believing what he sees or feels,' Reid wrote, 'and, if he did, it would be difficult to find one', but if 'Nature gives us information of things that concern us, by other means than by reasoning, reason itself will direct us to receive that information with thankfulness' (Reid, 1863, p.328).

Unlike Reid, Plantinga and Wolterstorff hold that belief in God is properly basic. By that they mean that belief in God may be immediate, the sort of belief that is not founded on inference and which need not and perhaps cannot be defended by reason. They argue that one's inability to know how to defend a properly basic belief does not itself mean that one's belief is not warranted. After all, how would you defend a belief that you have a book in front of you to a sceptic who distrusts sense perception? The inability to do so does not undermine your epistemic right to believe the book is indeed before your eyes. 'Why should we suppose,' asks Plantinga, 'that if the theist can't prove his contentions to the satisfaction of the skeptic, he doesn't know what he claims to know?' (Plantinga [1982] 1996, p.334). Plantinga and Wolterstorff propose that one may be warranted in believing one has a revelation from God while being unable to supply evidence for that belief. So Wolterstorff asks: 'Is not God's power and freedom such that God might well reveal something to some person without providing to that person satisfactory evidence on which it is probable that God has revealed that?' (Wolterstorff, 1996a, p.120). They reject the idea that the believer has some epistemic duty to ensure that she believes only those things for which she has evidence, especially where evidence is understood to be something that believers ought themselves to possess self-consciously. They want to allow that children and adults with respect to some beliefs in some circumstances can hold justified or warranted beliefs although they would not know how to offer reasons and evidence for them.

Warrant and Proper Function

Plantinga has developed, and Wolterstorff embraced, an externalist epistemology that holds warrant rather than justification as a necessary condition for knowledge. They say that theories of justification have tended to imply some duty on the part of the believer to hold beliefs only on the basis of evidence or states of which she is directly aware, and that fulfilling such duty is not sufficient or even necessary for knowledge or warrant. Not that an externalist epistemology necessarily commits one to warrant rather than justification. The externalist argues that justification does not depend on the believer being internally aware of conditions which justify a belief, for example, that the believer possess the premises upon which the belief relies, that the belief be justified by the reflections of the believer, or that it be based upon an internal condition about which the believer cannot be mistaken, such as feeling cold. Rather the externalist argues that beliefs are justified or warranted by factors which need not be internal to the believer's consciousness. I do not need to be conscious of how it is that I come to believe that I walked to work this morning, in order for that belief to be justified.

Reliabilism is a form of externalism. The reliabilist argues that a belief is justified if the processes by which it was formed are reliable. Hence the belief that you see a desk in front of you is justified by the reliability of your processes for forming perceptual beliefs: that usually you are correct in your judgments about what you see. Plantinga and Wolterstorff concur with reliabilists in pitching themselves against evidentialists: they deny that one is justified in one's beliefs only if one has the evidence to support them. Plantinga adds to reliabilism the criterion of proper functioning, because it is not enough to say that the belief-forming processes are usually reliable. They have to be functioning properly in the particular instance. You may usually be correct about what you see, but if your eyes are impeded in some way your belief about what you see will lack warrant. Thomas Reid, whose arguments concerning the immediacy of some convictions have so influenced Plantinga and Wolterstorff, would depart from them here. As we shall see later, he would not concur with reliabilists or Reformed epistemologists that the just grounds of a belief are the processes by which it is formed.

The proper functioning of belief-forming processes is central to Plantinga's account of warrant, which he summarizes like this: 'a belief has warrant if it is produced by cognitive faculties functioning properly (subject to no malfunctioning) in a cognitive environment congenial for those faculties, according to a design plan successfully aimed at truth' (Plantinga, 1993b, pp.viii–ix). Let me briefly explain each of these qualifying clauses. The faculties must be subject to no malfunction (this is how Plantinga claims to improve upon reliabilist accounts): a normally reliable short-term memory might fail to function properly because the subject knocks his head or experiences some trauma. The ensuing malfunction counts against warrant, and the degree of malfunction indicates the degree of warrant. Plantinga further adds that the cognitive environment must be congenial for the faculties in question. Some of our faculties might work well on earth but not on Mars, or well above water but not under water, or well in the light but not in the dark. Beliefs about what was seen in the dark or heard under water may lack warrant. Plantinga then specifies that, in order for a belief to have warrant, the faculties that formed it must be functioning according to a design plan successfully aimed at truth. Our belief-forming faculties are not always aimed at truth. A mother may remember childbirth as less painful than it really was, and this memory–belief may be important to her desire to have more children. The belief may be caused by cognitive faculties which are functioning properly in an environment congenial to the purpose of the continued survival of the human race. If so it is a natural and proper belief, but it is not warranted because in forming it the cognitive faculties were not aimed at truth about the way things are. They were operating according to a different purpose. One more qualification needs mentioning, for we might have cognitive faculties which aimed at truth but whose design plan was not reliable (Plantinga, 2000, pp.155–6). Therefore Plantinga adds the reliabilist criterion that, for a belief to have warrant, it must be produced by a design plan that is not only aimed at truth but is successfully so aimed (which arrives at true beliefs most of the time).

Situated Rationality

Having developed an account of warrant and a notion of proper functioning, Plantinga and Wolterstorff tend more than many philosophers of religion to acknowledge the significance of an agent's situation in the beliefs he or she forms. Properly functioning processes will yield different beliefs depending on how they have been modified by the life experiences of the believer. Plantinga takes account of a cognitive agent's 'maturation and learning' (1993b, p.43): 'Cognitive proper function at the age of three,' he says, 'is quite different from cognitive proper function at the age of thirty; a small child will have bizarre beliefs but not necessarily by way of cognitive malfunction.' His reaction to our situatedness is to propose that there is a master plan, and so we might say a vantage point by which and from which all age-relative beliefs may be assessed:

> There is that whole series of snapshot design plans, with a master design plan specifying which of them is appropriate at which age and under which circumstances. In addition there is also learning, which also, in a way modifies the design plan. More exactly, the design plan specifies how learning new facts and skills will lead to changes in cognitive reaction. (Ibid.)

The question then arises, how far do the Reformed epistemologists go in meeting the range of objections canvassed at the start of this essay. These objections revolve around a sense that philosophy of religion is detached from the lives we lead and from the ways that religious belief is shaped by people's circumstances and practices. Well, the Reformed epistemologists do not go as far as they might. In the extract just quoted, no sooner does Plantinga countenance our situatedness than he looks for ways to transcend it. This seems to justify Grace Janzten's charge that he works with the same 'untroubled idea of the rational, autonomous human subject' as other mainstream philosophers of religion (Jantzen, 1998, p.30). Moreover he screens out all variables other than age. The affects that our social, psychological and physical situations have on our beliefs go unrecognized in his epistemology. He is interested in the effects of people's religious (or non-religious) situations insofar as he defends the right of children who are raised in religious communities to believe in God, based on the testimony of their elders; hence his interest in age. But he does not develop a religious epistemology that reflects or engages with religious nurture within believing communities.

It is Wolterstorff more than Plantinga who notes variations in people's belief-forming mechanisms according to their social, psychological and previous epistemic backgrounds.[3] In his Gifford Lectures, delivered to the University of St Andrews in 1994–5, Wolterstorff explored the relation between our programming and our access to reality. He argued that sometimes our access to what is 'out there' requires more than just the hard-wiring of the human constitution, and more than the programming that normal human adults acquire. Sometimes it requires particularity of programming, or the gaining of a certain perspective. Objectivity, he argued, requires non-objectivity. It is apparent from the Gifford Lectures that Wolterstorff recognizes what feminist standpoint epistemologists and others who work on points of view (Moore, 1997) also recognize: that our social, psychological, physical or religious history enables us to become aware of things and to believe things that it is most unlikely someone without the same sets of experiences or situations would become aware of or believe. Wolterstorff suggests some preparedness to build into his epistemology the acknowledgment that persons who have lived under oppression are aware of social realities that those who have always had power are oblivious to; that women discern things that men are most unlikely to discern; that those who have lost children understand suffering in a way that those who have not experienced such loss rarely do. This last suggestion is a particularly personal one, Wolterstorff having lost a son in a climbing accident. In recording his grief he has put into words something of how this loss has shaped his understanding of God and his continuing Christian faith (Wolterstorff, 1987/1997). He also allows that religious contemplatives discern realities that the irreligious and activistic among us almost never do. This could lead to developing a religious epistemology with an eye on the practice

3   See esp. Wolterstorff (1987) and his Gifford Lectures for 1994–5, delivered to the University of St Andrews.

of spiritual disciplines, although Wolterstorff does not do this himself. How programming in religious practice and spiritual disciplines, such as prayer and contemplation, help us to become more competent knowers (or seers, or hearers or perceivers – no term is adequate) of religious realities is a project awaiting our attention.[4]

One might respond that this would take us beyond the proper work of philosophy. I have argued elsewhere that we should not expect philosophy of religion to do the full work of religion itself (Harris, 2000b, p.117). Wolterstorff himself writes from and about contemplation of the divine in his least philosophical works, notably *Art in Action* ([1980]1997) and *Lament for a Son* ([1987]1997). Arguably philosophy of religion performs its proper role when it attends primarily to the belief aspects of religion. However Wolterstorff has become aware that the justification or warrant of beliefs, perception of reality and even construction or transformation of reality are affected by agents' situations and experiences. It should follow that, in attending to beliefs, philosophy of religion can properly be developed to take on board how people's histories and current practices shape how they perceive and affect reality. The British philosopher Mark Wynn, who is interested in the emotions as data for philosophy of religion, has suggested recently that 'working through certain basic questions in [philosophy of religion] may require not just skills of abstract enquiry, but the cultivation of an appropriate moral personality, that is, one properly attuned to the recognition and making of value through forms of felt response' (Wynn, 2002, p.111). Wynn studies grief and other emotional processes, and proposes that emotions help both to reveal the character and extent of the world's goodness and to constitute that goodness. He says that emotions 'confer new meaning on people and things, and on our own lives as the source of that meaning' (ibid., pp.102, 105; cf. Nussbaum, 2001).

Wolterstorff posits that our particular programming can give us privileged access to reality, but he has not yet further clarified this account of realism, where reality is apprehended differently (and is also constitutively affected) through people's differently formed cognitive apparatus. Following Reid, he holds that ultimately we realize that belief in our access to reality is a matter of trust (Wolterstorff, 2001). As early as the 1980s, Wolterstorff was attributing to Reid the theory that 'Rationality is always situational, in the sense that what is rational for one person to believe will not be rational for another to believe' (Wolterstorff, 1983, p.65). To elaborate: 'we cannot inquire into the rationality of some belief by asking whether *one* would be rational in holding that belief. We must ask whether it would be rational for *this particular person* to hold it, or whether it would be rational for *a person of this type in this situation* to hold it' (cf. Wolterstorff, 1992). Wolterstorff is interested in the effect of learning upon the principle of credulity, that, through the acquisition of

---

4   Though see beginnings in these directions in McGhee (1992, 2000), Wood (1998), Coakley (2002), Hollywood (2004). Mark Wynn (2003) discusses Raimond Gaita's non-religious arguments for the way the lives of saints can improve our moral perception.

learning, people come to disbelieve things they once believed. For example, adults are more reliable processors of testimony than are small children who have not yet acquired a useful functioning array of doxastic inhibitors and abettors. One could see how this epistemological route could be diversified by taking into account the factors Wolterstorff mentions in his Gifford Lectures, that by going through various experiences we become more sophisticated at processing testimony and responding to other people's accounts of events. We also become more nuanced at appraising our own experiences and reactions to circumstances.

Wolterstorff himself has not developed his epistemology by taking fuller account of people's social and other circumstances. What he has done is relate the justification for a belief to the way its formation is affected by the experiences and circumstances of the believer. Thus he shifts attention away from evidence upon which a belief is based to the processes by which a belief is formed. The governance of our belief-forming mechanisms is affected by individual experiences (Wolterstorff, 1983, p.47). According to his interpretation of Reid, our intellectual responsibility lies not in a duty to find evidence, but in using our abilities, particular to each of us according to our experiences and stage of development, for controlling our belief-forming mechanisms (1983 ibid., p.46).

Back towards Evidentialism

A question that arises is whether we can offer normative accounts of justified or warranted beliefs while reckoning with the variables of situatedness. It is precisely this area that remains undeveloped and uninvestigated by the Reformed epistemologists. As we shall see, ultimately situatedness becomes uninteresting to them. Moreover they find it hard to resist the pull of evidentialism. They inevitably face the question, could a belief which is known to be wrong in one context, be warranted in another? A child's belief in God, based on the testimony of her elders, is something Wolterstorff and Plantinga are keen to defend. It is probable that belief in God for most people is acquired, at least in the first instance, through testimony (cf. Gellman, 1993). But would belief in Father Christmas be warranted when held by a three-year old whose entire adult world concurs in indulging this belief, whose cognitive faculties are behaving as they should in one so young, and are aiming at truth rather than wish-fulfilment, whose experience of receiving presents at the end of her bed is as she has been led to expect, who has been given no reason to doubt that she has sat on the knee of the very man in question, in Debenhams, and has had no experiences which should cause her to modify her belief?

Plantinga and Wolterstorff would say that belief in Father Christmas lacks warrant because the chain of testimony lacks warrant. If we tell children that Father Christmas exists we are deceiving them, even though we are acting with benign intentions. If there is deceit, false belief or lack of knowledge in a chain of testimony, then a belief resulting from that chain lacks warrant (Plantinga, 1993b, pp.84–6, cf. Wolterstorff, 1983, p.60).

This is not a fully satisfying solution. What about circumstances where the testifiers did not intend to deceive and were in no position to say that the chain of testimony was faulty? What if their testimony received the support of all rational adults in their acquaintance? This problem may signal an inadequacy with their externalist account of warrant. Plantinga tends towards the view, though he does not state it, that the degree to which a belief is warranted depends on how many people hold it.[5] Would it then be possible for an entire community to be functioning properly and yet its beliefs be wrong – such as a community of people who 1000 years ago believed the world to be flat? Plantinga suggests that it is possible to have justification (to be within your rights) without having warrant. A community that believed the world was flat, before it became possible to know what is known today, would be within its rights in holding this belief but would not be warranted in holding it. Is proper function, then, not sufficient for conferring warrant on beliefs formed on the basis of testimony?

Plantinga's move here resembles the distinction between weak and strong justification made by the reliablist Alvin Goldman. Goldman discusses the case of a 'benighted cognizer' who lives in a pre-scientific community which believes in oracles and omens and knows nothing of the experimental method. He suggests that the benighted cognizer may be justified in a weak sense in that he is not culpable, but not in the strong sense that the beliefs were arrived at by a reliable process. In response to Goldman, Susan Haack argues that the reason we feel pulled between the verdict that the benighted cognizer is and is not justified in his beliefs is that, intuitively, we feel he is not justified because 'his beliefs don't satisfy our criteria of evidence, don't meet what we take to be indications of truth' (Haack, 1993, pp.151–2). In a similar vain we might respond to Plantinga that the reason that his own examples are 'penumbral' cases, as he calls them, is that, while we may regard the believers as non-culpable, we intuitively feel that the warrant for a belief should be related to the evidence in favour of its truth, and that the proper functioning of belief-forming processes is not the relevant sort of evidence. We waver because we know the evidence points away from the earth being flat, not because we doubt the proper functioning of the believers' cognitive faculties. These faculties were functioning fine, but were not inhibited by evidence we now have against the earth's flatness.

---

5 He sets up the following scenario (1993b, p.86): you believe in Darwinian evolution on the basis of testimony, and then some experts give up their support of Darwinian evolution, but you do not hear about it. It turns out that Darwinian evolution is in fact true. Plantinga asks, did you know all along, or was the warrant that the belief held for you decreased by the fact that others (mistakenly) doubted? He regards this as a penumbral case, which suggests the possibility that a false belief may have the power to decrease the warrant of a true belief, in that the amount of warrant enjoyed by a belief depends on the general support for that belief.

Plantinga concedes that proper functioning is not sufficient for warrant in the case of beliefs formed on testimony. Testimony, he says, is a 'second-class citizen of the epistemic republic'. It is 'parasitic on other beliefs so far as warrant goes', and 'if no one has nontestimonial evidence for the facts in question, then none of our beliefs on this head has warrant, even though we are both justified in forming the beliefs and such that our faculties are functioning properly' (Plantinga, 1993b, p.87). However he makes this concession for the wrong reasons. Plantinga accepts Steve Wykstra's point that, if no one has non-testimonial evidence, for example if an entire cognitive community believes in quantum theory on the say-so of others, the community is in 'big doxastic trouble' (ibid.). But he does not follow up Wykstra's argument as it relates to religious belief, which is that derivational evidence is not sufficient where beliefs conflict, as do religious beliefs (Wykstra, 1989). Wykstra argues that, when faced with conflicting beliefs, we must discriminate between them inferentially, and then inferential evidence (not proper function) supplies warrant. Plantinga still attributes the lack of warrant to a problem in the cause, this time that the chain of testimony has no non-testimonial base. Testimony can provide warrant, says Plantinga, but a cognitively superior way is to come to see the truths for myself (Plantinga, 1993b, pp.87–8).

It is perhaps not surprising that the Reformed epistemologists cannot help bending in an evidentialist direction, however hard they try to avoid doing so. As the discussion of testimony suggests, externalists sometimes need internalist reliance on evidence to test the reliability of their belief-forming processes.[6] Plantinga and Wolterstorff have been heavily influenced by Reid in their work on the immediacy of beliefs and on belief-forming mechanisms, but Reid himself is more evidentialist than externalist on the matter of justification. As Wolterstorff and Plantinga acknowledge, for Reid it is always evidence, not the process of belief formation, that provides the just ground of belief: 'We give the name evidence to whatever is the ground of a belief. To believe without evidence is a weakness which every man is concerned to avoid, and which every man wishes to avoid. Nor is it in any man's power to believe anything longer than he thinks he has evidence' (Reid, 1863, p.328). Moreover Reid was evidentialist on the matter of belief in God, and did not hold that belief in God is a commonsense or immediate belief. He wrote of belief in God as though it were an inference drawn from more basic beliefs. He offered an evidentialist argument for God's existence from 'the marks of design and wisdom in the works of nature' (ibid., pp.460–61) and he urged that revelation be judged by reason in the matter of both Natural and Revealed religion.[7] Wolterstorff has proposed that a child's belief in God is justified on the grounds that it is natural for

---

6   I am grateful for conversation with Richard Swinburne for discussion of this point.

7   See Reid's *Lectures on Natural Theology* (ed. Elmer H. Duncan; University Press of America, 1981), pp.1–2, quoted in Wolterstorff (1983, p.63). Reid may also show sympathy for cosmological arguments when he writes that 'things cannot begin to exist, nor undergo change, without a cause that hath power to produce that change' (Reid, 1863, p.521), though he is not here positing a deity.

children to believe what their elders tell them. He has argued, plausibly, that Reid would 'agree that children often believe that God exists, that he is our Creator and beneficent Provider, etc., on the authority of some adult', and that 'when they do so, they hold these beliefs immediately'. He has suggested, less plausibly, that Reid might even say that 'the child would be *justified* in such beliefs' (Wolterstorff, 1983, p.62) on the basis of the workings of the credulity principle (that we are constituted to believe what we apprehend people as telling us), which Reid says is 'unlimited in children' (Reid, 1863, p.196).

On a more faithful reading of Reid, one would propose that a child who is told about God will accept that belief, at least in earliest life, but will at some point come to test whether there are good reasons for belief in God.[8] For Reid, if beliefs based on testimony lack justification, this is not because of faults in the chain of testimony, but because there is a lack of 'good reason' for believing the testimony in question, for as we mature our credulity is 'limited and restrained by experience', and 'we find good reason to reject testimony in some cases' and good reason to accept it in others (ibid., p.197). Reid implies that some beliefs are formed non-culpably in a natural way prior to the process of modification which puts a person's beliefs more in tune with reality. We might spare a thought for Plantinga's 14-year-old theist who is brought up in a community where everyone believes, and so is not 'violating an all-things-considered intellectual duty' by not basing his belief in God on evidence (Plantinga, 1983, p.33). Reid would expect a period of testing at some stage, but he seems to recognize a category of arational beliefs upon which reason needs to work and has not yet done so because of the stage of development of the subject.

Appeals to Spiritual Insight: a Wasted Opportunity

While the Reformed epistemologists are anti-evidentialist, the logic of their own lines of argument and those whose philosophies have influenced them lead in an evidentialist direction when it comes to belief in God. In particular, if they followed the philosophy of Reid more consistently, and of present-day influences such as Wykstra, they would be led to conclude that belief in God is properly based on evidence.

My purpose here is not to defend evidentialism. I regard evidentialists as less right than Plantinga and Wolterstorff concerning the proper grounds for belief in God, and less successful at conveying the ways in which people come to affirm religious beliefs. Both phenomenologically and theologically I hold that faith can often find and articulate points of contact with rational arguments and experiences, and with the role of testimony and of faith-shaping practices, but can also survive when all of

---

8   For a fuller explanation of the Reformed epistemologists' departure from Reid, see Harris (2000a).

these points of contact disappoint or fall away. Its existence and survival can seem inexplicable insofar as faith is itself groundless except for its grounding in God. While I hold this understanding theologically, I find that it fits with people's experience of faith. My wider concern, beyond the scope of this chapter, is to see philosophy of religion, and religious epistemology in particular, reflect more adequately this groundless nature of religious faith as well as the ways that faith is nurtured and its cognitive aspects enhanced. My purpose here, however, is to show up deficiencies in Reformed epistemology which incline it towards evidentialism when this is what Plantinga and Wolterstorff most wish to avoid. It is then to argue that their attempts to avoid evidentialism show potential to take into account the significance of moral and spiritual development in influencing our ability to think well and improve our understanding, but that, sadly, this potential is not realized.

Ultimately the way that Plantinga and Wolterstorff avoid evidentialism in religious belief is by appealing to the *sensus divinitatis* in fitting us for belief in God, and to the inner testimony of the Holy Spirit on matters of specific Christian doctrine, both of which are claimed to produce beliefs in us immediately (esp. Plantinga, 2000, Pt III). Their theological appeal to the *sensus divinitatis* and work of the Spirit accords with the position that faith is groundless except for its grounding in God, which Plantinga and Wolterstorff would probably uphold. It could open the way for epistemological attention to the development of our attunement with the *sensus divinitatis* and testimony of the Holy Spirit. Or, if that is too theological for a philosophy of religion, it could promote epistemological enquiry akin to Pierre Hadot's interest in spiritual exercises that constitute philosophy as a way of life, or McGhee's exploration of philosophy and the spiritual life (Hadot, 1995; McGhee, 1992, 2000). It could provoke development of Wolterstorff's hint in his Gifford Lectures that religious contemplatives discern realities that others of us are unable to discern, or of Plantinga's acknowledgment that faith 'isn't merely a cognitive activity; it also involves the will, both the affections and the executive function' (Plantinga, 2000, p.247). However Plantinga confines his attention to faith as a cognitive activity and does not expand his notion of cognitive activity in a way that recognizes the constitutive roles of affections or the intelligence of emotions (contrast Wynn, 2002, 2003; Nussbaum, 2001). His appeal to the *sensus divinitatis* and to the Spirit turns out to be disappointing, as he treats each flatly as further cognitive faculties and omits the role of the will in his analysis of their cognitive functioning.

Potentially insights about situatedness could feed discussion of the workings of the *sensus divinitatis* and testimony of the Holy Spirit, but what Plantinga and Wolterstorff say about these natural and supernatural gifts is devoid of much sense of the development or context of cognitive subjects. Plantinga issues mechanical and repetitive statements about the functioning of belief-forming mechanisms, such as 'there is a kind of faculty or cognitive mechanism, what Calvin calls a *sensus divinitatis* or sense of divinity, which in a wide variety of circumstances produces in us beliefs about God' (Plantinga, 2000, p.172); and 'the internal instigation of the Holy Spirit working in concord with God's teaching in Scripture is a cognitive process or belief-forming mechanism that produces in us the beliefs constituting faith' (ibid., p.284). He reduces assessment of both the *sensus divinitatis* and operations of the Holy Spirit to a process of assessing the functioning of cognitive faculties in producing particular beliefs. The beliefs they produce will have warrant for believers because 'they will be produced in them by a belief-producing process that is functioning properly in an appropriate cognitive environment (the one for which they were designed), according to a design plan successfully aimed at the production of true beliefs' (ibid., p.246).

Nor does Wolterstorff integrate situatedness significantly into his epistemology, despite his appeals to Reid's principle of credulity to argue that children are justified in believing what they are told about God. He ultimately seems to argue that what does justify a child's belief in God is not the principle of credulity, but a belief disposition endowed by our creator and triggered by our awareness of the world. This disposition is shared by all, although dulled to different degrees in different people by the workings of sin. At this point Wolterstorff would not want to make a virtue of situatedness: that the sinner's belief-forming processes are functioning as we would expect, for a sinner does not provide for situated warrant. Both he and Plantinga hold that God fits us so as to believe immediately, but sin gets in the way (for example, Wolterstorff, 1992). But neither of them explores ways in which we counteract the noetic effects of sin and develop virtuously functioning cognitive faculties for discerning religious truths. Ultimately the Reformed epistemologists wish to do without situatedness in their account of rationality, and they have not further developed this aspect of their account.

This is a wasted opportunity. Their limited interest in the role of communities in shaping people's beliefs, and in the situated nature of rationality, provides a potential point of contact with virtue epistemology (especially as pointed out positively by Wood, 1998, but also negatively by Swinburne, 2001, p.190), but not one that either Plantinga or Wolsterstorff have explored. They remain focused on isolated belief formation, and they provide a mechanistic model of the way our faculties function, rather than an organic model of the way people develop virtuous intellectual habits or mature in their religious outlook (cf. Zagzebski, 1996, pp.321, 325). They put their energy into defending the child or teenage theist who has been brought up to believe in God and would not know how to defend that belief if interrogated by a J.L. Mackie enthusiast. They are interested in situated rationality as it bears on the religious nurture of such a child. However they consider religious nurture almost exclusively in relation to testimony, and not to religious practice, and on the matter of testimony they find that their theory of warrant and proper function is insufficient. They struggle to resist returning to a need for evidence-based means of distinguishing between justified and unjustified beliefs. Their way of avoiding evidentialism in religious belief is to propose that the individual forms beliefs immediately, through the workings of a natural sense of the divine, or through being convicted by the Holy Spirit. At this point, they disregard rather than build on insights they had begun to develop regarding our situatedness and cognitive development. They argue that warrant is derived from the proper functioning of a natural disposition to believe or an inner working of the Spirit, and they do not explore how this proper functioning is aided by the development of our cognitive faculties through communal, moral or spiritual nurture. Despite introducing into their epistemology the *sensus divinitatis* and the testimony of the Holy Spirit, neither Plantinga nor Wolterstorff develops a discourse about growing in spiritual discernment. According to the theological framework that they deploy, there is a struggle in us to be shaped by the Holy Spirit and conformed to God's way of thinking, but we cannot find that sense of struggle in their religious epistemology.

The Reformed epistemologists have a specific agenda: to uphold the right of theists to believe in God even when they do not know how to defend the rationality of that belief. But, working within that agenda, they have not escaped that mentality of ensuring that believers have done what they need to have done in order to avoid epistemic blame (cf. Zagzebski, 1996, p.28). Their epistemology is a rather unambitious one, primarily concerned with escaping the need for evidence, which they do not fully achieve, rather than with cultivating good habits in the formation of belief and understanding. What Plantinga (2000, p.285) claims for his model 'is that there aren't any successful philosophical objections to it'. And while Wolterstorff is interested in our steering our belief-forming practices as best we can, the main philosophical point he aims to make is that, having done that, we have fulfilled as much epistemic duty as can reasonably be required of us, and have earned an entitlement to believe: 'What we can do is steer our belief-dispositional nature: go out and acquire additional experiences, attend more carefully and in different ways to the experiences we are having, reflect more carefully on the things we already know and believe and how they fit together, and so forth. Beyond that there's nothing we can do, nothing at all' (Wolterstorff, 1995, p.279). A more ambitious religious epistemology would consider what promotes wisdom, and how a religious habitus develops. One can envisage a richer theory for what the Reformed epistemologists themselves are wishing to achieve, one which enables them to develop a (theologically informed) account of how the *sensus divinitatis* and testimony of the Holy Spirit work in people to develop their understanding and instil wisdom in them.

What I am calling a lack of ambition is something that many in the analytical tradition regard as a proper modesty with respect to the philosophical task, and an appropriate prizing of the intellectual virtue of rigour in breaking down arguments and propositions for careful analysis. But such a narrow conception of the philosophical task, combined with a flat account of the functioning of cognitive faculties, undermines what philosophers of religion can achieve. It perhaps also distorts their accounts of what is involved in believing in God by averting their attention away from questions about faith development, from nurture within communities of faith, from the role of ritual and practice in shaping our understanding, and from the relation between the development of intellectual virtues, spiritual development and growth in wisdom.[9]

---

9   I am grateful to Pamela Sue Anderson, Chris Insole, Ann Loades and Mark Wynn for comments on this chapter during its preparation.

CHAPTER 8

Analytical Thought and the Myth of Anglo-American Philosophy

G.W. Kimura

'Anglo-American philosophy.' The term has grown far beyond the philosophers' vocabulary into a commonplace, indicating a logico-empirical, analytical way of thinking. Yet at the same time that it has grown commonplace the term has become one of philosophy's greatest myths. The presumption of 'Anglo-American philosophy' as a shared analytical-style philosophy ignores vast differences in the way Anglophone thought has developed across the Atlantic for the last 50 or so years.

What sense can the term 'Anglo-American philosophy' hold in light of the history of these two fiercely distinctive philosophical cousins before that period? How can they understand their relationship today? This chapter turns the tables on the notion of Anglo-American philosophy as analytical. It applies to the term itself some of the techniques analytical philosophy champions. The aim here is to take apart the term, to analyse so-called Anglo-American analytical-style thinking, not because the term in this sense has lost all usefulness (referring to an historical window from the 1930s to the mid-1950s, for example), but in order to redraw the parameters of the term's reference. The aim of this chapter is to recover and reconstruct an earlier and deeper Anglo-American philosophical tradition for a post-analytical world. The aim is to *de*mythologize the analytical connection and *re*mythologize the notion of Anglo-American thought along Romantic–neopragmatist lines.

This chapter argues that, if a continuous and live tradition of Anglo-American philosophy exists, it is best conceived along the Romantic–neopragmatist trajectory, rather than the now largely defunct analytical genealogy. This trajectory extends through such diverse Romantics as Blake, Coleridge, Arnold and Wordsworth through transcendentalists and classical pragmatists such as Emerson, Peirce, James and Dewey, to the growing circle of neopragmatist-influenced philosophers, including Richard Rorty, Hilary Putnam, Stanley Cavell and, recently, Charles Taylor (cf. Taylor, 2002). This tradition recovers elements lost or rejected by philosophical analysis that are revitalizing current philosophical discourse, from epistemological holism to methodological fallibilism, to the literary–autobiographical voice. But, of all these elements, the most significant for this chapter is the renewal of philosophical interest in religious faith.

The methodology of this chapter is not deconstructive or merely historical. It is, pragmatically-speaking, reconstructive. It is to reconstruct and remythologize the notion of Anglo-American thought via a philosophical distinctiveness that earlier Romanticism and classical pragmatism held, and now versions of neopragmatism are coming to hold, with respect to religious belief and, even, to God. It is to account for an intellectual openness, seriousness really (sometimes in spite of itself), that this tradition of Anglo-American thought contains. It is a seriousness that cannot be sustained by the typical analytical view of Anglo-American philosophy that has in large part sought to marginalize, refute or wholly ignore the religious question (analytical philosophers of religion included in this volume notwithstanding).

It is important to recall that the period when philosophical analysis dominated the Anglo-American philosophy faculty coincides with the most damning criticism and, increasingly, self-criticism of that faculty. It was the period when philosophy grew overly technical, arcane and insular. It severed connections not only to wider university and culture, but even to lived experience. In short, the criticism is that, in becoming analytical, Anglo-American philosophy had cut itself off from its proper subject matter. It had, in a real sense, ceased to be philosophy.

Part of that history involves reckoning the failure of analytical thought, especially its failure to take seriously the religious dimension of life. It involves holding the tradition accountable to questions of whether something in the method of analytical philosophy lends towards such an anti-philosophical tendency. Part of that history also involves a final laying to rest. Analytical philosophy is all but abandoned by today's post-analytical Anglo-American faculty. Reconstructing and remythologizing Anglo-American philosophy along Romantic–neopragmatist lines, therefore, speaks to its vindication over the analytic tradition, especially in philosophy of religion.

The purpose of this chapter is not to draw exhaustively the history of British Romanticism through American transcendentalism to pragmatism and neopragmatism. Nor is it to define all aspects of what British Romanticism is: Isaiah Berlin has shown the impossibility of such tasks (Berlin, 2000). Rather the purpose is to posit significant epistemological features of this trajectory of Anglo-American thought. It is to examine how they allow neopragmatism to accomplish what philosophical analysis could not. By describing traits such as epistemological holism, fallibilism and a peculiar literary–autobiographical voice, the purpose is to show how neopragmatism, like classical pragmatism, transcendentalism and Romanticism before it is philosophically reconnecting to *pragma*: to practical, lived experience.

Neopragmatism is now forcing Anglo-American philosophy to confront areas of life that in large part did not register philosophically for analytical thought. It is even engaging religious concepts and religious experience, in a way that analytical philosophy never did and, frankly, probably never could. Neopragmatism is now returning to religious faith as a genuine philosophical theme. Thus, in an Anglo-American philosophy faculty that was not just indifferent, but even antagonistic, towards the religious question, neopragmatism is now ushering in something not seen since before the ascendancy of analytical thought: the return of religion in Anglo-American philosophy.

The term 'Anglo-American philosophy' is invoked most frequently to identify an epistemological alliance. Like its political one, the alliance may share history, but it also lives in constant tension. This tension expresses itself in the way the alliance is described. Often it is characterized in terms of a common rejection of what it is not (or at least what it imagines it is not), rather than a positive identification of what it actually is. Anglo-American philosophy in this sense indicates a general mood or a style of philosophizing even more than the continuity of method, set of epistemic problems or textual canon.

Anglo-American philosophy is thus portrayed as half of a binary that, whether explicit or not, it always partners: 'Continental philosophy.' The two names, 'Anglo-American' and 'Continental', describe a philosophical world in which each side in large part indexes itself against the other. The difference here is more than the *prima facie* case that something like a common tongue unites Anglo-American philosophy. Continental thought is traditionally portrayed as foundational, aesthetico-political, anti-representational and synthetic. Anglo-American thought is portrayed as substantively different. It is mainly characterized as empirical, scientifically rigorous, positivistic and, of course, analytical. Certainly these are clumsy generalizations, but that is part of the point of any mythology. Such generality is what has allowed the division to be sustained, from the empiricist/rationalist debates of three centuries ago to the realist/anti-realist and deconstructionist debates today.

Writing in a theological context, Graham Ward describes the Anglo-American/ Continental difference in terms of the hermeneutical/critical:

> In brief, the hermeneutical tradition sought, in various ways, to define the methods and processes whereby what is meaningful is made meaningful *for us* (whether by 'meaningful' we refer to a text or our experience of the world). The critical tradition, on the other hand, sought to develop critiques of these methods, theories and politics of these appropriators of the meaningful. ... To sharpen the edge of the conflict, we could say, generally, the presupposition of the hermeneutical tradition is a holism which guarantees that meaning can be discovered. On the other hand, the presupposition of the critical tradition is that meaning is always historically embedded, is always caught up with the exercise of individual and institutional 'will-to-power'. (Ward, 1996, p.6)

The distinction between the hermeneutical and critical, of course, is usually gauged as an internal Continental binary. But Ward's reading of it as a general philosophical division illustrates another feature of such characterizations. Those qualities appealing to the Anglo-American 'analytical' sensibility are not necessarily absent from Continental 'synthetic' thought, or *vice versa*. They are embedded in the tradition, secondary or, to borrow a favourite Foucault-*cum*-Radical Orthodoxy trope, 'subterranean'. If they are implicit, they are still present, and therefore recoverable.

Truth, in Ward's view of the 'hermeneutic' strain, is, as it were, received. It is made meaningful 'for us' rather than *by* us, as appropriators of the meaningful. This strain describes the Anglo-American philosophical tradition from logico-empiricism to Utilitarianism to philosophical analysis. The opposite strain follows the

Continental sensibility from rationalism through Marx and the later Heidegger to the French Nietzscheans. They describe the 'critical' strain. Truth in this conception (if there is any value to maintaining such a notion at all in some versions) is 'historically embedded', shot through with human interest and implicated in 'individual and institutional' contexts of 'will-to-power'.

This division, Ward says, operates whether one is speaking about a 'text' or an 'experience of the world'. Thus it is more than a simple juxtaposition or opposition of the Anglo-American and Continental view. The two approaches exhaustively describe two ways of doing philosophy, setting them in clear and irreconcilable camps. Richard Rorty similarly characterizes the Anglo-American/Continental difference, albeit with Nietzschean flourish. He traces back the origin further than Ward:

> Within Philosophy, there has been a traditional difference of opinion about the Nature of Truth, a battle between (as Plato put it) the gods and the giants. On the one hand, there have been Philosophers like Plato himself who were otherworldly, possessed of a larger hope. They urged that human beings were entitled to self-respect only because they had one foot beyond space and time. On the other hand – especially since Galileo showed how spatio-temporal events could be brought under the sort of elegant mathematical law which Plato suspected might hold only for another world .... In the nineteenth century this opposition crystallized into one between 'the transcendental philosophy' and 'the empirical philosophy', between the 'Platonists' and the 'positivists'. To be on the transcendental side was to think that natural science was not the last word – that there was more Truth to be found. To be on the empirical side was to think that natural science – facts about how spatio-temporal things worked – was all the Truth there was. (Rorty, 1982, p.xv)

In Rorty's view, like Ward's, Anglo-American philosophy as typically understood flows from the 'meaning can be discovered', 'empiricist', 'scientific', positivist' source: 'the giants'. The Continental camp flows from the 'meaning is always historically embedded', 'transcendental', 'Platonist' source: 'the gods'.

For Rorty, this Manichean philosophical world continues to play out and its effects are still felt today in the philosophy faculty. The result has been professional disaster.

> Philosophy in the English-speaking world became [in two generations] 'analytic', anti-metaphysical, unromantic and highly professional. Analytic philosophy still attracts first-rate minds, but most of these minds are busy solving problems no nonphilosopher recognizes as problems: problems which hook up with nothing outside the discipline. So what goes on in Anglophone philosophy has become largely invisible to the academy, and thus to the culture as a whole. (Rorty, 1998b, p.129)

Perhaps this is not so striking an admission for Rorty, until one recalls that he, like most of his generation, grew to prominence as an analytical philosopher. Hilary Putnam expresses the same sentiment. After becoming disenchanted with A.J. Ayer and other dominant Anglo-American philosophers of the day, Putnam converted to the view that most of the problems raised by logical analysis were 'pseudo-problems' entertained solely by professionals and irrelevant outside the field (cf. Putnam, 1994, p.99). By the 1980s, Putnam became the premier American philosopher of his generation trained and tenured in analytic philosophy to make the Romantic–neopragmatic turn.

The difficulties Rorty and Putnam identify in analytical thought arise precisely out of its most self-congratulatory aspect: a science-like style or mood. Philosophical analysis modelled itself along mathematical principles and mimicked the intellectual rigour of the natural sciences. It fashioned itself as logical, disinterested and apodictically certain.

Ignoring for a moment that this idol of science has been breaking down at least since Planck, Einstein and Schroedinger from *within* science, and ignoring the fact that analytical positivism failed to deliver on lawlike rules of inference, Rorty grants its success aping the style. No doubt analytic philosophers took this route with the best intentions, to keep philosophy relevant in an environment so driven by the success of the sciences. Unfortunately for philosophy, just the opposite occurred. The issue, rather the self-indictment on Rorty's part, is that, by following the analytical path, Anglo-American philosophy 'in two generations' brought about the institutional and cultural marginalization in which it is now stuck.

Rorty should go even further, because the problem is far more serious than a mere professional dilemma, especially if one believes that philosophical reflection truly matters for the orientation of life. Anglo-American philosophers abjectly failed philosophy by marching it off into the technical obscurity of logical analysis. They exiled philosophy from its necessary Socratic consideration of lived experience and the integrative life. The failure occurred on many levels, from the moral to the political to the aesthetic. But especially, given analytical philosophy's reticence if not outright antipathy towards religion, the greatest victim was the life of religious faith.

Now those two generations of which Rorty speaks have spent themselves, and the Anglo-American philosophy faculty continues to struggle. It struggles to situate itself not only in the university, but in the larger intellectual discourses of modernity/postmodernity. Earlier it fought for its place against the rising authority of the natural sciences. Now its subject matter has been colonized by other areas of study, from psychology and sociology to, most recently, literary theory.

Yet, out of the post-analytical environment a new autobiographical–literary voice is emerging in philosophy. Drawing on the tradition that extends at least from British Romanticism to neopragmatism, it is directing Anglo-American philosophy back to its proper subject matter. This autobiographical–literary voice is developing in American thinkers of the stature of Rorty, Putnam, Taylor and Cavell, all of whom cut their teeth on philosophical analysis and have now abandoned it. This shift in voice, in mood or style, is as telling as the ostensible return of interest in pragmatism that it is supposedly bringing about. Drawing on this voice, these thinkers are drawing on the British Romantic and American transcendentalist sources behind the classical pragmatists themselves.[1]

The adoption of the autobiographical–literary, rather than the scientifico-logical mode, is more than a mere complaint against the excesses of philosophical analysis. It is an admission tinged with confession now that analytical thought has run its course. In fact, this new voice/mood/style resembles Anglo-American philosophy's putative opponent, Continental thought:

> The arrogance of philosophy is not one of its best kept secrets. … A formative idea in planning these lectures was to pose the question whether, or how, philosophy's arrogance is linked to its ambivalence toward the autobiographical. … After some years of graduate study in which philosophy interested me but seemed unlikely to be moved by anything I had to say, or by the way in which I seemed to be fated to say it, I began finding my intellectual voice in the work of the so-called philosophers of ordinary language, J.L. Austin at Oxford and the later Wittgenstein; and, as it turns out, but took me years to recognize usefully, importantly because their philosophical methods demand a systematic engagement with the *autobiographical*. (Cavell, 1994, pp.3–6)

Cavell's statement that it was reading Austin and the later Wittgenstein that delivered him from analytical thought to the autobiographical–literary for which he is now famous, is instructive. Both Austin and Wittgenstein were in their own way tied to philosophical analysis, but also prime figures in the turn to ordinary language and, in some interpretations, neopragmatic realism.[2] But the transition from analytical philosophy proper to an ordinary language more oriented towards the autobiographical–literary is not only Cavell's story. It is the story of Anglo-American philosophy, at least from the US side, since the early 1950s.

The greatest US philosopher of the immediate past generation, W.V.O. Quine (with whom Cavell also studied at Harvard), is most commonly identified as the herald to analytical philosophy's demise. Quine's refutation in 1953 of the analytic/synthetic distinction in 'Two Dogmas of Empiricism' undermined a notion central to analytical thought. Later, with J.S. Ullian in *The Web of Belief* (1970), Quine moved further away from the scientific idiom. He began adopting literary–naturalistic epistemological metaphors such as 'web' and 'organism', displacing analysis's favoured technical/mechanical tropes. Following Quine, J.L. Austin was also sceptical of the analytic/synthetic distinction, but he was suspicious of other supposedly absolute notions that analytical philosophy operated with. With his *How to do Things with Words* (1962), he developed a speech-acts theory that rejects the constative–performative distinction likewise basic to philosophical analysis.

---

1 Cornel West was the first neopragmatist explicitly to make the Romantic/transcendentalist connection (West, 1982).
2 Cf. Crary and Read (2000), where thinkers such as Stanley Cavell, John McDowell, James Conant and Hilary Putnam, all leading neopragmatists, put the later Wittgenstein into a realist genealogy.

The work of these early post-analytical Anglo-American thinkers undermined the very reason that philosophical analysis was attractive in the first place. It was supposed to be logical, disinterested and apodictically certain. But Wittgenstein, Quine and Austin showed that the precise logical distinctions it used were charged with interest and that what language operated with looked more like rules in 'games' than mathematical laws. The emphasis in Anglo-American philosophy now began to shift. It moved away from logical analysis to ordinary language, epistemology, philosophy of action and critical and literary theory. In general, it moved to more holistic and literary styles of philosophizing that can trace their heritage to classical pragmatism and an earlier counterscientific movement: Romanticism.

In spite of this trend, analytical thought still entertains 'hold-outs': even, contra-intuitively, in philosophy of religion. Richard Swinburne is the most important representative of the resistance to analysis' decline. His trilogy *The Coherence of Theism* (1977), *The Existence of God* (1979) and *Faith and Reason* (1981) is the benchmark for incorporating analytical-style reasoning in philosophy of religion. Swinburne is vigorously anti-pragmatic in these volumes. He argues against what he fashions the 'Pragmatist View of Faith' by the final book.

Swinburne rejects pragmatist-influenced Wilfred Cantwell Smith and John Hick in particular for appealing to holistic accounts of belief. He accuses them of the logical–genetic mistake of confusing 'belief-that' statements with 'acting-as-if' statements. He criticizes them for refusing to boil down their accounts of belief to the 'propositional', 'logical probability' idiom of analytical thought. Then he applies that idiom and picks apart the 'Pragmatist View of Faith' with analytical methodology (Swinburne, 1981, pp.115–17).

Yet, even in the first volume, Swinburne recognizes he is caught in a methodo-logical dilemma. He is stretched between his strong fidelity to analytical notions and the awareness, post-Quine (a neopragmatist he clearly admires), that analytical notions have come under fire. Swinburne even seems to acknowledge Quine's argument against the absolute division between the analytic and synthetic:

> Sometimes it can be said that a proposition is analytic if and only if it is a truth of logic or can be reduced to one with the help of definitions (which correctly report the meanings of the words defined). [Footnote: 'An example of such a definition is provided by W.V.O. Quine in "Two Dogmas of Empiricism". ... A definition of this type is suggested by Frege'.] ... This definition can, however, be of use if there is an agreed set of truths of logic. There is not. Further, it does not seem at all obvious that many propositions which many philosophers would wish to classify as analytic can be shown to be so on this definition. (Swinburne, 1977, p.16)

The point of Quine's remarks, of course, was to nullify the conception of the 'analytic' and 'synthetic' as aprioristically distinct. For Quine, in practice the terms of propositions are shifted around in such a way that the very distinction itself becomes gossamer. But, even before Quine, the difficulties of the analytic/synthetic division were identified by Kant: 'The distinction between analytic and synthetic propositions begins with Kant', according to Swinburne (1977, p.16). Kant was forced into the *tertium aliquid* of the synthetic a priori to overcome the logical problems of treating knowledge as either synthetic or analytic. Kant himself effectively modified what was supposed to be an exhaustive and nomological distinction. He recognized the weakness of what would come to be inherited by Anglo-American analytical methodology, and reconstructed around it.

Swinburne's strategy is to acknowledge the force of Quine's critique (and Kant's), in purely logical terms, then to transfer consideration of the concept of 'the analytic' to the arena of language. Instead of scrapping the apodictic view of the analytic/synthetic distinction, he proceeds Kant-like, even pragmatist-like, to revise the understanding of the analytic in order to preserve it in another form:

> A more hopeful approach to a definition of 'analytic' is one which defines an analytic proposition in terms of getting its truth from the meaning of words [rather than the validity of logic]. Thus one might wish to say loosely that what makes 'all bachelors are unmarried' true is simply the fact that the words 'all', 'bachelors', etc. mean what they do. Whereas what makes 'my desk is brown' true is not merely the fact that 'my', 'desk', etc. mean what they do, but something else, 'how the world is' [i.e. synthetic]. (Ibid., pp.16–17)

It is clear that Swinburne's 'linguistic' characterization of the analytic will be forced at some point beyond language alone. It will have to move beyond tautology or 'synonymy' of terms to at least a basic transcendental logic of, for example, the excluded middle. It also will need to rely upon some formal rules or guidelines (if not full-blown inferential laws) for determining problematic cases of what fits in a particular class of statements as part of its 'analysis'. Even then, such an account also eventually requires a theory of reference as to how such words hook up to 'how the world is'.

This issue of reference, of course, has been the thorn in the side of analytical thought. The failure to address it adequately has in large part led to analytical philosophy's demise. History has seen philosophical analysis move from defending a positivist picture of correspondence to multiple versions of verificationism, in order to salvage privileged notions like the analytic and synthetic distinction. For the most part, neopragmatism has followed Quine in jettisoning the distinction and its myriad epistemological and referential problems. However, at least one important pragmatist retained it. The great middle pragmatist C.I. Lewis, following Peirce's 'pragmaticism' (Peirce dubbed it thus to differentiate it from James's 'pragmatism'), held fast to an absolute division between the analytic and synthetic (Lewis, 1946, pp.45f).

Like the analytical philosophers, Lewis thought that 'what is knowable *a priori* is certifiable by reference to meanings alone' and that the linguistification of the analytic/synthetic definition abrogates the need for a metaphysics. Swinburne would perhaps dispute Lewis's identification of the a priori with the analytic exclusively, nonetheless Lewis shares the same propensity for analytic/synthetic division. Lewis, however, goes further than Swinburne. Lewis requires a non-magical theory of reference in order to avoid what he saw as a tendency of linguistic accounts of the distinction to fall away from realism into nominalism.

Certainly, if he was alive, this would be Lewis's criticism of neopragmatists like Quine and Rorty. (Rorty especially has been accused of anti-realism, the modern version of nominalism.) Might Lewis hold a similar view of Swinburne's linguistic redescription of the division?

> However, in the repudiation of this kind of rationalistic realism, current empiricism [*sic*] sometimes goes to the opposite extreme of a nominalism which regards meanings as no more than the creatures of linguistic convention. The truths of logic may then be taken as relative to the language-system, and the analytic in general may be delimited as the syntactically derivable. But if analytic truth 'says nothing about' an independent reality, it likewise 'says nothing about' and has no dependence on language. (Ibid.).

Lewis anticipated the logical problems of retaining traditional analytical notions like the analytic/synthetic division in a post-analytical *milieu*. Even in the 1940s, he recognized the need for a strong non-metaphysical realist defence if the division was to be viable. Neopragmatists have not, by and large, taken Lewis's route.[3] Perhaps, like Putnam, they might be non-metaphysical realists, but they follow Quine and Austin in rejecting traditional analytical notions, like the analytical/synthetic distinction.

In one sense, Swinburne misses Quine's (and Kant's) point by continuing to draw such a clear analytic/synthetic distinction in language, if not beyond it. Yet, in another sense, he confirms Quine's larger pragmatic reasoning. In fact, Swinburne's linguistification of the distinction is an oddly pragmatic move.

The reason for maintaining the division between the analytic and synthetic is precisely because of the certitude it brings. Its incorrigibility is precisely what allows analytical philosophers to make strong claims on truth and value. But Swinburne is forced into a revision of the supposedly incorrigible notion. The conception of the division is modified in the very least by the transfer from the logical to the linguistic. The so-called 'absolute division' between the analytic and synthetic changes. But if the epistemological Archimedean point moves, then it is no longer Archimedean. In the moving, it loses its rationale for certainty in the first place.

Lewis understood this predicament. That is why he refused the linguistic move and insisted on the absolute logical distinction. Quine, on the other hand, jettisoned the absolute distinction altogether. For Quine, where one draws the line between 'matters of meaning' and 'matters of fact', rather than being independent of interest, is very much informed by it. Any movement of that line works itself out in the 'web' of practice where experience occurring on the 'edges' of knowledge ripples through and affects even that knowledge and belief thought to be the most rationally stable.

---

3   The British neopragmatist Susan Haack is an exception that proves the rule (Haack, 1998).

For Swinburne, the difference also works itself out in language, apparently stopping short of certain basic formal truths on which language functions and providing a kind of stability. Yet even moving into the arena of language transforms that division in order for it to be conceived as stable in the relevant understanding. Swinburne then reinserts the reconstructed analytical/synthetic distinction in his philosophy of religion in order to underpin the rational stability of key Christian concepts.

Rorty's solution to the problems of analytical thought is to complete the so-called 'Wittgensteinian linguistic turn' and make philosophy 'literary' and 'autobiographical'. The recent development of Continental thought is his model and, whilst much of his recent work has been devoted to the recovery of Hegel, Nietzsche and Heidegger (figures more or less associated with the Continental–Romantic trajectory of thought), the contemporary thinker he is most impressed with is 'Derrida, that extraordinarily imaginative, poetic, inventive, ingenious, funny, flesh-and blood writer' (Rorty, 1998a, p.349). For Rorty, he is 'the most intriguing and ingenious of contemporary philosophers', a figure for whom even the term 'deconstruction[ist] is inadequate' (ibid., p.307).

Indeed Rorty fancies himself an Anglo-American analogue to Derrida, and his neopragmatism an Anglo-American parallel to Derridean deconstruction. However one of their greatest, if least remarked upon, differences is in approach to religion. Derrida has enjoyed a career-long serious engagement with the religious question. This is because of his criticisms of 'logocentrism', 'essentialism' and 'presence' that Christianity, in his view, bequeathed to philosophy. This is one reason why theologians and philosophers of religion, from those of a so-called 'postmodern' bent to neo-Thomist apophatic thinkers, have found Derrida valuable.

Rorty, on the other hand, is well-known for his rebarbative attacks on religion. Theologians and philosophers of religion have thus found him a much less productive resource and remain largely absent from the philosophical conversations he has started. This is an understandable, if regrettable development, especially considering how enormous Rorty's influence has been in other areas of the academy, especially literary criticism. Recently, though, Rorty has given up his knee-jerk atheism. He is adopting, at least on the surface, explicitly theological language to describe his version of neopragmatism. Rorty now calls his philosophy '*pragmatism as romantic polytheism*' (Rorty, 1998b, pp.20f).

This radical change has come out of his exploration of the connection between classical pragmatism and Romanticism. His particular philosophical interest is in what he sees as the incipient anti-logocentrism of the Romantics, especially British Romantics. Rorty admires their recovery, in his words, of the 'literary–autobiographical' voice and the language of 'poetry'. These, rather than the notion of a monotheistic 'God' or other 'transcendentals', provide an immanent source of ideals by which to live (ibid.). As a result, Rorty is now fashioning his own Romantic/pragmatist/neopragmatist genealogy. It is a broad lineage, accounting for a common immanent view of human teleology he claims is found in thinkers like Nietzsche, Coleridge and, especially, J.S. Mill, and which extends through James and Dewey to himself.

Many serious problems trouble Rorty's neopragmatic genealogy, so much so that he is the only one who recognizes it. On the one hand, he entirely avoids the most obvious Ralph Waldo Emerson transcendentalist/Romantic connection, probably on the grounds that Emerson was too metaphysical to fit his model. On the other, he completely ignores Peirce, whom even James credited with founding pragmatism, because Peirce was too logic- and scientifically-oriented. Furthermore Rorty is also the only thinker I know, neopragmatist or otherwise, who considers Nietzsche a pragmatist. (Ironically, the one bit of thin historical support comes from the fact that Nietzsche's title, *The Gay Science*, is a reference to an Emerson essay, but Rorty disallows Emerson.) Numerous other historical problems exist as well. Rorty incorrectly imputes non-theism to the originally Unitarian, then Trinitarian Coleridge. Rorty also controversially claims Mill as the most philosophically significant of all British Romantics.

Rorty's neopragmatist genealogy is certainly not plausible. Yet it is not that Rorty gets the figures of the Romantic inheritance mostly wrong, but that he gets the connection at all. The upshot of his 'pragmatism as romantic polytheism', despite its faults, is important in three ways. First, 'pragmatism as romantic polytheism' is the *apotheosis* of the anti-representationalist turn Rorty made in *Philosophy and the Mirror of Nature* (1982). That text is one of the most influential philosophy books of the past 25 years, even if that influence has been mainly outside the philosophy faculty. Rorty at once completes the linguistic turn he made in *Mirror* and moves beyond any residual analytical scientism to the autobiographical–literary idiom of 'poetry'. In this respect, Rorty joins Cavell and, increasingly, Putnam. Second, Rorty, the best-known of the three, is also, with them, moving closer in philosophical style to what was before understood as Continental.

Third, the transition to poetical, Continental-style philosophy undercuts the rigid logical–linguistic divisions on which analytical Anglo-American philosophy typically prides itself. The hallmark of Rorty's neopragmatism, for which it truly is indebted to Romanticism, is that poetic sensibility which allows him to move freely across such divisions – not only divisions in language, but divisions conceived within the rational subject itself. The Romantic–neopragmatic poetical imagination travels across Kantian divisions between the speculative, practical, aesthetic and (if one reads *Religion within the Limits of Reason Alone* (1960) as a fourth critique) the religious. As it travels, it problematizes those divisions, calling the distinctions themselves into question.

An unintended consequence (no doubt a painful one for Rorty) is that, in claiming the Romantic legacy, he is forced to accept the Romantic tradition that prevents the religious understanding being rationally cordoned off from the subject. The great irony now played out upon the liberal ironist par excellence is that, in reconstructing his neopragmatism as an updated, atheistic version of Romanticism, Rorty has discovered that he cannot exclude consideration of religious faith. He cannot exclude consideration without resorting to the very type of a priori distinctions that such a view rejects. Far from excluding religion, Rorty has settled into a version of theism himself.

Rorty is not avoiding religious themes any more. He is writing about them more than at any point in his career. He considers his theological position 'polytheistic'. It is polytheistic in 'think[ing] there is no actual or possible object of knowledge that would permit you to commensurate and rank all human needs'. It is also immanentist, believing that there are 'no nonhuman persons with power to intervene in human affairs'. Romantic polytheism, in Rorty's conception, is a wholly privatized version of religious faith.

> For human perfection becomes a private concern, and our responsibility to others becomes a matter of permitting them as much space to pursue these private concerns – to worship their own gods, so to speak – as is compatible with granting an equal amount of space to all. The tradition of religious toleration is extended to moral toleration. This privatization of perfection permits James and Nietzsche to agree with Mill and Arnold that poetry should take over the role that [traditional] religion has played in the formation of individual human lives. (Rorty, 1998b, pp.22–3)

Rorty reconstructs his pragmatism as romantic polytheism to fit with the 'Jeffersonian compromise' on religion. In that compromise, the religious beliefs and practices of individuals are granted a place in the private sphere if and only if those beliefs and practices are subordinated to the rational justification procedures of the democratic community in cases where they conflict (Rorty, 1991). This position has developed in recent published arguments he has had with, amongst others, neopragmatist Yale law professor and novelist Stephen L. Carter and literary critic Stanley Fish. At issue in the debate was the proper public role of religion in US political discourse.

Rorty has also been engaging the theological tradition as well, lately associating his religious understanding with the demythologizing of Paul Tillich, the Social Gospel of Walter Rauschenbusch and the liberation theology-influenced documents of the Vatican (Rorty, 1998a, pp.45–6, 59–60; 1999, p.206). Rorty's transition from bald atheism to 'pragmatism as romantic polytheism' is eccentric. Like his neopragmatist genealogy, it is a not altogether successful attempt to reconstruct his philosophy as a public theology. Despite the lack of credibility, the reconstruction is remarkable for a couple of reasons. First, through his provocative suggestions, Rorty has now gained access to the public debate over religion in his capacity as a philosopher.[4] Second, and more important for philosophy itself, is his linking of Romanticism and neopragmatism.

Making this connection between Romanticism and neopragmatism has forced

---

4   Rorty, and Cornel West in the area of race relations, are possibly the first two academic philosophers to have such a wide impact in the USA since John Dewey.

Rorty not only to engage religion seriously for the first time; it has propelled him into an outright reconstruction of religious belief. Rorty's neopragmatism, in his own characterization, is a theology. It is a theology operating according to the Jeffersonian compromise; it is a theology describing an entirely privatized faith life; it is a theology where private faith is subordinated to public faith in the democratic process; it is a theology that, unlike monotheism in Rorty's view, allows for religious pluralism. In this sense, Rorty's pragmatism as romantic polytheism is not far from that of his classical pragmatist predecessors. William James, in *A Pluralistic Universe*, and John Dewey, in *A Common Faith*, delivered similar reconstructions. Both privileged the autobiographical Romantic aspect of Anglo-American thought in their philosophical theology. Both emphasized private religion in a theologically plural society. And, like Rorty, both have been accused of secularizing or polytheizing faith.

Again Rorty is not the only neopragmatist philosopher dealing with religious belief, as it were, from the inside of the tradition. Stephen Mulhall (1994, p.285) holds that Stanley Cavell's Romantic notion of 'Emersonian perfectionism as redemption' contains significant 'structural analogies' to the 'Christian story of redemption'. According to Mulhall, in spite of Cavell's renunciation of religious faith as a competitor to pragmatic 'Emersonian perfectionism', 'it could be well argued that the question of Cavell's understanding of his relationship with religion is not merely one element amongst others in his work, but the most fundamental and so the most revealing of his preoccupations'.

It is no surprise that Cavell's engagement with Emerson has led to the question of religious faith. It was the former Unitarian minister Emerson's chief intellectual preoccupation. Cavell's casting of Emersonian perfectionism in secular terms contains another glaring irony. The paradigmatic experience of perfectionism, in Emerson's own view, is mystical religious experience. Emerson's description of this experience is probably the most famous in all of US literature: 'I become a transparent eyeball; I am nothing; I see all; the currents of the Universal Being circulate through me; I am part or parcel of God' (Bode, 1981, p.11).

Cavell's autobiographical–literary philosophical voice, which he attributes to the Romantic influence, also leads him to engage religion. In recent material, Cavell is self-revelatory about the connection between his struggles as a philosopher and as a Jew, specifically 'the ways my Jewishness and Americanness inflect each other' and his surprising religious feelings upon visiting Israel. He refuses to write these feelings off 'as a clinical issue', seeing them as 'a critical issue' colouring 'certain forms taken by my devotion to Thoreau and to Emerson as expressions of that issue' (Cavell, 1994, p.xv).

Completing the triumvirate, Hilary Putnam has also begun to write seriously on religious themes. Considering his earlier career in analytical positivism, of all three he would seem the most unlikely to end up a neopragmatist, let alone someone raising faith issues in his work. In a fascinating autobiographical admission in his Gifford Lectures, he says:

As a practising Jew, I am someone for whom the religious dimension of life has become increasingly important, although it is not a dimension I know how to philosophize about except by indirection; and the study of science has loomed large in my life. ... Those who know my writings from that [earlier] period may wonder how I reconciled my religious streak, which existed to some extent even back then, and my general scientific materialist worldview at that time. The answer is I didn't reconcile them. I was a thorough-going atheist, and I was a believer. I simply kept these two parts of myself separate. (Putnam, 1992, p.1)

Now that Putnam has forsaken philosophical analysis and adopted a neopragmatic voice, he has begun philosophizing about religion with a little more direction. As early as *Meaning and the Moral Sciences* (1978) he explored the literary–religious relationship to a realist ethics. More recently he wrote an introduction to a reprint of Jewish theologian Franz Rosenzweig's *Understanding the Sick and the Healthy: A View of World, Man and God*. In it he places Rosenzweig in the intellectual company of Buber and Levinas. Putnam considers what Rosenzweig was doing in theology parallel to what Wittgenstein accomplished with his later philosophical work (Rosenzweig, 1999, p.1f).

But the best example of Putnam's philosophical engagement with religion is a paper he read at the annual inter-faith gathering of scholars at the Shalom Hartman Institute in Jerusalem in 1999. That paper was a response to Hindu scholar Diana Eck's defence of the religious notion of idolatry. She argued that the western monotheistic prohibition of idolatry offers a position from which to advocate religious pluralism.

Putnam's response is interesting. He echoes James, Dewey and Rorty by questioning a pluralism based on the traditionally exclusionary language of monotheism. He is critical of words like 'idolatry' that have 'a triumphalist assumption built in'. He also argues against what he considers the soft modernist view of pluralism of Eck and his other interlocutor, Catholic theologian Francis Schüssler Fiorenza:

> Not only do I believe that no religion has a monopoly on religious value; I also reject the 'containment' model, the model on which the value and one virtue that the pluralist finds in other religions are all supposed to be already 'contained' in one's own religion (or one's own religion at its best, anyway). One reason this model is wrong is that all perception, including religious perception, is depending on concepts, and concepts, as we have learned from Wittgenstein, depend on practices and on whole ways of life. ... There is no one religion whose value, to use the economists' term, 'dominates' all the others. On the other hand, being a religious pluralist does not mean that one has to give up one's own tradition or one's own views as to how that tradition is to be interpreted, unless those views are themselves inherently intolerant. If it did, religious pluralism would just be a new universalistic religion. For example, belief in a single personal God is dear to me (a fact that shocks some members of my minyan). (Putnam, 2000, p.19)

This passage is fascinating because it suggests a neopragmatic reconstruction of Jewish religion. It suggest reconstructing it without those notions which, in

Putnam's view, are 'triumphalistic' and dominating (such as 'idolatry'), or which hold a theology of 'containment'. The *ethos* in this case is the same as Rorty's romantic polytheism in excluding by *fiat* religious views that are 'inherently intolerant'. Yet Putnam goes further. By the end of the passage he makes a not-so-veiled swipe at Rorty's polytheistic pantheon. He criticises the creation of 'a new universalistic religion' based solely on 'religious pluralism'. Putnam is doubtful of the wholesale reconstructive approach. He is unapologetic about maintaining his own tradition's belief in 'a single personal God'.

For all the shared history, the relationship between British and US philosophy has proved difficult to pin down. In 1968, A.J. Ayer published *The Origins of Pragmatism*, in which he surveyed the thought of Peirce and James (but, tellingly, not Dewey), with respect to British philosophy. His desire was to situate pragmatism in the logico-analytical mould. *Origins* was supposed to be accompanied by 'a comparable study of Moore and Russell at a later date' to draw the Anglo-American parallels from the British side (Ayer, 1968, p.20). Ayer never wrote it, apparently abandoning the project.

This chapter has argued that, if an 'Anglo-American' philosophical connection is to be found, Ayer was simply looking in the wrong place. It is not in the pragmatism–philosophical analysis connection, but in the tradition extending from Romanticism to pragmatism, and now neopragmatism. Bertrand Russell understood this fact earlier. In the chapters on pragmatism in his *History of Western Philosophy* (1945), he entertained no illusions that James and Dewey were indebted to the British empiricist–positivist–analytical school. He thought they owed much more to Continental figures, specifically Romantic-influenced ones.

This was especially true when it came to religion. Most of Russell's chapter on James, for example, denigrates him as a philosopher of religion, whose 'superstructure of belief ... is dependent on fallacies'. Pragmatism, according to Russell, is 'a form of subjectivistic madness which is characteristic of most modern [that is, Continental] philosophy' (ibid., p.846). For Russell, the heritage of the main trajectory of US philosophical thought runs through 'Bergsonianism' and 'romanticism', not British 'empiricism' or 'logical analysis'.

Despite such reservations, the myth of Anglo-American thought as philosophical analysis prevailed. Analytical philosophy did hold sway on both sides of the Atlantic, if only for a slice of the twentieth century, but now that time is past. Seen in historical perspective from the American side, analytical thought was preceded by pragmatism that hearkens back to British Romanticism. Now it is superseded by neopragmatism discovering those same roots. Despite this fact, analytical thought has proved surprisingly robust. Like existentialism, it clings on to a commonplace reputation far exceeding its substantive philosophical legacy. To that extent, this chapter confirms both Russell's and Ayer's assessment of the vast distance between the dominant US philosophical thinking and the type of philosophy they considered 'Anglo-American' and subsequently bequeathed to other analytical thinkers.

This chapter maintains that there is a living tradition of so-called 'Anglo-American philosophy'. It is not philosophical analysis. It is the autobiographical–literary tradition of Romanticism, specifically British Romanticism, and its current reconstructions in neopragmatism. This Romantic–pragmatic tradition was vilified not only by Russell, but by analytical thought in general as 'Continental'. But this tradition also has an indigenous, rich and long-standing claim in the history of Anglophone philosophy. Neopragmatists like Rorty, Cavell and Putnam are now recovering and incorporating that tradition in their philosophy.

The end of the analytical reign and the specific rise of Romantic-influenced neopragmatism is good news for theology and philosophy of religion. It opens up manifold creative possibilities. These possibilities did not exist in an academic environment where non-analytical thinking was derided for its lack of mathematico-scientific sensibility. Nor did they exist in a faculty where philosophers exercised themselves on spent philosophical notions like the absoluteness of the analytic/synthetic division.

Now that the connection to Romanticism has been established, even when it is drawn in zigzagging genealogies such as Rorty's, neopragmatists are finding themselves heir to a philosophical tradition that has always grappled seriously with the religious question. Whether they ultimately follow Coleridge in affirming religious faith (like Rorty and Putnam), or Wordsworth and do not (like Cavell), the fact is that religious faith is still being raised as a philosophical concern. This did not occur and probably could not have occurred, when they were analytical philosophers. It only happened after their conversion to neopragmatism.

In fact the centrality of the religious question to the tradition has now delivered neopragmatism to the point where its principal philosophers are adopting and adapting theological language and concepts. Rather than dismissing faith simplistically as illogical supernaturalism in the mode of Russell's oddly unsophisticated yet revealing essay 'Why I am not a Christian' (Russell, 1957), or Rorty's own earlier reactionary atheism, neopragmatist philosophy is now actively engaged in theological reconstruction.

The problem for Anglo-American thought under the analytical regime is that it dealt faith a worse blow than Nietzsche did (troping Hegel, troping the Lutheran Good Friday hymn) in pronouncing God dead. These declarations are meant to be theologically provocative. Invariably such provocativeness keeps God-talk in intellectual play.

For analytical philosophy, on the other hand, it was not that God was dead. It was that God did not even register. Its major philosophers, from the early Moore and Russell to those anachronistically flying the banner today, have by and large not considered religious faith worthy of genuine philosophical consideration. Borrowing Swinburne's term, religion has mostly been 'unintelligible' to analytical philosophy.

The real question now is, why should theology and philosophy of religion continue to utilize the analytical mode at all? Swinburne's trilogy, along with the work of other current analytical philosophers of religion, argues for a type of philosophy that for the most part has not been interested in religion. Contrast this stance with the rise of neopragmatism in the past few years. Neopragmatist philosophers like Rorty, Cavell and Putnam are not only creating a revival of interest in the classical pragmatists (cf. Menand, 2002), they are creating a new Romantic–neopragmatic myth of Anglo-American philosophy. They are returning the religious question to the Anglo-American philosophy faculty after its long banishment. And, in doing so, neopragmatists keep Anglo-American philosophy faithful to the Socratic responsibility to examine the full range of human life; life that in the post-analytical world continues to entertain varieties of religious belief.

CHAPTER 9

Philosophy of Religion:
Its Relation to Theology

Ann Loades

Philosophy of religion as we know it is a phenomenon of the last half-century, though it has different locations in academic settings which affect what counts as philosophy of religion, as we shall see. 'Theology' also may be found in the context of 'religious studies', so both 'philosophy of religion' and 'theology' are contested notions, as indeed is 'religion' (Griffiths, 1997). For our purposes, 'philosophical theology' is a phrase which usefully indicates attempts to relate one to the other, though both philosophy and theology may be remarkably resistant to such attempts, depending on how each is construed. 'Analytic' philosophy is a way of doing philosophy which has had profound effects on philosophy of religion, as Basil Mitchell explains in his contribution to this volume, but there is no single comparable mode of theological reflection, given the great variety of the ways in which theology itself has developed in the last 50 years. Theologians might indeed benefit from attention to the analysis of the very conditions of the meaningfulness of their differing discourses, but are notably resistant to engaging in the mode of reflection so characteristic of much philosophy of religion, as well as regarding it as mere 'prolegomenon' to theology proper.

It is unsurprising that it has taken time for the very possibility of re-establishing and exploring relationships at least in respect of some topics in each broadly construed discipline to come back on the agenda. This is despite the substantial evidence of interrelationship between philosophy and theology which is deeply rooted in western intellectual traditions both Greek and Latin, and profoundly influenced by argument with philosopher-theologians of Judaism and Islam such as Maimonides, Avicenna and Averroes (Burrell, 1986; Leaman, 1997, 1998; Seeskin, 2000). Philosophy of religion as we know it takes its rise from the 'Enlightenment' and its production of 'theism'. Theism is an understanding of reality which has at its core belief in one deity who has certain attributes and is of a certain character. One obvious problem with the study of 'theism' is that it has been studied quite apart from the monotheistic traditions which have given rise to it. Fifty years ago, however, it might well have been thought that the discussion of theism itself would be conclusively ruled out of court and it is helpful to have a reminder of the challenges of that time if we are to understand features of the present situation.

John Lucas (one of the Oxford 'Metaphysicals') gave in 1992 a lecture on the anniversary of C.S. Lewis's Riddell Memorial Lectures on 'The Abolition of Man', which had originally been given in King's College, Newcastle on Tyne in 1942 (Lucas, 1995). The popularity of Lewis's argumentative polemic for the truth of Christianity has sometimes been a source of exasperation for philosophers and theologians, but it is still a widely read and influential form of apologetics in the United States (Farrer, 1965), where philosophy of religion can be undertaken as a mode of apologetics. And John Lucas explains why that is, for what he himself found so moving in Lewis's work overall was his preoccupation with the nature of God, and what God's love is like; how values collapse unless we put first things first; how prayers should be prayed and what things we ought to ask for. In 1942, in a university in which a philosopher such as Dorothy Emmet had published her *Philosophy and Faith* (1936; cf. Emmet, 1945), it was still eminently possible to give public and academic lectures on such explicitly theological topics. By contrast, recalling his own experiences as an undergraduate matriculating in Oxford in 1947, Lucas has written that the philosophical climate which he encountered there was one of 'extreme aridity'. Much prized was the ability not to be convinced; a competent tutor could disbelieve any proposition, no matter how true, and 'the more sophisticated could not even understand the meaning of what was being asserted' (Lucas, 1976, p.ix). Undergraduates (and not only those reading philosophy) were avidly reading A.J. Ayer's *Language, Truth and Logic*, finished in 1935, just before Ayer's twenty-fifth birthday, which had the singular advantage of being both short and clear. Ayer's position required the rejection of authority in both knowledge and morality, and had politically radical implications (Rogers, 1999). It is obvious that those convinced by it would have considerable difficulty in taking seriously religious traditions and their appeal to revelation, and the institutional mediation of such traditions. Well discussed in professional journals, the influence of Ayer's book was long-lasting, but those interested in the continued engagement of philosophy with theology were by no means defeated, not least in Oxford. In noting various responses to the challenge particularly associated with Ayer's name, we can also attend to the legacy of those responses in present-day debate within Anglophone culture.

Exercises in large-scale understandings of reality and human relationship to the divine continued, such as Austin Farrer's (1943) *Finite and Infinite*, in which he argued from the analysis of the experience of finitude to indirect knowledge of an infinite God, source of all there is. Farrer's wide-ranging series of publications, including his *The Freedom of the Will* (1958, cf. Conti, 1995), constituted one form of direct riposte to those who thought theological language to be meaningless nonsense. His work on the freedom of the will was crucial, since for him understanding the nature of human persons was central, because 'person' was a key analogy for some measure of apprehension of the activity and nature of the God of theism (Farrer, 1967; cf. Hebblethwaite and Henderson, 1990). And Farrer went further, exploring topics important in philosophical theology such as the role of imagination in thinking (cf. Brown, 1999, 2000), as well as the relation between divine and human activity in the world as understood by a range of sciences. His work has been more widely appreciated by philosophical theologians than by biblical scholars, central though his work must be to the understanding of both scripture and liturgy.

Eric Mascall was an equally tough polemicist on behalf of Christian 'orthodoxy' with his publication of *He Who Is* (1943) and its sequel, *Existence and Analogy* (1949). Both of these books appropriated what was then thought to be the theology and philosophy of St Thomas Aquinas for explicitly Christian belief. Although 'Thomists' refuse appeal to theological premises in their project of 'natural theology', 'Thomism' is itself clearly a 'confessional' form of philosophy of religion (Haldane, 1999; cf. Hughes, 1995). And the issue of the propriety of the 'confessional' character of some forms of philosophy of religion remains alive and well, especially in the USA, depending on location, as we shall see. It can of course also be argued that western philosophy of religion, preoccupied with 'theism' as the core of the monotheisms of Christianity, Judaism and Islam, is itself 'confessional' as compared with the philosophy of religion which might explore non-theistic religion, as is more likely to be undertaken under the aegis of 'religious studies' than philosophy (Helm, 2000; cf. Cooper, 1996).

A quite different perspective on the relationship between philosophy and theology was connected with Donald MacKinnon, a Scottish Episcopalian layman. He was tutor in philosophy in Oxford (1937–47) before he returned to Aberdeen as professor of moral philosophy, and was then appointed to a chair in divinity in Cambridge. Almost uniquely amongst theologians, he endeavoured to take the measure of Kant's philosophical work on theology (cf. Hebblethwaite and Sutherland, 1982; Murray, 2004), not least the Kant of the second part of the 1790 *Critique of Judgement*, and the later, short essays of the 1790s as well as of *Religion within the Limits of Reason Alone*. In Kant, MacKinnon found the 'transcendent' presence of the divine impinging on us in morality and politics in an inescapable and unmistakable way. MacKinnon apart, we can locate in the Kantian tradition those who think that understanding the rationality of religion in terms of 'belief' is mistaken, and that it is Kant's sense that religious conviction is a matter of hope that needs evaluation and development (Pojman 1986; Audi, 2000; Wainwright, 1995). Also standing in a 'Kantian' tradition are those who give weight to the argument that all our experience is 'interpreted' experience, and who are severely critical of those philosophers of religion who ignore their own social and political context, and the varied phenomena not only of non-monotheistic forms of religion but of modern/postmodern thought and culture. This group are very critical of the 'analytic' way of philosophizing, and not only about religion.

Whilst philosophy of religion from 1950 and for the next 20 years was to some extent developed by philosophers with theological interests, it was largely dominated by preoccupation with the cognitive status and function of religious language, such as in Ian T. Ramsey's *Religious Language* (1957), to be followed by a book he edited, *Prospect for Metaphysics* (1961). The most significant collection of essays, however, was *Faith and Logic* (1957), edited by Basil Mitchell, which included work by John Lucas, R.M. Hare, I.M. Crombie, M.B. Foster and Christopher Stead as well as Austin Farrer. Mitchell's introduction gives an account of the parting of the ways between philosophers and theologians in his time, but reminds his readers that the central question being asked about the possibility of human thinking about God had a recognizable ancestry. Theologians should be grateful for any assistance in getting clear about ways of answering the question, formulating argument with care. It is also important that he notes that a Christian philosopher is committed 'to a certain agnosticism both by the demands of his profession and by his Christian vocation' (Mitchell, 1957, p.8), a commitment certainly shared by MacKinnon and, amongst pure philosophers, Anthony Kenny (Kenny, 1987, 1992). Mitchell himself contributed an essay to *Faith and Logic* on 'The Grace of God', a topic almost wholly neglected in explicit theological reflection to this day despite its centrality to Christian theology.

Beyond *Faith and Logic*, Mitchell has not allowed himself to be narrowly confined in the way he construes his task. His first major book was *Law, Morality and Religion in a Secular Society* (1967), and besides making a major contribution to the work of the Doctrine Commission of the Church of England (1978–84) he has also contributed to its reports on the issues of the 1960s and 1970s, such as abortion, sterilization and the medical care of the dying. In *Morality, Religious and Secular* (1980) he critiques (amongst others) the religious perspective of Iris Murdoch (cf. Emmet, 1966, 1979, 1994), sometime member of the 'Metaphysicals' from whom she had necessarily to part company as she developed her own 'Platonist' metaphysic of an impersonal 'Good', as represented in *The Sovereignty of Good* (1970b) and through some of her novels. Iris Murdoch's work could not become central to philosophy of religion in its theistic form, yet she never saw philosophy as just an intellectual exercise. It has taken time for some of her insights to impinge on philosophy of religion of a certain kind (cf. Hadot, 1995; Sarot, 1999), but already in her work it is possible to explore connections between philosophy and spirituality or, more precisely, what may be called a spirituality of renunciation – of power and personal fantasies. This may lead to our 'inhabiting a spiritual world unconsoled by familiar religious imagery' (Murdoch, 1970a), such as may be found in the arguably anthropomorphic deity of theism. One does not have to follow her in her metaphysic of an impersonal 'Good' to see how the defence of theism produces its own mirror-image in atheism, the denial of the deity of rational theism (cf. Martin, 1990; Le Poidevin, 1996).

To return to Basil Mitchell's work, his achievement is especially associated with what is known in some quarters as 'soft rationalism'; that is, an approach that recognizes the variety and subtlety of arguments and patterns of inference (none of them of a knock-down character) which make sense in discussing religion. It is an approach whose arguments may be complex, involving personal judgment and interpretation in establishing a case for religious belief and adjudication between its various forms, and one which remains open to critical objections against theism as well as advancing argument for theism. Its publicly shared criteria of rationality may include accuracy, fruitfulness, simplicity and scope available to believer and non-believer alike; and believer and non-believer must be prepared sympathetically to engage with each other's position (Mitchell, 1973, 1990a, 1994; cf. Abraham and Holtzer, 1987). Theologians have much to learn from this mode of argumentation, and some have taken it on board to good effect, as exemplified in David Brown's *The Divine Trinity*. Here Brown challenges the preoccupation of philosophy of religion with undifferentiated 'theism' by analysing the specifically Christian concept of God, as well as risking engagement with biblical theology – a rare venture for philosophical theologians (Brown, 1985; cf. 1987). Brown recovers religious sensibility in respect of a wide range of human creativity (such as architecture, pilgrimage and gardens). His work is both analytic in its origins and engaged with human culture, fully alert to the merits of the varieties of philosophy of religion while by no means restricted to its familiar topics (Brown, 2004).

Before turning to other emphases in philosophy of religion we may observe the institutional importance of the fact that Oxford University supports the Nolloth Professorship in the Philosophy of the Christian Religion, which was held by Ian T. Ramsey before Basil Mitchell, and then by Richard Swinburne. The existence of this professorship and the distinction of those who have held the chair undoubtedly have had an important influence on the shifts in philosophy of religion away from its preoccupations of the 1950s to 1970s with the cognitive status and function of religious language to the new topics, methods and range of interests characteristic of the period from 1980 onwards (Soskice, 1985, 1987). Ian T. Ramsey founded the Christian Philosophers Group which flowered into the British Society for the Philosophy of Religion, which despite its name is an international society. Basil Mitchell saw the establishment of the Joint Honour School of Philosophy and Theology in Oxford in the 1970s, a combination successfully followed in some other universities where both disciplines flourish. Before turning to Richard Swinburne's philosophy of religion, it is also important to notice some other features of the period.

Some rapprochement between philosophy and theology in the United Kingdom has been signalled by publications arising from conferences sponsored by the Royal Institute of Philosophy: *Talk of God* (Royal Institute of Philosophy, 1969); *Reason and Religion* (ed. Brown, 1977); *The Philosophy in Christianity* (ed. Vesey, 1989); *Religion and Philosophy* (ed. Warner, 1992); and, perhaps most significantly, *Philosophy, Religion and the Spiritual Life* (ed. McGhee, 1992). The third, *The Philosophy in Christianity*, re-explored some features of the relationship between the two disciplines throughout the centuries. And we note especially by this time that philosophy of religion in the USA had produced at least interest in re-examining the work of philosopher-theologians of the past. Such thinkers as Norman Kretzmann and Eleonore Stump can be thought of as 'evidentialists' in agreeing that it is irrational to believe something on insufficient evidence, and that rationality expressed in argument must be used by those who have a confessional commitment as well as by those who do not. Hence the importance of examples such as

Augustine, Anselm and Aquinas, and their redeployment by philosophers of religion such as Kretzmann and Stump in their essays in *The Philosophy in Christianity* and in many other publications (Kretzmann and Stump, 1993, 2001; Kretzmann, 1999; cf. Stump, 1993; MacDonald and Stump, 1998).

One major achievement in reconnecting philosophy of religion to biblical theology was the conference held at the University of Notre Dame, Indiana in 1990 on the relationship between biblical exegesis and philosophical theology, published as *Hermes and Athena* (Stump and Flint, 1993), a conference which included Richard Swinburne. Some of the exchanges were heated, but not since the days of Austin Farrer had such discussion been possible, and Farrer, of course, had engaged in such discussion in his own person, as it were. The publication of *Philosophy, Religion and the Spiritual Life* indicated that the engagement of analytic philosophers with hitherto neglected areas of religion need not be impossible, as Iris Murdoch had suggested in her own way.

Further constructive engagement with the interrelationship of philosophy and a more generous understanding of religion than theism has most notably been undertaken by Stephen R.L. Clark with his roots in the Neo-Platonism which has served a variety of religious traditions remarkably well (Clark, 1984, 1986, 1991). And, in engagement with Buddhism, Michael McGhee (of the same Liverpool department) has risked writing on philosophy as spiritual practice (McGhee, 2000). We may also note in passing the importance of the European Conference on the Philosophy of Religion, which brings together thinkers from both philosophy and theology faculties (Roman Catholic and Protestant) and from the confessionally 'neutral' faculties of state universities such as exist in the UK. Philosophy of religion in mainland Europe may be found in one form or another in a variety of locations, and be characterized by analytic or non-analytic methods and topics, though the analytic is much less common. Philosophy of religion is conducted differently according to whether it works in tandem with interests in hermeneutics, existentialism, phenomenology or, nowadays less frequently, Marxist philosophy, and attendance at such gatherings is an important reminder that, so far as philosophizing about religion is concerned, whatever the merits of the analytic tradition, much may be learned from other ways of thinking about religion.

To return to the Nolloth succession, however, its most powerfully influential representative in recent years has been Richard Swinburne. Along with others he holds that a central function of philosophy of religion is to assess the rationality of religious faith, assuming universal forms of rationality which may establish, not merely the rationality of theism, but also its intelligibility when the concept of God is being discussed, and without appeal to any one particular religious tradition. That said, this notion of theism has identifiable religious roots, as we have seen. They are the roots to which Norman Kretzmann and Eleonore Stump, amongst others, recall us. What is distinctive about Swinburne's approach is that he unambiguously advances arguments for the accumulation of evidence to support the truth of theism. Further his inductive and probabilistic argument for theism as the best explanation for the way things are takes the formal modes of argument and analysis of evidence current in some sciences as the pattern to follow. The existence of the world is then best explained, he suggests, in terms of the intentional action of a rational, personal God: a position directly counter to the arguments of some philosophers who have held that we cannot draw any such conclusion, given the limitations of our knowledge and our understanding of our own experience. Theism for Swinburne thus has the status of an explanatory hypothesis, relating evidence which provides some support for theism to other evidence (particularly religious experience) which provides strong support (Swinburne, 1993, 1996; cf. Brümmer, 1992; Ward, 1995). He exemplifies in his own person a rigorously intellectual engagement with the dominant scientific rationality of our time, and demands comparable engagement of theologians. He has also moved into territory which theologians might have thought to be their province: writing on the soul, on atonement and moral responsibility, providence, the 'person' of God, divine predicates (eternal, perfectly free and good, omniscient, omnipotent, creator and so on) and the truths of revelation including Trinity and Incarnation, addressing all the consequences for oneself in terms of the worship of God and the relationships that such beliefs will require if personal commitment to these beliefs is actively chosen (Swinburne, 1989, 1992, 1994, 1997, 1998; cf. Padgett, 1994). Philosophy of religion is no 'merely intellectual' matter on this view, for its conclusions exhibit an understanding of reality which cannot be ignored or its consequences neglected. While not complete in its range of topics, Swinburne's work is both a considerable stimulus to those philosophers and theologians thinking about the intelligibility of central Christian doctrines and a standing invitation to them to produce work of comparable intellectual stature in respect of issues with which he has not so far chosen to engage, such as the mediation of grace in the sacramental patterning of human life, which is to say that interesting work might come from the pen of a more 'Catholic' writer who has learned from the rigour of his methods.

Impressive though Swinburne's philosophy of religion is, in the USA his is not the only mode of engagement, least of all among those committed to the values of the analytic tradition: its consistent concern for clarity, for the weighing of carefully formulated objections to one's own position, for what can be made of available evidence, what counts as evidence and so forth. So far as context is concerned, one needs to note that, in the USA, departments of religious studies are most likely to house non-analytic philosophers of religion who may attend to religions other than those of the western intellectual theist. Unlike the UK case, it is in departments of philosophy that analytic philosophy of religion more or less closely associated with confessional commitment flourishes. Members of The American Philosophical Association themselves keep philosophy of religion on the agenda of philosophers to a degree which has not yet been established in the UK. And there is the remarkable phenomenon of the Society of Christian Philosophers, founded on the initiative principally of William Alston in the late 1970s, and its distinctive journal, *Faith and Philosophy* (Alston, 1989, 1991, 1996; cf. Senor, 1995). There are many outlets for writing in philosophy of religion based in the USA, and the wealth of material produced there largely dominates even the pages of the UK's *Religious Studies*, as a glance at its contents and contributors reveals.

Unique to the USA has been the mode of philosophy of religion often referred to as 'anti-evidentialism', especially advanced by Calvinist philosophers of religion since the late 1970s, most notably by Alvin Plantinga and Nicholas Wolterstorff. The significance of their Calvinist commitments will shortly be noticed at two points. Their anti-evidentialism does not mean that they think that religious belief is irrational, but that theism does not have to do with explaining reality by modes of argument analogous to scientific explanation, in the manner of Swinburne's reasoning. Nor is it to be limited by appeal only to natural theology as a Thomist would argue. Rather theism requires all that we can know in order to understand reality, so revelation and its truths may properly be brought into play in philosophy of religion. Like Swinburne, however, Plantinga and Wolterstorff think that we require intellectual engagement with religious faith, but more, they think that philosophical problems and questions should be thought through from an explicitly theistic and indeed Christian point of view. Just what sort of difference this would make to philosophy of religion cannot be predicted, but it might well be of the greatest importance in resisting views of reality which compete with Christianity, such as materialism. That said, Calvinist anti-evidentialists undercut debates about whether or not theism can be counted as basic, foundational for us, if that means that it must be supported by argument and evidence which can be given unambiguous propositional form. That is not to say that they will entirely ignore inductive argument which may shift someone into recognizing the truth of theism, but they require us to see that, since there are many beliefs which are neither self-evident nor incorrigible or evident to the senses, such as our knowledge of ourselves and others, or our knowledge of the past, in holding such beliefs we are not being irrational. So we can count theism as 'basic' to human beings, taking as a premise their 'natural knowledge of God', as did Calvin.

Plantinga has advanced the criterion of 'warrant' to distinguish personal knowledge from the merely holding of true belief (Plantinga, 2000; cf. Kvanvig, 1996). This is not to be assimilated to the concept of the justification of belief, that is to say, belief which is epistemically permissible. Rather 'warrant' has to do with the proper functioning of our faculties of cognition, and so Plantinga has a strongly teleological and normative view of human beings, from roots which lie deep in Greek philosophical theology mediated via Augustine and Aquinas. In other words, he takes as a presupposition that we are creatures made with a certain capacity, however limited, to understand what we mean when we speak of God's knowledge of things, and this depends upon the fully integrated functioning of a believer's capacities for knowledge. Wolterstorff's contribution to 'Reformed epistemology' (McLeod, 1993, Zagzebski, 1993) is subtly different, since he does not preoccupy himself overmuch with distinctions between basic and non-basic beliefs, arguing rather that, of whatever kind, we are equipped with a variety of 'cognitive dispositions', thus emphasizing the importance of these as the source of our beliefs. We can and must check that we have no reasons against the beliefs that we hold, and we can examine their coherence, but we also have to reckon with the resistance of our sinful dispositions to the truths we find ourselves faced with – another Calvinist point which we would not expect to find made except coming from someone representing an explicitly confessional form of philosophy of religion (Wolterstorff, 2001). As a philosopher of religion, we can also attend to the way in which Wolterstorff has extended the agenda of topics, as he has explored the possibility of a specifically Calvinist aesthetics, and Calvin's understanding of the Eucharist as compared with Aquinas's with the aid of modern philosophy. He has also published a major book on the issue of the interpretation of Scripture (Wolterstorff [1980]1997, 1996b, 1995).

It is Plantinga, however, who successfully threw down a particular gauntlet to philosophers of religion in the USA with the publication in 1984 of his 'Advice to Christian Philosophers' (Cf. Beaty, 1990, Wainwright, 1996). In his view, philosophy of religion should be based on and related to topics on the Christian agenda, or on topics on the Jewish or Muslim agenda, and philosophers of religion have a positive duty to serve their respective communities in this way. The relationship between churches and higher education is different in the USA from what it is in Britain (where former church-related universities and university colleges are not conspicuous in philosophy of religion). Melissa Raphael in England is something of an exception, in being a philosopher of religion in a former church-based college (now the University of Gloucester). Raphael is Jewish and her work includes writings on Otto and religious experience (Raphael, 1997), suffering and the construction of feminist theology or thealogy.

We have not yet seen in the UK the very close alliance between a conservative, Protestant Christian agenda and philosophy of religion quite comparable to what we may find in the USA, irrespective of whether one falls in with the evidentialists or the anti-evidentialists. For instance, in the preliminary 'invitation to Christian philosophy' to be found in J.P. Moreland and William Lane Craig's *Philosophical Foundations for a Christian Worldview* (2003), the authors claim that 'one of the awesome tasks of Christian philosophers is to help turn the contemporary intellectual tide in such a way as to foster a sociocultural milieu in which Christian faith can be regarded as an intellectually credible option for thinking men and women'; and, 'since philosophy is foundational to every discipline of the university, philosophy is the most strategic discipline to be influenced for Christ' (ibid., p.2). The book covers topics in epistemology, metaphysics, philosophy of science, ethics and philosophy of religion, as well as philosophical theology: Trinity and Incarnation, and a relatively new topic in philosophy of religion, that of 'Christian particularism', the consistency between 'the facts of God's existence and the perdition of the unevangelized'. John Hick's arguments for the studies of religious pluralism and the understanding of the part played by religion in human life have clearly cut little ice in the context from which the authors write, and they fail to appreciate the connection between his philosophical position and the fact that he was stimulated into finding it by his reflections on the multi-ethnic and multi-religious character of the city of Birmingham in which his university department was situated (Hick, 1993; cf. Hewitt, 1991; Sharma, 1993).

Nor would Moreland and Craig be sympathetic to the position of, for example, Jacques Dupuis and his argument as a theologian towards a specifically Christian theology of religious pluralism. He argues from theological premises that Christians would receive not only the enrichment of their own faith but its purification from understanding other religious traditions in their approach to God – a process of mutual evangelization (Dupuis, 1997). It should be noted that Dupuis's theology has not been received with unqualified enthusiasm by some of the authorities of the Roman Catholic Church, his own communion. Amongst British theologians, only Keith Ward has risen to the challenge of thinking through a theology of revelation in the world's religions (Ward, 1994). This is a bold and risky exercise, given the dearth of conceptual work on mainstream religions currently undertaken, in Britain at any rate, where forms of Buddhism receive some attention, but both Islam and Hinduism are treated more as sociocultural phenomena as yet.

Given the particular turn in philosophy of religion illustrated by Moreland and Craig, it may be that we can appreciate afresh another perspective in philosophy of religion, that associated with the name of Wittgenstein, before venturing some concluding comments on the very recent phenomenon of 'Radical Orthodoxy' in theology. It cannot be asserted too often that Wittgenstein himself did not produce a philosophy of religion. The point, rather, is that Wittgenstein's shift in philosophical position from the publication of his *Tractatus* (1921) to *Philosophical Investigations* (1953) as well as his brief *Lectures on Religious Belief*, remarks on *Culture and Value* and on Frazer's *Golden Bough* (Wittgenstein, 1953, 1966, 1972, 1979, 1980; cf. Pears, 1971; Phillips, 1993; Malcolm, 1994) has been appropriated by some philosophers of religion and theologians, though not always in the same way (Sutherland, 1984; Kerr, 1986; Putnam, 1992; Tilghman, 1994; Clack, 1998). The major player in the Wittgensteinian field remains D.Z. Phillips, whose perceptive analyses of religion always repay attention by theologians as well as philosophers, as with, for example, his writing on prayer or death and immortality (Phillips, 1965, 1970). Phillips has found a place to stand which is that of neither the evidentialists nor the anti-evidentialists. He does not think that belief in God needs supporting evidence (*contra* Swinburne, for example); nor does he think that Reformed epistemologists are correct in arguing that believers may properly locate belief in God in their structures of knowing. He argues rather for the 'groundlessness' of religious belief, on the one hand, and, on the other, denies that religious belief can be construed as a source of information about reality. Christianity in his view does not have at its core theism in the sense of philosophical belief in the existence of one God with certain philosophically understood attributes and character, nor is it a metaphysical worldview. This is not to say that it is irrational, but that we should examine the kind of rationality religion has as expressed in its languages and practices (Phillips, 1988; Phillips and Tessin, 1997, 2001; cf. Whittaker, 2002). It is certainly not the business of a philosopher of religion to 'influence philosophy for Christ' or to advance religious conviction in respect of any other religious tradition than the Christian. In principle, of course, his pursuit of clarity about concept formation and the elimination of confusion in the analysis of religious language could be applied to any form of religion.

Philips's particular achievement has been to advance the exploration of the language of religion as the irreducible and irreplaceable phenomenon it is, and its relationship to cultural change, especially as this is exhibited in literature, both prose and poetry, taking his readers away from preoccupation with 'science' as the pattern for the understanding of human reality (1982, 1991). This renders him almost unique amongst philosophers of religion and theologians in taking artistic forms of human culture seriously (Basil Michell and David Brown also deserving mention on this count). He is also one of the few British philosophers of religion to have addressed himself to the work of the French philosopher–theologian, Simone Weil, not least perhaps because her own extreme, and one might say Kantian, religious austerity is akin to his own conviction that language presents God to us as a hidden God – not the God of theism, clearly (Bell, 1993; Rhees, 2000). Were he a theologian, he would be a theologian of the 'negative way', one of those more clear about what we cannot know and say about God than about what we can (Turner, 1995).

In conclusion, we turn briefly to comment on the very recent intellectual phenomenon of 'Radical Orthodoxy' which originated in Cambridge, a fact which deserves the attention of a sympathetic sociologist of religion, despite the antipathy of Radical Orthodoxy to sociology, an antipathy shared with philosophy and much theology, though theologians receptive to its insights will continue to read at least the work of David Martin, himself both sociologist and theologian (Martin, 2002; cf. Flanagan, 1996; Ward, 2000). Radical Orthodoxy has precipitated itself, as it were, into debate about whether we can any longer be confident about the western Enlightenment project and its confidence in universally applicable reason; and into the postmodern argument with such analytic philosophy of religion as is still committed to theism, to the effect that such theism is no longer credible as a worldview (Andersen, 1994; Charlesworth, 2002; Murphy, 1996, 1997). Radical Orthodoxy also thinks that philosophy of religion's project of theism is a mistake; to that extent it finds both evidentialism and anti-evidentialism vulnerable to the same range of criticism. More positively, as a movement it exhibits a kind of confidence in both learning from and critiquing manifestations of modern culture almost unique in present-day theology, without allowing Christian theology to be overcome by such culture and its theories. It is deeply resistant to some forms of knowledge, such as sociology of religion insofar as the latter tries to 'reduce' religion to something which robs it of its content, or recasts it in inappropriate terms. It insists on the irreducibility of religious language, as does a Wittgensteinian philosopher of religion. It is characterized by its immersion in non-analytic, post-Hegelian, 'Continental' philosophy, and is short on the clarity of the analytic tradition and its careful attention to the strength of objections to its positions. It is a political as well as academic movement in that Radical Orthodoxy makes a bid for the intellectual hegemony of orthodox Christianity in constructive critique of science, philosophy and ethics, politics, modern culture and aesthetics.

One might say that Radical Orthoxy has some affinities with Plantinga's encouragement to Christian philosophers to precipitate into public debate discussion of Christian doctrines, though it goes much further than Christian philosophers in the USA have done by making a bid, not just for re-establishing a relationship between philosophy and Christian belief, but for whole disciplines from which theological perspectives have long been excluded. It is unambiguosly ambitious in its aspirations, for it is 'radical' not merely by working from Christian dogmatic 'roots' ('radix' means 'root' in Latin) but in arguing for specifically theological knowledge to mediate all other forms of knowledge. Its epistemology is Augustinian, conceiving knowledge as the illumination of the intellect by divine being, with specifically theological knowledge made possible by participation in the Church and its gift to humanity of incorporation into divine life, a gift which then suffuses all life. Not its least important feature is the attention given by Catherine Pickstock to the language of liturgy, though Pickstock does not attend sufficiently to the enactment of liturgy, nor to the well-developed field of liturgical theology found in the USA, which is disastrously almost wholly neglected in the UK (Pickstock, 1993, 1998). Its theological ethos is 'Catholic' rather than Protestant, its main representatives being Anglo-Catholic. It has generated much criticism, and is arguably the most stimulating and exasperating single movement in philosophical theology in Britain and the USA at the present time. So far as analytic philosophy of religion is concerned, Radical Orthodoxy's associates will not be allowed to escape questions about just how they understand publicly shared criteria of rationality (O'Grady, 2000). Those who appeal to Augustine and Aquinas among the philosophers can hardly do less.

Overall, however, it is clear that we are a very long way from realizing the claim made by Benjamin Whichcote, that 'there is nothing true in divinity which is false in philosophy, or the contrary' (Hedley, 2000, p.298).

CHAPTER 10

Modernism and the Minimal God: On the Empty Spirituality of the God of the Philosophers

Giles Fraser

For a period of some months in the late 1980s I spent several afternoons in the Rothko Room of the Tate Gallery and thought about becoming a priest. I would walk to the Tate past dozens of churches to seek enlightenment amidst the brooding maroon and black shapes of high Modernism. Churches were places of dogma, boredom and intolerance, or so I thought. Here was spirituality without doctrine and mysticism without superstition. And it was not just my faith, it was evidently the faith of thousands. The gallery (cathedral-like in its scale) was filled with hushed reverence, the sort associated with visiting a church itself. The silence of art contemplation had a distinctly religious seriousness about it, a sort of secular prayerfulness. This was the new religion.

On reflection, it strikes me as significant that the search of my former self for this secular religiosity was also the search of an undergraduate studying philosophy. For the concept of God that was at the centre of my burgeoning interest in the philosophy of religion was of a piece with the secular religiosity of the Modernist art gallery. Indeed both of these interests I now recognize as secular attempts to articulate the nature of the divine. Whether it be the galleries of the Upper East Side, or the lecture halls of secular university, in both instances notions of God that were formed within faith communities are reinterpreted for a secular environment. In both the gallery and the university, the language of God is taken out of the churches. It is the purpose of this chapter to offer some doubt as to the degree to which this process can ever be successful.

'Central Core' Philosophy of Religion

At my local hospital there are two chapels. At least, one is obviously a chapel – the other is a 'meditation space'. The first of these is a familiar, overly elaborate Christian chapel. It has a huge painting of the Resurrection over the altar. The iconography throughout makes constant appeal to the narratives and historical consciousness of the Christian faith. The chapel is full of stories, with multiple references to real or fictional heroes of the Christian faith. In contrast, the other chapel is totally plain. It is a place to go and find God (or a sense of God, or a sense of what is often called 'peace') for those uncomfortable with the very specific references of the Christian chapel. This second chapel is wholly ecumenical and neutral between the various different faith traditions. It is there for everybody, not just for Christians. So, for example, it gives us God but not Jesus or Mohammed or Krishna. Paintings on the wall are wholly abstract, suggesting no stories or historical references that might tip the carefully balanced neutrality of the space. The assumption being made in the provision of the 'meditation space' is that it is possible, albeit in some minimal way, to characterize the basics of *religion in general*.

The God of this space is also the God of the Modernist artwork, the God of a certain sort of apophatic spirituality and also the God of analytic philosophy of religion. Consider the following, from Richard Swinburne:

> By a theist I understand a man who believes that there is a God. By a 'God' I understand something like a 'person without a body who is eternal, free, able to do anything, knows everything, is perfectly good, is the proper object of human worship and obedience, the creator and sustainer of the universe'. Christians, Jews, and Muslims are all in the above sense theists. Many theists hold further beliefs about god, and in these Christians, Jews and Muslims differ amongst themselves ... With beliefs of this latter kind this book is not concerned. It is concerned with the central core of theistic belief, that God exists, that there is a God. (Swinburne, 1993, p.1)

The feature of this passage I want to emphasize is the idea that there is a central core notion of God. On this model there are primary, central core attributes to God common to many different faith traditions. Differences between these faith traditions are to be accounted for in terms of secondary attributes that are, as it were, 'add-ons' to the central core. The philosophy of religion, as practised by analytic philosophers like Swinburne, takes this central core notion of God to be what the subject is all about.

But, clearly, this line only works if one accepts that there is such a thing as a central core to these different faith traditions. There are major difficulties with the very idea of an agreed central core. What, for example, of the claim made by Muslims that Christianity is not a genuinely monotheistic religion and that its conception of the Trinity leads to tritheism? Here the fundamental ontology of God is being contested at the most basic of levels. This is no secondary concern, for it is *essential* to the Christian conception of God that God manifested himself in the person of Jesus Christ and that He died and rose again to save us from our sins. It is not possible, for instance, for a Christian to answer the question posed by the so-called 'problem of evil' without speaking of the cross. And yet an analytic philosophy of religion that is concerned with the generic God of the philosophers expects an answer to this question within terms that exclude such soteriological considerations as secondary and not concerned with 'the central core of theistic belief'. Despite all this, the central core approach to God functions in the same way as the meditation space: it offers a sense of the divine that can be shared by people of very different faith traditions. In the secular university, it is a device to articulate a subject of study that is not specifically indebted to the Christian story – at least that is the intention. It is supposed to be God with those elements that are specific to any one faith tradition‍ carefully subtracted. It is an approach to God that is characteristically Modernist.

The Modernist artwork represents the authentic spirituality of this 'central core' approach to God. For the crucial feature of Modernist artworks, characteristic of the work of Mark Rothko, as well as that of artists like Barnett Newman and Clifford Still, is that they are wholly abstract and empty of any suggestion of figuration of narrative. Indeed, following the enormously influential theorist Clement Greenburg, these became the defining features of high Modern painting. And if these were to become the emblems of a new spirituality it was to be a spirituality with which no one could disagree, for, so it seemed, there was nothing 'in them' with which one could agree or disagree. They were spiritually intense and doctrinally inert, the perfect combination for this new religion. The great Christian mystics of the past had employed emptiness and absence as means of approaching God. The emptiness of the desert, the dark night of the soul, the emptiness of the Modernist canvas: these are all features of the same phenomenon. What Rothko offers is a *via negativa* for the twentieth century.

The ascription of mystical or spiritual qualities to artworks, like those of Rothko, has become a prominent idea amongst many of the artists, critics and theorists of the mid to late twentieth century. Indeed we have come, in a way previously unimaginable, to think of spiritual experience as being something along the same lines of aesthetic experience. But what, for instance, is to be made of invitations to view these artworks as spiritual while rejecting any sort of meaningful connection with the narratives and practices embodied by organized and public religion?

The Aesthetics of Modernity

The debate between John Ruskin and James Whistler, which culminated in the notorious court case of 1877, was, at least as far as Ruskin was concerned, not so much about aesthetics but principally about morality. Whistler claimed that Ruskin had libelled him by referring to the 'cockney impudence' whereby 'a coxcomb could charge two hundred guineas for flinging a pot of paint in the public's face' (a reference to Whistler's 'abstract' painting *Nocturne in Black and Gold: A Falling Rocket*). For Whistler, art was understood as something purely aesthetic: 'in essence, a matter of retinal and auditory effects produced for their own sakes' (Wilenski, 1993, p.198). In this Whistler is adopting a position that can be seen as characteristic of modernity. Ruskin, on the other hand, adopting a position that one might call 'pre-modern', argued that art had to be a great deal more than 'mere sensual perception': 'I wholly deny that the impressions of beauty are in any way sensual: they are neither sensual nor intellectual but moral' (Ruskin, 1920, vol.IV, p.42). The court, who evidently found it difficult to decide the matter, eventually found in favour of Whistler, though awarding him the minimum damages of a farthing. Ruskin resigned his professorship at Oxford.

According to Habermas in *The Philosophical Discourse of Modernity* (Habermas, 1987), modernity can be characterized as that discourse which tends towards the categorical separation of art, truth and morality. It is worth unpacking this just a little. For modernity, art, truth and morality are obliged to define themselves wholly in their own terms and without reference to each other. One might point to the tripartite separation of Kant's critiques – of pure reason (truth), of practical reason (morality) and of judgment (art) – as illustrative of this understanding of modernity. For Kant, of course, the appreciation of artworks must be disinterested; considerations of truthfulness, of ethics, even of pleasure, are irrelevant in making an aesthetic judgment. It is indeed no coincidence that the great theorists of the Modernist aesthetic, in particular Clement Greenburg, looked back to Kant as providing the philosophical grounding for their criticism. From this perspective the whole Modernist revolution in art, and one thinks in particular of the art-for-art's-sake movement, can be seen as the consequences of a series of exclusions that originate in the philosophical foundations of modernity.

Of course there are many other important consequences of this series of exclusions: in particular, one notes the extent to which 'truth', from the perspective of modernity, comes to be understood as the domain of instrumental reason; hence the characteristically modern emphasis on technology and efficiency. Similarly morality estranged from questions of truth leads to a slide into extreme forms of moral subjectivity which, as Charles Taylor has warned, can narrow and trivialize public debate to such an extent that moral goodness comes to mean simply 'good for me' and requires no further justification. For Christianity, truth and moral goodness are, at a fundamental level, indivisible; for modernity, they are necessarily separate. Interestingly, Habermas's definition of modernity suggests a potential affinity between the concerns of Christianity and those of postmodernity. For, whereas a definition of modernity in terms of meta-narratives seems to bring postmodernity (understood as 'incredulity towards meta-narratives': Lyotard) and Christianity (a meta-narrative, if ever there was one) into conflict, the idea of postmodernity as that which issues from the collapse of categorical separations invites the thought of a potentially fruitful mutuality of interest.

One of the consequences of the modernist separation of art, truth and morality is that those concepts that necessarily contain elements of each came to be torn apart and discarded. Take, for instance, Ruskin's concern for beauty. For the most part, modernism has found little use for the concept of beauty, suggesting, as Ruskin argues, both moral and aesthetic dimensions. A term like 'beauty' manifestly transgresses the injunction for categorical separation. Indeed it is often still the case that to ask after the beauty of a particular work of art is perceived as something reactionary. Nonetheless there are increasingly voices that seek to highlight the damaging consequences of the modernist *sporagomos* (death by pulling apart). Take, for example, the Catholic theologian Hans Urs von Balthasar's attempt to reinstate beauty in *The Glory of the Lord: A Theological Aesthetics*. He writes:

> In a world that no longer has the confidence in itself to affirm the beautiful, the proofs of the truth have lost their cogency. In other worlds, syllogisms may still dutifully clatter away like rotary presses or computers which spew out an exact number of answers by the minute. But the logic of these answers is itself a mechanism which no longer captivates anyone. The very conclusions are no longer conclusive. (Von Balthasar, 1982, p.19)

The idea that our 'conclusions are no longer conclusive' sounds a bit like a definition of nihilism. And this prompts the question as to the viability of speaking about a modernist *sporagmus* of God. Certainly I find that, in teaching the philosophy of religion in Oxford, I continue to be stymied by the modernist division of labour. For under these conditions the question of God can only ever be posed in such a fashion that it becomes all but impossible to explain the way in which (say) Christianity functions in the life of a believer or how people ever came to believe in Christianity at all. If any attempt to speak of 'the beauty of holiness', for example, is deemed inadmissible under the terms set up by secular modernity, one is led to conclude that the way subject boundaries have come to be drawn leads to an inevitable misrepresentation of the subject being studied. An academic complaint, no doubt, but there is a larger point: in what way does theology in particular and Christianity in general suffer through being asked to play according to a set of rules that militate against its own nature? And this is why postmodernity can be seen as some sort of ally for theology.

The problem, I think, is not that the religious instinct is quashed by modernism, but rather that it is all too often forced to try and express itself in wholly inappropriate ways. And, by 'inappropriate' I mean in ways that render its expression either nonsensical or, at least, incredibly awkward: like being made to walk in shoes that are too small, to borrow an image from Wittgenstein.

The Ascription of Mysticism

Although God may have died in the twentieth century, 'spirituality' remains alive and well. Or so it might seem. People who no longer go to church or feel any sense of loyalty to the narratives of the Christian tradition (or indeed to those of any other major tradition of world faith) nonetheless frequently want to describe themselves as 'spiritual'. If the cultural stock of words like 'religious' or 'theological', or 'Christian' even, have plummeted in places like Britain in the mid-to-late twentieth century, there has been an equivalent upturn in the fortunes of ideas such as 'spirituality' or 'the mystical', understood, roughly speaking, as the innate human aspiration to that which is ultimate.

It is important to note, however, that a description of spirituality as 'the innate human aspiration to the ultimate' would have been wholly foreign to the early Church. As John Zizioulas has argued, for the early Church spirituality was that which was made possible through the sacrament of baptism. To be baptized was to be reborn in the spirit.

> The deeper meaning of baptism for Christian existence involved on the one hand a death of the 'old person', that is, of the way in which personal identity was acquired through biological birth; on the other hand it involved a birth, that is, the emergence of an identity through a new set of relationships, those provided by the church as the communion of the Spirit. (Zizioulas, 1987, p.28)

This understanding of 'spirituality' is entirely different to that which comes about under the auspices of modernity. For the early Church spirituality was expressed as the way in which a new sort of life was made possible by participating in the body of Christ: that network of reformed relationships constituting the Church. The human orientation towards the divine was therefore not a matter of subjective experience or inner states of consciousness. Rather it concerned being the people of God, living a new sort of life, and thus was something fundamentally public, something shared with others and, in a sense that the modern understanding of spirituality is not, something open to view.

The story of the shift of emphasis in which spirituality becomes increasingly associated with the private world of the individual is clearly one in which modernity has had a prominent, if not decisive, role. The 'turn to the subject' so characteristic of modernity is one of the fulcrums around which the term 'spirituality' has become twisted and reshaped. Various cultural forces are responsible for this. One could argue that an 'increasingly rigid clericalization, begun after the Councils of Constance and Basel ... drove many devout believers toward a more internal, hence more personal, religious practice' (Dupré, 1989, p.xiv). One might point to the decline in the political authority of the Church or to the reaction against the idea that the Church mediates the relationship between the individual believer and God associated with the Reformation. However one describes it, it seems clear that, in the early modern and modern periods, private religious practices begin partially to disengage themselves from the life of the Church corporate. The defining feature of 'modern' spirituality is surely that it seeks a new language of the inner, a discourse that is freed from the perceived constraints of the ecclesiastical establishment. In this way the modern redefines the relationship between the public and the private, in a sense creating both out of the distinction it creates between them. A new contrast is generated: public worship and private prayer.

What then of Modernist art? Looking at a number of the things said about it, by both art critics and the artists themselves, it does seem that Modernist art exists in some sort of continuity with this drive towards inner spirituality. Furthermore with Modernist art this private spirituality of experience is crossed with the general secularization of art that accelerated in the twentieth century. For one of the most obvious, but nonetheless important, features of Modernist paintings is that, by and large, they came to be celebrated as peculiarly American as opposed to European. For many, it is through the work of these painters that New York wrests cultural supremacy away from Paris, hence the interest of the CIA in helping to promote their work, and the subsequent suspicion that some form of cultural imperialism is being played out. But, for many of the artists themselves, what was important about America was that it provided a climate 'free from the weight of European culture', as Barnett Newman put it. America provided the opportunity to reinvent art outside those highly developed cultural structures (including, of course, the Church) which had so shaped the course of European art and which, for many, were implicated in the atrocities of two world wars. What happened in the trenches of northern France, in the carpet bombing of many European cities and in the death camps of Poland was bound to have a dramatic effect upon the way in which the artistic project was conceived. From as early as 1915, Dadaist artists were declaring art to be dead. It had sold its soul to the bourgeoisie and now required a radically new raison d'être. Those artists who emigrated from Europe took with them a sense of the need for this new start. And though the denial of any continuity with the traditions of European art was often something of a pose, nonetheless the American context encouraged the drive for aesthetic innovation.

It was Clement Greenburg's philosophy of art that came to exert such an influence upon both the artists themselves and the way in which the artworks they produced were understood. Greenburg saw himself as an aesthetic revolutionary and the rallying cry of his revolution was that of purity. Painting, he insisted, had to rediscover its essential nature. It had to purge itself of those features that were extraneous to itself and through a rigorous process of self-definition seek to ground itself upon those features which are unique to painting alone. 'The history of avant-guard painting,' Greenburg insists, 'is that of a progressive surrender to the resistance of its medium; which resistance consists chiefly in the flat picture plane's denial of efforts to "hole through" it for realistic perspectival space' (Greenburg, 1992, p.558). Painting must remain totally loyal to itself, to the bare essentials of paint upon flat canvas. Painting denies itself in seeking to impose a pseudo three dimensionality upon the two-dimensional picture plane. Hence a commitment to the 'shallowness' of painting and a rejection of, for instance, any sort of shading that may suggest sculptural form. So too, painting must forswear any suggestion of narrativity; it must stop trying to tell stories, which, so says Greenburg, are the business of literature. This, I take it, is the icy logic of pure modernity.

This, then, is the extent to which I want to cast the work of these artists as 'secular': they rejected any meaningful relationship with the narratives of the Christian tradition, indeed they programmatically rejected the suggestion of any sort of narrativity at all. These were works of art self-consciously styled in opposition to the Christian art of the European past. The new patrons were the galleries of the Upper East Side; no more would the Church have any major role in influencing the direction of the artistic enterprise.

Nonetheless, however 'secular', these galleries became the new temples of the spirit. Those who enter them behave in the hushed and respectful ways strongly reminiscent of visitors to a holy shrine. The architecture of major modernist art galleries often seeks to echo the architecture of cathedrals. What is even more surprising is the extent to which the artists who painted modernist artworks invite their audience to look for a spiritual dimension in their paintings. Barnett Newman writes:

> We are reasserting man's natural desire for the exulted, for a concern with our relationship to the absolute emotions. We do not need the obsolete props of an outmoded or antiquated legend. … We are freeing ourselves from the impediments of memory, association, nostalgia, legend, myth, or what have you, that have been the devices of Western European painting. … The image we produce is the self-evident one of revelation, real and concrete, that can be understood by anyone who will look on it without the nostalgic glasses of history. (Newman, 1992, p.574)

The theologian Mark C. Taylor describes the purpose of Newman's work thus:

> The goal of Newman's artistic endeavour is to provide the occasion for the experience of the sublime. To experience the sublime is to enjoy the fullness of Being Here and Now – in the Moment. This moment is the Eternal Now, which, paradoxically, is simultaneously immanent and transcendent. It can only be reached through a process of abstraction in which the removal of figuration or representation creates the space for presentation of the unfigurable or unrepresentable. (Taylor, 1992, p.13)

Taylor goes on to associate this attempt to present the unrepresentable through abstraction with the Christian tradition of the *via negativa*. He speaks of the immediacy of the abstract painting as 'the aesthetic version of the unitive experience that is the telos of negative theology' and says that 'Newman's theoaesthetic project is … one type of negative theology' (ibid., p.15).

Arguably the best example of this sort of spirit can be perceived in the work Rothko produced for a Catholic chapel in Houston, Texas during 1965–7. Rothko's relationship to organized religion was altogether more complex than that of Newman. Brought up a Jew, Rothko came, through an extensive engagement with the writings of Nietzsche, to adopt a position which, on one level, looked very much like philosophical humanism, but which, as with Nietzsche, contained within it a great deal of existential passion which both men associated with Christianity. It is not that Rothko was specifically anti-religious – indeed, far from it. Eric Heller's description of Nietzsche might be said to apply equally to Rothko:

> He is, by the very texture of his soul and mind, one of the most radically religious natures that the nineteenth century brought forth, but is endowed with an intellect which guards, with the aggressive jealousy of a watchdog, all approaches to the temple. (Heller, 1988, p.11)

Rothko accepted the death of God as the condition of modern humanity, yet nonetheless sought to construct a sense of religiosity upon precisely this most barren of theological landscapes. In thinking about and painting the work of the Rothko chapel he put himself, in the words of Doré Ashton, in 'the psychological condition of religiousness'.

Ashton goes on to compare Rothko and the young Malevich, 'whose spirit he most nearly resembles': 'Rothko sought a godless expression of godliness. He too had emotional responses that, as Malevich said, led to the desert of pure feeling. The kind of universe Malevich had in mind was boundless, yet encompassable or "felt" by the imagination which could intuit its very boundlessness. Malevich built for himself an objectless world. Swept clean of centuries of painterly clutter, Malevich's world, famously expressed by him in the form of a black square on a white ground, was a world secure from the ravages of daily life', a conception which coheres with the extensive rejection of 'byt' (everyday-ness) in much Russian thought and literature of the time. Ashton goes on to trace this spirit throughout the work of Rothko's contemporaries: 'Eventually his project was confirmed: generations of artists were at home in this objectless language of pure feeling. It became one of the available idioms for Rothko's generation' (Ashton, 1993, p.178).

Rothko's 'theoaesthetic project' is, however, a great deal darker than that of Newman. For in Rothko, the (Newman's?) *via negativa* falls over into *Deus absconditus*: 'a far more troubled and modern conception of the fled deity,' says Ashton (ibid., p.81). The dark brooding shapes that inhabit Rothko's paintings reflect something of the increasing despair in his life and, with hindsight, can be seen to anticipate his eventual suicide. They can also be interpreted as reflecting a specifically religious form of darkness, as if an aesthetic rendition of the dark night of the soul. There is undoubtedly a subtle and complex relationship between these paintings and the experience of the loss of faith: the death of God in its many manifestations. Nonetheless I think the idea that here we see religion reinvented for a secular age (an idea with which Taylor is sympathetic), and reinvented as aesthetic spirituality in particular, just will not do. Subject to a bit of philosophical pressure, these sorts of claims all but fall apart.

To a considerable extent, the desire to wrest the 'mystical experience' away from its narrative frame is of a piece with the tendency of much late nineteenth- and twentieth-century thinking which tends to regard 'the mystical' as something essentially separable from its embeddedness in any particular religious form of life. The desire to be ecumenical, like the desire to isolate a core of religious experience that is common to all religious systems, inevitably severs the mystical from the specific practices and beliefs that give it its sense. This is one of a number of important conclusions made by the influential *Mysticism and Philosophical Analysis* (ed. Katz and Moore, 1978). For Katz the problem with the idea of a basic mystical core to religion – 'an inward, personal experience that people in all religions have in common, though it is overlaid with culture-specific beliefs and practices' (Jantzen, 1995, p.9) – is epistemological. For Katz, there can be no epistemological sense made of the idea of unmediated experience. All experience is necessarily the experience of a particular person, in a particular place and time, and embedded within a particular context. Similarly the idea of a pre-linguistic, pre-cultural form of mystical experience can be seen as subject to the withering logic of Wittgenstein's 'private language argument', the conclusion of which asserts the (logical and epistemological) priority of the public, in particular public language, over the private and the inner. Public language and all the cultural forms and practices that shape it are not premised upon the private and the inner, but in fact, the other way around.

Likewise Denys Turner has recently emphasized that mysticism makes sense only within the context of a pattern of religious life. 'No mystics (at least before the present century) believed in or practiced "mysticism." They believed in and practiced Christianity (or Judaism, or Islam, or Hinduism), that is, religions that contained mystical elements as parts of a wider historical whole' (Turner, 1995, pp.260–16). This insight has been generally accepted in the area of spirituality. Generally speaking, philosophers of religion of the analytic school have not appreciated its force or significance.

In studying any subject 'Philosophy of X', it is crucial that one first learns something about X. The problem with the religion in philosophy of religion is that it is the religion of no particular person at no particular moment in time. There is no such thing as religion as such: people are Christians or Muslims or Hindus or Jews and so on. To presume that they all believe in roughly the same thing (with a few minor differences that occur on the conceptual fringes) is to impose uniformity where there is none.

CHAPTER 11

Political Liberalism, Analytical Philosophy of Religion and the Forgetting of History

Christopher J. Insole

The distinction between analytical and non-analytical approaches to philosophy of religion has a place in the 'ordinary language' of universities, albeit sometimes a less than honourable one in marking opposing and hostile tribes. Against this, a good case can be made that the distinction buckles upon serious investigation, revealing that positions assumed to characterize Continental approaches can be found in analytical thinkers, and vice versa. In this chapter I will attempt to show both the difficulty and the possibility of an analytical/non-analytical distinction. First of all, I will acknowledge the difficulty of drawing the distinction too substantially, which is to say in terms of substantial philosophical doctrines. I will concede that it is very hard to find a philosophical position in Continental philosophy which has not been, or could not be, expressed by an analytical thinker. I will go on to suggest that the difference is more at the level of a methodological commitment to what analytical philosophers call 'clarity'. 'Clarity', I will show, is supposed to enable any individual reader who is clever enough to see that what is being argued is so, whatever their attachments to history, society or tradition. I will argue that this studied and deliberate bracketing of history in the interest of transparency to the individual can be traced back to the shared origins of analytical philosophy and political liberalism, using the writings of John Locke to make this connection. I conclude that this structurally similar forgetting of history, shared by political liberalism and analytical approaches to philosophy of religion, could be a source of strength and renewal to the discipline, but only if the attendant limitations of the project are understood also.

The Impossibility of Substantial Distinctions between Analytical and Non-analytical Approaches

Sometimes it can be heard that analytical philosophy is 'logocentric', lacking a sense of the indeterminacy and construction of meaning, and so of the constructed and/or indeterminate nature of pivotal philosophical concepts such as 'truth', 'reality' or 'God'. So, for instance, Grace Jantzen argues that one of the (many) things that analytical philosophy ignores is 'the continuous play of signifiers in an ever shifting constellation of meaning, and therefore the problem of reference or relation to the signified' (Jantzen, 1996, pp.435–6). This blindness is sometimes put down to being captivated by the 'myth of presence', whereby the meaning of a term is in some sort of pristine way 'present to the mind' (Wheeler, 2000, p.3). It is certainly true that a critique of the myth of presence is to be found in continental philosophers such as Derrida, who is convinced that the myth of a self-interpreting 'magic-language' (ibid., p.4) was the foundation stone for philosophy since Plato. At the same time, it is also to be found (and this scuppers the search for the golden distinction) in resolutely 'analytical' philosophers, such as W.V. Quine and Donald Davidson. As Samuel Wheeler, in his comparative study of analytical and continental approaches, observes:

> Both Davidson and Derrida are committed to the textuality of all significant marks, whether in neurons or on paper. Further, they are committed to the idea that how an expression is to be interpreted is in principle epistemologically indeterminate. For Davidson and Derrida, the context of a speech act does not suffice to choose one interpretation over another. That is, epistemologically … neither representations nor the context in which they take place can determine which of several interpretations is correct. (Ibid.)

It may be true that no prominent analytical philosopher *of religion* has pursued this line, but the crucial point is that, if they did, they would be recognizably working from within an analytical position (a position developed by philosophers whose works would by anyone who used such vocabulary be called 'analytical').

Other candidates for being the 'difference' between analytical and non-analytical approaches fare equally badly. Suggestions that analytical philosophy of religion is intrinsically absolutist about truth, realist or wedded to a foundationalist or evidentialist epistemology may work as a description of broad tendencies about existing analytical philosophers of religion (in fact they do not), but it is clear that analytical philosophy can be relativist about truth (Goodman, 1978), anti-realist (Dummett, 1993; Wright, 1992), coherentist in epistemology (Bonjour, 1985) and anti-evidentialist in their epistemology (Plantinga, 2000).

Analytical Philosophy, Kant and the Lack of Intellectual Givens

The last name in the list above, Alvin Plantinga, is particularly to the point. Plantinga launches his challenge against the evidentialist approach, which he characterizes as involving the 'claim that religious belief is rationally acceptable only if there are good arguments for it' (Plantinga, 2000, p.82). Strikingly this insistence is seen as being a case, not of Plantinga moving away from analytical philosophy, but rather of making a move within the analytical discourse against other analytical philosophers such as Richard Swinburne. Now we should pay close attention to what happens next in Plantinga's argument; it both reveals the extent to which analytical approaches can be strongly and surprisingly anti-evidentialist/rationalist, and perhaps gives the first hint at what might be a core feature of analytical approaches. Plantinga describes the classical foundationalist position as involving the following claim:

> (CP) A person is justified in accepting a belief p if and only if *either* (1) p is properly basic for S [where S denotes a subject], that is self-evident, incorrigible, or Lockeanly evident to the senses for S,
>
> *or*
>
> (2) S believes p on the evidential basis of propositions that are properly basic and that evidentially support p deductively, inductively, or abductively. (Ibid., p.94)

Plantinga launches his critique on CP by showing that it fails to attain the very standards for rationality which it sets up within its own terms: 'Now consider CP itself. First, it isn't properly basic according to the classical foundationalist's lights. To be properly basic, it would have to be self-evident, incorrigible, or Lockeanly evident to the senses' (ibid.).

As Plantinga points out, CP is neither self-evident, incorrigible (which is to say, simply reporting mental states) nor evident to the senses. So CP is not properly basic. The only other option, on the classical foundationalist approach, is for CP to be believed 'on the evidential basis of other propositions – propositions that *are* properly basic and that evidentially support it' with 'good inductive, deductive or abductive arguments to CP from propositions that are properly basic according to CP'. Plantinga reports that there are, as far as he is aware, no such arguments, concluding that 'one who accepts CP does so in a way which violates CP':

> CP lays down a condition for being justified, dutiful, which is such that one who accepts it probably violates it. If it is true, therefore, the devotee of CP is probably going contrary to duty in believing it. So it is either false or such that one goes contrary to duty in believing it; either way, one shouldn't accept it. (Ibid., p.95)

Notable about Plantinga's approach here, and something characteristic of the analytical approach, is the way in which all the premises, moves in argument and conclusions are supposed to be visible and transparent in the text. Even where the argument is moving towards a position which plays down the role of intellectual/rational adjudication of evidence, it is done so in such a way that the individual is supposed to be able to see for themselves, out of a rational self-sufficiency: reason comes to rationally accept its own boundaries. In Plantinga's case, the individual can *see* that CP is self-referentially incoherent. There is a constant avoidance of any hint that the individual reader needs to assent to any special initiation, or be *au fait* with some particular tradition, hidden knowledge or mystical erudition. Consider any analytical philosopher listed above and one will find the same characteristic. So the relativism of truth, as argued for by Nelson Goodman, is something we are just supposed to see when presented with a certain argument, which shows that two incompatible statements cannot be rendered compatible in higher terms without changing the original content of the statements (Goodman, 1978, pp.109–20). Anti-realism, with Michael Dummett, is something which we are supposed to have the resources to assent to just from reading Dummett and considering with him the nature of mathematical inquiry: that mathematical truths are not 'discovered', but constructed internally within the discipline and practice of mathematics (Dummett, 1993, pp.230–76). In each case, we are supposed to be able to go from not accepting a certain position and not knowing anything in particular about history, culture, society, authority or literature, but by just being clever enough and skilled enough in a certain vocabulary to *see* that certain things hold.

This is not to deny that analytical philosophy can in practice be extremely hard to follow, cramped and tied up in internal debates; but the (in principle) dedication to a certain notion of 'clarity' and 'rigorous argument' is symptomatic of an ideal of analytical philosophers, which is that anyone intelligent enough could read their work and see that the argument they are putting forward is valid. The sense of independence from history and authority is reflected in the slightly high-handed manner in which canonical writers are treated. So we have Richard Swinburne congratulating John Locke for recognizing in 'a vague way' (Swinburne, 2001, p.187) insights about internalist justification which are developed in his own work, *Epistemic Justification*. Although Locke's 'general approach ... was the correct one', we are told that 'of course Locke missed a lot' (ibid., p.188), which Swinburne is able to fill in. Historical texts are explored, not in terms of what they say, and their location within history and space, but in terms of how well they forward the argument. When trained in analytical philosophy we are taught to look at what the text should have said to convey an argument, glossing over the complexities and flaws of what is actually said. On a personal note, I have never forgotten my first graduate tutorial in Oxford with Richard Swinburne. As I sat nervously in a warm office at the top of an Oriel stairway, with bookshelves far more populated by the most recent journals than by ancient texts (suggesting that philosophy – like quantum physics – has a cutting edge), Swinburne (as it turned out an exemplary supervisor) explained that my approach was needlessly historical and interpretative, commenting that 'at Oxford we are interested in the truth, not in who says it'.

The importance and role ascribed to Kant would seem a good candidate for being the litmus test of a thinker's deference to philosophical history, and so to analytical approaches. Theologians have a tendency to show an overwhelmed reverence for Kant, with a sense that Kant demonstrated once and for all that our concepts cannot apply to God. Wolterstorff complains of just this attitude, commenting that 'Kant is a watershed in the history of theology':

> Ever since Kant, the anxious questions, 'Can we? How can we?' have haunted theologians, insisting on being addressed before any others. This is the agony, the Kantian agony, of the modern theologian. Since Kant, a good many of our theologians have spoken far more confidently about the existence of The Great Boundary (between our concepts and God) than about the existence of God. (Wolterstorff, 1998, pp.15–16)

In the present volume Swinburne takes a similar line to Wolterstorff, commenting that 'philosophies ... which are often lumped together as "continental philosophy", have in common an allegiance to Kant's claim that investigation of the nature of the world can discover only patterns in phenomena, not their unobservable causes; and hence "ultimate questions" are beyond theoretical resolution' (p.67). This is ascribed to the historical limitations of Kant's knowledge:

> Kant lived before the establishment of the atomic theory of chemistry, the first scientific theory to purport to show in precise detail some of the unobservable causes of phenomena – the atoms whose combinations give rise to observable chemical phenomena. No one in the twenty-first century can seriously doubt that, what chemistry purported to show, it really did show, and that we now know a very great deal about the unobservable causes of things and the framework of the universe far beyond observation by the naked eye. The Kantian doctrine about the limits of human knowledge was a big mistake; and analytic philosophy, unlike Continental philosophy, has liberated itself from that doctrine. (p.39)

Although very different from Swinburne in overall approach, Plantinga shares the 'analytical' assessment of Kant, commenting:

> It doesn't look as if there is good reason in Kant or in the neighbourhood of Kant for the conclusion that our concepts do not apply to God, so that we cannot think about him. Contemporary theologians and others sometimes complain that contemporary philosophers of religion often write as if they have never read their Kant. Perhaps the reason they write that way, however, is not that they have never read their Kant but rather that they have read him and remain unconvinced. They may be unconvinced that Kant actually claimed that our concepts do not apply to God. Alternatively, they may concede that Kant did claim this, but remain unconvinced that he was *right*; after all, it is not just a given of the intellectual life that Kant is right. Either way, they don't think Kant gives us reason to hold that we cannot think about God. (Plantinga, 2000, p.30)

The crucial phrase here is that it is 'not a given of the intellectual life that Kant is right'; this could be generalized to give us the crucial feature of the analytical approach as a whole, that there are no givens, no authorities, no history (there are arguments which happened to have been written in the past, but which are treated with a methodology identical to present-day arguments). Contrast this with the way in which theologians write, and one is struck by the difference in atmosphere. Depending on the position of the author, one is frequently told that certain statements or propositions are no longer possible 'after Kant', 'after Wittgenstein', 'after Foucault', 'after Hegel'. Thinkers are allowed to settle and accumulate upon a sea bed, gradually changing the contours of the landscape; the analytical philosopher would rather dig up the skeleton and re-arrange the bones more coherently. The texts produced by so-called 'radically orthodox' theologians are illuminating in this respect. A large part of the famous difficulty of the writing is the long lists and genealogies of authorities, involving or excluding the reader, depending upon one's access to a rather daunting and laterally imaginative erudition. Open *Theology and Social Theory* and one is swept up into historical whirlpools such as the following:

> The conversion of gnosticism into nihilism is already firmly in place in Heidegger, and in this respect Derrida and Deleuze merely add refinements. ... In particular, they both suggest ... that not Heidegger, but Duns Scotus, was the inventor of a fundamental ontology, and that Heidegger is pursuing an essentially Scotist line of thought. (Milbank, 2000, p.302)

Something actually happens in the history of thought: here gnosticism is 'converted into nihilism'. Milbank is dealing with a history which is not just a repository for stronger or weaker arguments, but for a past which shapes the very conditions of possibility for thought and social reality. Thought is the history of the critique of the Greek *logos*, 'a discourse that "theoretically" secures a self-identical, transcendent reality undergirding "propositions" concerning an objective "truth"'; this critique is 'carried forwards', and then we have a list of intellectual ancestors, evoking irreversible changes in the landscape: 'Martin Heidegger, and in his wake ... Jacques Derrida, Gilles Deleuze and Jean-François Lyotard' (ibid., p.294).

The attitude of analytical philosophers to history is symptomatic of the aspiration, argued for in this collection by Charles Taliaferro, to achieve the 'view from nowhere'. The criticism of this position is so well-rehearsed that it only needs to be briefly evoked. The critique would be that analytical approaches do violence to the way in which the subject is not so much a rational observer of the world, but rather a complex site where a raft of historical and social discourses meet which shape the very possibilities of thought, perception and feeling. On this view, analytical philosophy does not even get started in understanding the lived human condition. Analytical philosophy of *religion* can be judged particularly harshly, as religion is precisely one area where the existential and lived dimension of faith is important, and therefore its neglect so damaging; something like this is being said in this collection by Giles Fraser, where he argues that the abstract, non-narrative and non-figurative pretensions of modern analytical philosophy are part of a wider modernist ambition which can also be seen at work in the art of painters such as Rothko.

I want to suggest a different story, where analytical philosophy is understood as important precisely because of its studied and deliberate lack of interest in the complex discourses which constitute our various roles and identities in the world. I will argue that this passionate lack of interest in history is itself shaped by historical factors which surrounded the birth of both liberal political philosophy and analytical philosophy in the seventeenth century.

Clarity and the History of Analytical Philosophy of Religion

This deliberate lack of interest in history, tradition and society (and the elimination of the polyvalent resonances which concepts can enjoy when used with such an awareness) manifests itself in terms of analytical philosophy's stated ideal of 'clarity'. Something being 'clear' can be cashed out entirely in terms of the individualism outlined above; if a text is 'clear', it can be understood by any individual who is 'reasonable' and intelligent enough, self-sufficiently on the basis of the argument presented.

What emerges from other studies in this collection, particularly those by Burns, Mitchell and Swinburne, is something of a consensus concerning the development of 'analytical philosophy'. This history could be divided into three stages, which we might call the empiricist, the positivist and the analytical. The empiricist period covers the British empirical tradition originating in Locke, Berkeley and Hume. The crucial feature of this movement was its interest in clarifying the meaning of words, by determining which ideas, simple or complex, words signified. There was then the further task of assessing the relationship (if any) between these ideas and objects in the world, with Locke claiming that some of the ideas (of extension and solidity) resembled objects, Berkeley insisting that 'objects' were just systematically conjoined ideas, and Hume doubting both these solutions, but finding that nature 'has esteem'd it an affair too serious' to give much space to systematic sceptical doubts in everyday life.

The positivist period originated in Oxford in the 1950s, going on to influence the wider philosophical academy in Britain and America throughout the 1950s and 1960s. This movement explicitly looked back to its empiricist roots. So Burns draws our attention, in this collection, to A.J. Ayer's proclamation that the origins of logical positivism may be found in the eighteenth century. To establish this claim, Ayer quotes Hume's *Enquiry Concerning Human Understanding*:

> If we take in our hand any volume; of divinity or school metaphysics, for instance; let us ask, *Does it contain any abstract reasoning concerning quantity or number?* No. *Does it contain any experimental reasoning concerning matters of fact and existence?* No. Commit it then to the flames: for it can contain nothing but sophistry and illusion. (Quoted by Ayer, 1971, p.72)

This movement was guided by the verification principle, which saw only two types of statement as meaningful: analytical statements of logic and mathematics and those verified by sense-experience. Here the same preoccupations as moved the empiricist movement are at play: primarily a desire to clarify the meaning of words (with a greater emphasis on the context of the whole proposition) and then to consider how these words attained this meaning, in terms of the relationship between the asserted proposition and the world (which entered the philosopher's consideration as a verifiable sense-experience).

The climate of opinion towards philosophy of religion in the positivist movement was hostile, pushing those who wished to continue to use religious language to the various revisionist verificationist interpretations of religious language, which were motivated, as Swinburne puts it, by the desire 'not to be too disreputably metaphysical' (p.35). Burns explores, in this connection, the work of Braithwaite, who reinterprets religious assertions in terms of their use as moral assertions, which in turn are analysed as expressive of an attitude, which in turn is understood as an intention to act in a certain way. In this way the religious assertion is analysed in broadly verificationist terms, where the content of verification is not given by an experimental procedure, but rather in terms of the 'use principle: the meaning of any statement is given by the way it is used' (Braithwaite, 1971, p.77), where 'use' can include a wide range of social behaviour. Arguably something like this liberalized verificationism is behind Wittgensteinian approaches to philosophy of religion, as defended in this volume by Cyril Barrett.

The post-positivist analytical period began to gain momentum in the 1970s. In this collection Swinburne comments that 'the metaphysical urge which has dominated western philosophy quickly returned in the 1970s to Anglo-American philosophy departments, leading most philosophers in those departments to pursue once again the traditional task of seeking a true metaphysical account of the world' (p.35). Something of this sentiment is borne out by the biographical experiences related in this volume by Basil Mitchell. Teaching philosophy at Oxford after the Second World War, Mitchell found that it 'was being strongly argued by A.J. Ayer, and tacitly assumed by others, that metaphysics was impossible and *a fortiori* so was theology' (p.21). What flourished in the 1970s as a renewed philosophical interest in metaphysics may have some of its roots in the actions of philosophers and theologians, related by Mitchell, in the Oxford heart of positivism:

> It was to combat this pervasive assumption that in 1946 the philosophical theologian Eric Mascall gathered together a small group of philosophers and theologians who came to call themselves 'the Metaphysicals' (Basil Mitchell, Austin Farrer, Michael Foster, Ian Crombie, Dennis Nineham, Richard Hare and Iris Murdoch). (Mitchell p.21)

The interest in metaphysical questions, and religious language 'traditionally understood', fell foul of the 'positivist' commitment to what Mitchell calls 'minute philosophy' (small-scale and manageable problems, with little existential import) and the fact/value dichotomy (an aversion to realist construals of evaluative statements). Nevertheless the philosophical movement to which both Mitchell and Swinburne belong deserves to be called 'analytical' and placed in the same genealogy, in that both see a continuity in the enduring commitment to *clarity*. So Mitchell comments that 'we remained committed to saying clearly whatever could be said clearly and to formulating arguments with as much rigour as the context allowed' (p.26). He relates with pride 'an occasion when I was about to give a lecture in a Dutch university and the professor of philosophy who introduced me said, "One thing we have learned when we have a lecturer from England is that it will at any rate be entirely clear what it is that he is saying"'(p.26). Swinburne is in agreement here, commenting that even after the 'metaphysical turn' of the 1970s 'The Anglo-American tradition retained from its "ordinary language" [my "positivist"] period a high valuation of clarity and coherence' as well as reacquiring 'from the earlier British empiricist tradition of Locke, Berkeley and Hume awareness of the need to take serious account of the empirical discoveries of modern science (now especially, neurophysiology, Quantum and Relativity theories)' (p.35).

What emerges from this historical survey is that clarity is seen as a defining ideal of the analytical approach, originating in the British empiricists, and remaining with the movement even after the positivist excesses of the 1950s have been left behind. 'Clarity' has something to do with the transparency of words, so that their meaning and the work they do is on the surface for all to consider. Texts influenced by Continental thinkers will tend to enjoy language more: playing with the resonances and allusions of concepts, multiplying and harnessing ambiguity and polyvalence in the circling around an argument or suggestion. Texts informed by the analytical tradition will show more distrust of language, and attempt to pin it down, isolating meanings, listing ambiguities and eliminating every association except the one which is intended for the thesis being constructed. This is not to say that analytical texts cannot, at their best, have a lean and austere beauty, with the precision enabling a nuance and a comprehension which is almost poetic in itself; but it is arrived at through a subtle slicing, exposing and dissemination of language.

John Locke and the Clarification of Words

If one attends to one source of the analytical project, in the British empiricism of John Locke, one finds that this clarification of the meaning of words is a direct response to the European wars of religion, and the English Civil War, which Locke considered was brought about by doctrinal and theological conflict. For our purposes, two things are of central interest here, First of all, we should observe the explicit and principled attempt to bracket out of the philosophical task all those things which are the cause of conflict and miscomprehension. Theological, historical and traditional presuppositions are to be laid aside in the philosophical task of clarifying which words stand for which ideas. Secondly, we note that the 'clarification of words' is not motivated by a lack of awareness of how we are involved as full-blooded subjects in complex historical situations with substantial commitments concerning the nature of truth and the good: quite the opposite. It is *because* Locke is aware of our complex human involvements and vulnerability to irrational factors that he is motivated to attempt the artificial exercise of clarifying the meaning of words as if we were not so involved. As I will go on to suggest, the clarification of words is motivated by the same impulse that generates a strand of political liberalism, of which Locke is also a founding figure.

Locke understands language to have a dual usage, one 'civil' the other 'philosophical'. By the 'civil' use of words he means 'such a communication of thoughts and *ideas* by words as may serve for the upholding of common conversation and commerce about the ordinary affairs and conveniences of civil life in the societies of men one amongst another' (Locke, 1975, III, ix, 3). By the 'philosophical' use of words, Locke intends 'such an use of them as may serve to convey the precise notions of things, and to express in general propositions certain and undoubted truths which the mind may rest upon and be satisfied with in its search after true knowledge' (ibid.).

In an ideal world this association between ideas and thoughts, in both the civil and philosophic realms, should enable thoughts to be 'made known to others, and the thoughts of men's minds be conveyed from one to another' (ibid.). In our actual fallen state, we find that there is a parallel breakdown in both the civil and the philosophic use of words:

> The chief end of language in communication being to be understood, words serve not well for that end neither in civil nor philosophical discourse, when any word does not excite in the hearer the same *idea* which it stands for in the mind of the speaker. Now, since sounds have no natural connexion with our *ideas*, but have all their signification from the arbitrary imposition of men, the *doubtfulness* and uncertainty of *their signification*, which is *the imperfection* we here are speaking of, has its cause more in the *ideas* they stand for than in any incapacity there is in one sound more than another to signify any *idea*, for in that regard they are all equally perfect. (Ibid., III, ix, 4)

Where there is this gap between the articulated sounds and the thoughts they convey, there is scope for disagreement about the meaning of (for instance) scripture and Christian doctrine:

> Where shall one find any either *controversial debate* or *familiar discourse* concerning *honour, faith, grace, religion, church,* etc., wherein it is not easy to observe the different notions men have of them; which is nothing but this: that they are not agreed in the signification of those words nor have in their minds the same complex *ideas* which they make them stand for, and so all the contests that follow thereupon are only about the meaning of a sound. And hence we see that, in the interpretation of laws, whether divine or human, there is no end: comments beget comments, and explications make new matter for explications ... Many a man who was pretty well satisfied of the meaning of a text or scripture or clause in the code, at first reading has, by consulting commentators, quite lost the sense of it, and by those elucidations given rise or increase to his doubts, and drawn obscurity upon the place. (Ibid., III, x, 22)

Such disagreement leads to political disputes, which can and did lead to the religious wars of Europe and the English Civil War, in whose wake Locke is writing. It is clear what political importance the philosophical clarification of words has when the 'multiplication and obstinacy of disputes', as Locke puts it, owes 'to nothing more than to this ill-use of words' (ibid.). Owing to the historical accumulation of imprecise and misunderstood associations between words and ideas, Locke feels called upon – we might say obliged by the troublesome course of history in Europe – to take an uncompromising and determined hold of language. This involves sitting lightly to the source of conflict (history, authority and tradition) in order to facilitate the dual civil and philosophical goal of concordance and toleration.

Perry Miller has drawn attention to the parallel between Locke's theories of government and theories of language, both of which are geared towards achieving peaceful and tolerant consensus and contractual negotiation:

> The essence of Locke's theory is that language, like government, is artificial; it rests upon contract, and neither vocabulary nor syntax have any inherent or organic rationale. By themselves, words are only noises, having no transcendental or preternatural correspondence with what they name; there is no 'natural connexion ... between particular articulate sounds and certain ideas', and a specific word serves as the sensible mark of a particular idea only 'by a perfect voluntary imposition'. Meaning is arbitrary, the result of social convention ... They are related to reality according to nothing more than their conscious designation by society, and no utterance can convey meaning to anyone who does not accept, who is too boorish or too eccentric to accept, the manners of society. (Miller, 1956, pp.168–9)

So the plot draws together. Locke stands as a dual founding father of political liberalism and of analytical philosophy; his analytical commitment to the clarification and analysis of the meaning of words is intrinsically related to his liberal project of the bracketing of history and authority in the interests of public concordance and toleration.

Political Liberalism and Analytical Philosophy of Religion: a Fruitful Relationship?

'Analytical' political philosophers, in contrast to analytical philosophers of religion, are arguably more aware of the nature and purpose of the bracketing of history which goes on in their discipline, tracing its ancestry back to figures such as Locke. My suggestion here is that philosophers of religion may have something to learn from the awareness shown by political philosophers of the specific purposes and limitations of forgetting history. We will take the political philosopher John Rawls as our test case. Rawls suggests, in *A Theory of Justice* (Rawls, 1971), that in framing laws the correct approach is for interlocutors to imagine themselves behind a 'veil of ignorance'; they must imagine that they are in a sort of 'pre-born' state and know nothing about what position, gender, role or gifts they will be 'born with'. The subjects behind the veil of ignorance are also to imagine an ignorance about what their conceptions of the good will be, which is to say, that the individuals behind the veil of ignorance will not know what their beliefs are regarding how they should lead their lives.

Now there is a critique of Rawls which goes something like this: the hypothetical contract drawn up behind the veil of ignorance is neither possible nor desirable because it overlooks the extent to which people are (i) shaped by their circumstances, and (ii) identified by their conceptions of the good. This critique is made forcefully by Charles Taylor, who argues that Rawls's approach represses the dependence of conceptions of the good and the self upon social matrices (Taylor, 1999, pp.289–317). In a more theological register the critique against Rawls is that he has a faulty anthropology, ignoring the extent to which people are thrown into their embodied and created situations, complete with both fatal limitations and immortal longings. We have, in effect, structurally the same criticism that is launched against analytical philosophy of religion.

But this critique would not have got Rawls quite right. As becomes clear in his *Political Liberalism* (Rawls, 1993), it is not that Rawls is somehow unaware of our social and historical conditioning, but rather that he is all too aware of it, and the difficulties it engenders when trying to frame laws of fairness within a diverse and pluralistic culture. Just as Locke was, Rawls is aware of our constructedness within discourses. It is precisely this awareness of individuals as sites for intersecting discourses which motivates the artificial exercise of attempting to abstract from those thicker discourses *when, and only when, framing the laws of the polis*. We might say that it is because of Rawls's sense of the frailty, createdness and complexity of human agency that he sees the need for the artificial exercise of framing laws behind the veil of ignorance; it is because the imagined life behind the veil of ignorance is so *unlike* our actual condition that it can help us (heuristically) to frame laws and institutions which facilitate a diverse and pluralistic society, with voluntary public association between people who share comprehensive and substantial conceptions of the good.[1]

The more comprehensive conceptions of the good held by citizens have a role to play, in that 'all those who affirm the [liberal] political conception start from within their own comprehensive view and draw on the religious, philosophical, and moral grounds it provides. The fact that people affirm the same political conception on those grounds does not make their affirming it any less religious, philosophical, or moral, as the case may be, since the grounds sincerely held determine the nature of their affirmation' (ibid., p.148). So, although the political conception is explicitly and deliberately rather thin and abstract, it is designed this way so as to be acceptable to those who approach it from a diversity of thicker, more committed, discourses.

We can see that both analytical political liberalism and analytical philosophy of religion theory are both weaker and stronger than they initially appear: weaker in that it they are not really representative of a universal rationality independent of history, tradition and authority, but stronger in that (*contra* their critics) they are themselves part of an historically legitimate and principled tradition of sitting lightly to history and authority. Political philosophers such as Rawls show themselves, at

---

1   Cf. Insole (2004), for a full theological defence of political liberalism, in both historical and conceptual terms.

points, to be well aware of this; the suggestion might be that, the more philosophy of religion can be aware of itself within this tradition, the stronger it can become. We might discover that there are powerful historical and anthropological motivations – when dealing with situations in which human diversity, plurality, conflict and frailty are to the fore – for attempting to bracket out certain forms of historical conditioning, authority and substantial notions of the good, not because we are not historically conditioned with substantial views of the good, but precisely because we are, and this can lead to intolerance, violence and mutual incomprehension.

Political liberalism is invoked to enable us to live together in pluralistic and diverse societies. Analytical philosophy is best understood as being an expression, a philosophical corollary, of this political project. One is supposed to be able to approach an analytical text and, whatever one's background or presuppositions, to see that the argument stands or falls. There is (in aspiration at least) an egalitarianism, a democratic, undogmatic and liberal spirit to this ideal. Analytical philosophy is 'best understood' in this light in several senses: first of all, in the sense that this is the most charitable interpretation of what otherwise can appear to be an idiotic lack of historical awareness and respect; secondly, in the sense that analytical philosophers of religion would do well to do what they rarely do, which is to tap into this historically rooted justification for their sitting light to history, tradition and authority. In situations marked by diversity, pluralism, misunderstanding, fear and frailty, the liberal commitment to concordance, peaceful coexistence, communication and clarification has a valuable political contribution.

The world we are faced with at the beginning of the twenty-first century is perhaps more like seventeenth-century Europe than the nineteenth and twentieth centuries. No longer facing the clash of empires or totalizing humanist ideologies, we live in the midst of a fraught and messy mixture of politics and religion. America seems to an extent motivated by Christian evangelism, and evangelism about the religion of liberalism, with the two, at times, being conceived as intimately related. Britain and America, lest they forget it, the two cradles of political liberalism and analytical approaches to philosophy, seem committed to taking an increasingly assertive and provocative course in their relations with Islamic regimes and groups which are portrayed as theocratic and fundamentalist. In such a context, analytical philosophy of religion – which, by virtue of being analytical, involves a studied bracketing of divisive authority, tradition and history – may have more of a political contribution to make towards mutual comprehension and toleration than any of its practitioners or detractors have yet realized.

Bibliography

Abraham, William J. (1985), *An Introduction to the Philosophy of Religion*, Englewood Cliffs, NJ: Prentice-Hall.

Abraham, William J. and Holtzer, Steven W. (eds) (1987), *The Rationality of Religious Belief: Essays in Honour of Basil Mitchell*, Oxford: Clarendon.

Almond, Brenda (1992), 'Philosophy and the Cult of Irrationalism', in A. Phillips Griffiths (ed.), *The Impulse to Philosophise*, Oxford: Oxford University Press, pp.201–17.

Alston, William P. (1989), *Divine Nature and Human Language: Essays in Philosophical Theology*, Ithaca: Cornell University Press.

Alston, William P. (1991), *Perceiving God: The Epistemology of Religious Experience*, Ithaca: Cornell University Press.

Alston, William P. (1996), *A Realist Conception of Truth*, Ithaca: Cornell University Press.

Andersen, Svend (ed.) (1994), *Traditional Theism and Its Modern Alternatives*, Aarhus: Aarhus University Press.

Anderson, Pamela Sue (1998), *A Feminist Philosophy of Religion: The Rationality and Myths of Religious Belief*, Oxford: Blackwell Publishers.

Anderson, Pamela Sue (2001), 'Standpoint: Its Proper Place in a Realist Epistemology', *Journal of Philosophical Research*, **xxvi**, 131–53.

Anderson, Pamela Sue (2003), 'Autonomy, Vulnerability and Gender', *Feminist Theory*, **4** (2), special issue on *Agency, Feminism and Ethics*, ed. Sasha Roseneil and Linda Hogan, pp.149–64.

Anderson, Pamela S. (2004a) 'An Epistemological–Ethical Approach to Philosophy of Religion: Learning to Listen', in Pamela Sue Anderson and Beverley Clack (eds), *Feminist Philosophy of Religion*, pp.87–102.

Anderson, Pamela Sue (2004b) '"Moralizing" Love in Philosophy of Religion', in Jeremiah Hackett and Jerald T. Wallulis (eds), *Philosophy of Religion for a New Century*, *Studies in Philosophy and Religion*, **25**, Dordrecht: Kluwer Academic Publishers, pp.227–42.

Anderson, Pamela Sue and Clack, Beverley (eds) (2004), *Feminist Philosophy of Religion: Critical Readings*, London and New York: Routledge.

Antonaccio, Maria (2000), *Picturing the Human: The Moral Thought of Iris Murdoch*, Oxford: Oxford University Press.

Arendt, Hannah (1968), 'The Crisis in Culture: Its Social and Its Political Significance', *Between Past and Future*, 2nd edn, New York: Viking, pp.197–226.

Arendt, Hannah (1982), *Lectures on Kant's Political Philosophy*, ed. Ronald Beiner, Chicago: University of Chicago Press.

Arendt, Hannah (2001), Beiner, Ronald and Nedelsky, Jennifer (eds), *Judgment, Imagination and Politics: Themes from Kant and Arendt*, Oxford: Rowman & Littlefield, pp.3–26.

Arrington, Robert L. and Addis, Mark (eds) (2001), *Wittgenstein and Philosophy of Religion*, London and New York: Routledge.

Ashton, Doré (1993), *About Rothko*, Oxford: Oxford University Press.

Athanasius (1971), *On the Incarnation*, trans. R.W. Thomson, Oxford: Clarendon Press.

Audi, Robert (2000), *Religious Commitment and Secular Reason*, Cambridge: CUP.

Audi, Robert and Wolterstorff, Nicholas (1997), *Religion in the Public Square: The Place of Religious Convictions in Political Debate*, Lanham, MD: Rowman & Littlefield.

Ayer, A.J. (1936), *Language, Truth and Logic*, London: Macmillan.

Ayer, A.J. (1968), *The Origins of Pragmatism*, London: Macmillan.

Ayer, A.J. (1971), *Language, Truth and Logic*, Harmondsworth: Penguin Books.

Ayer, A.J. (1986) *Ludwig Wittgenstein*, Harmondsworth: Penguin.

Barr, J. (1993), *Biblical Faith and Natural Theology*, Oxford: Clarendon Press.

Barrett, Cyril (1991), *Wittgenstein on Ethics and Religious Belief*, Oxford: Blackwell.

Bartell, T.W. (2003), *Comparative Theology: Essays for Keith Ward*, London: SPCK.

Beaty, Michael D. (ed.) (1990), *Christian Theism and the Problems of Philosophy*, Notre Dame, IND: University of Notre Dame.

Bell, Richard H. (ed.) (1993), *Simone Weil's Philosophy of Culture*, Cambridge: Cambridge University Press.

Benhabib, Seyla (1992), *Situating the Self: Gender, Community and Postmodernism in Contemporary Ethics*, London: Routledge.

Berlin, Isaiah (2000), *The Roots of Romanticism*, ed. Henry Hardy, London: Pimlico.

Beversluis, John (1995), 'Reforming the "Reformed" Objection to Natural Theology', *Faith and Philosophy*, **12** (2), 189–206.

Blanshard, Brand (1962), *Reason and Analysis*, London: George Allen and Unwin.

Bode, Carl (ed.) (1981), *The Portable Emerson*, New York: Penguin.

Bonjour, Laurence (1985), *The Structure of Empirical Knowledge*, Cambridge, MA: Harvard University Press.

Braithwaite, R.B. (1966), 'Response to discussion of his lecture', in Ian T. Ramsey (ed.), *Christian Ethics and Contemporary Philosophy*, London: SCM Press, pp.88–94.

Braithwaite, R.B. (1971), 'An Empiricist's View of the Nature of Religious Belief', reprinted in Basil Mitchell (ed.), *The Philosophy of Religion*, Oxford: Oxford University Press.

Brandt, Richard B. (1979), *A Theory of the Good and the Right*, Oxford: Clarendon Press.

Brown, Andrew (2003), 'Profile: the practical philosopher' (an interview with Mary Warnock), *The Guardian Review*, 19 July, pp.16–19.

Brown, Colin (1978), *Philosophy and the Christian Faith*, Downers Grove, IL: InterVarsity Press.

Brown, David (1985), *The Divine Trinity*, London: Duckworth.

Brown, David (1987), *Continental Philosophy and Modern Theology: An Engagement*, Oxford: Blackwell.

Brown, David (1999), *Tradition and Imagination*, Oxford: Clarendon.

Brown, David (2000), *Discipleship and Imagination*, Oxford: Clarendon.

Brown, David (2004), *God and the Enchantment of Place*, Oxford: Oxford University Press.

Brown, S.C. (ed.) (1977), *Reason and Religion*, London and Ithaca: Cornell University Press.

Brümmer, Vincent (1984), *What Are We Doing When We Pray? A Philosophical Enquiry*, London: SCM.

Brümmer, Vincent (1992), *Speaking of a Personal God*, Cambridge: Cambridge University Press.

Brümmer, Vincent (1993), *The Model of Love: A Study in Philosophical Theology*, Cambridge: Cambridge University Press.

Burns, Elizabeth (1997), 'Iris Murdoch and the Nature of Good', *Religious Studies*, **33**, pp.303–13.

Burns, R.M. (1989), 'The Divine Simplicity in St Thomas', *Religious Studies*, **25**, 271–93.

Burrell, David B. (1986), *Knowing the Unknowable God: Ibn-Sina, Maimonides, Aquinas*, Notre Dame, IND: University of Notre Dame.

Byrne, Peter (1998), *The Moral Interpretation of Religion*, Edinburgh: Edinburgh University Press.

Calvin, J. (1960), *Institutes*, ed. J.T. Mitchell, trans. F.L. Battles, Philadelphia: The Westminster Press.

Carson, Thomas L. (2000), *Value and the Good Life*, Notre Dame, IND: University of Notre Dame.

Cavell, Stanley (1994), *A Pitch of Philosophy: Autobiographical Exercises*, London and Cambridge, MA: Harvard University Press.

Charlesworth, Max (2002), *Philosophy and Religion: From Plato to Postmodernism*, Oxford: Oneworld.

Charry, Ellen T. (1997), *By the Renewing of Your Minds: The Pastoral Function of Christian Doctrine*, Oxford and New York: Oxford University Press.

Clack, Beverley and Clack, Brian R. (1998), *The Philosophy of Religion: A Critical Introduction*, Oxford: Polity.

Clack, Brian R. (1998), *Wittgenstein, Frazer and Religion*, Basingstoke: Macmillan.

Clack, Brian R. (1999), *An Introduction to Wittgenstein's Philosophy of Religion*, Edinburgh: Edinburgh University Press.

Clark, Stephen R.L. (1984), *From Athens to Jerusalem: The Love of Wisdom and the Love of God*, Oxford: Clarendon.

Clark, Stephen R.L. (1986), *The Mysteries of Religion. An Introduction to*

Philosophy through Religion, Oxford: Blackwell.

Clark, Stephen R.L. (1991), *God's World and the Great Awakening*, Oxford: Clarendon.

Clement (1968), 'First Epistle to the Corinthians', trans. M. Staniford, *Early Christian Writings*, Harmondsworth: Penguin.

Coakley, Sarah (1992), 'Visions of the Self in Late Medieval Christianity: Some Cross-Disciplinary Reflections', in Michael McGhee (ed.), *Philosophy, Religion and the Spiritual Life*, Royal Institute of Philosophy Supplement **32**, Cambridge: Cambridge University Press, pp.89–103.

Coakley, Sarah (1997), 'Feminism', in Phillip L. Quinn, and Charles Taliaferro (eds), *A Companion to Philosophy of Religion*, Oxford: Blackwell, pp.601–6 (revised and reprinted in Coakley, 2002).

Coakley, Sarah (2002), *Powers and Submissions: Spirituality, Philosophy and Gender*, Oxford: Blackwell.

Code, Lorraine (1991), *What Can She Know? Feminist Theory and the Construction of Knowledge*, Ithaca: Cornell University Press.

Code, Lorraine (1992), 'Feminist epistemology', in Jonathan Dancy and Ernest Sosa (eds), *A Companion to Epistemology*, Oxford: Blackwell, pp.138–42.

Conti, Charles (1995), *Metaphysical Personalism: An Analysis of Austin Farrer's Metaphysics of Theism*, Oxford: Clarendon.

Cooper, David E. (1996), *World Philosophies: An Historical Introduction*, Oxford and Cambridge, MA: Blackwell.

Copleston, Frederick (1967), *A History of Philosophy*, **8**, New York: Image Books.

Crary, Alice and Read, Rupert (eds) (2000), *The New Wittgenstein*, London: Routledge.

Crites, Stephen (1998), *Dialectic and Gospel in the Development of Hegel's Thinking*, University Park, PA: Pennsylvania University Press.

Crombie, Ian (1957), 'The Possibility of Theological Arguments', in Basil Mitchell (ed.), *Faith and Logic*, London: Macmillan.

Cusa, Nicholas (1928), *The Vision of God*, trans. E. Salter, New York: Frederick Ungar.

Davies, Martin (1994), 'The mental simulation debate', in Christopher Peacocke (ed.), *Objectivity, Simulation and the Unity of Consciousness*, Oxford: Oxford University Press.

Dewey, John (1977), *A Common Faith*, New Haven, CT: Yale University Press.

Dickstein, Morris (ed.) (1998), *The Revival of Pragmatism: New Essays on Social Thought, Law, and Culture*, Durham, NC: Duke University Press.

Dray, William H. (1957), *Laws and Explanation in History*, Oxford: Oxford University Press.

Dummett, Michael (1993), *The Seas of Language*, Oxford: Clarendon Press.

Duns Scotus (1950), 'Ordinatio', Prologue, *Omnia Opera*, **1**, Vatican City: Commissio Scotistica.

Dupré, Louis (1989), 'Introduction', in Louis Dupré and Don E. Saliers (eds),

Christian Spirituality: Post-Reformation and Modern, London: SCM Press.

Dupuis, J. (1997), *Towards a Christian Theology of Religious Pluralism*, Maryknoll: Orbis.

Emmet, Dorothy M. (1936), *Philosophy and Faith*, London: SCM.

Emmet, Dorothy M. (1945), *The Nature of Metaphysical Thinking*, London: Macmillan.

Emmet, Dorothy M. (1966), 'Why Theoria?', *Theoria to Theory*, **1**, 10–18.

Emmet, Dorothy M. (1979), *The Moral Prism*, London: Macmillan.

Emmet, Dorothy M. (1994), *The Role of the Unrealisable*, Basingstoke and New York: Macmillan and St Martin's.

Engelmann, Paul (1967), *Letters from Ludwig Wittgenstein With a Memoir*, Oxford: Blackwell.

Fairweather, Abrol and Zagzebski, Linda (2001), *Virtue Epistemology: Essays on Epistemic Virtue and Responsibility*, Oxford and New York: Oxford University Press.

Farrer, Austin M. (1943), *Finite and Infinite*, London: Dacre.

Farrer, Austin M. (1948), *The Glass of Vision*, Westminster: Dacre Press.

Farrer, Austin M. (1958), *The Freedom of the Will*, London: A. & C. Black.

Farrer, Austin M. (1965), 'The Christian Apologist', in J. Gibb (ed.), *Light on C.S. Lewis*, London: Bles, pp.23–43.

Farrer, Austin M. (1967), *Faith and Speculation: An Essay in Philosophical Theology*, London: Black.

Firth, Roderick (1952), 'Ethical Absolutism and the Ideal Observer', *Philosophy and Phenomenological Research*, **12** (3), 317–45.

Flanagan, Kieran (1991), *Sociology and Liturgy: Re-presentations of the Holy*, Basingstoke: Macmillan.

Flanagan, Kieran (1996), *The Enchantment of Sociology: A Study of Theology and Culture*, Basingstoke: Macmillan.

Flanagan, Kieran and Jupp, Peter C. (eds) (1996), *Postmodernity, Sociology and Religion*, Basingstoke: Macmillan.

Flanagan, Kieran and Jupp, Peter C. (eds) (2001), *Virtue Ethics and Sociology: Issues of Modernity and Religion*, Basingstoke: Palgrave.

Flew, Antony (1955), 'Theology and Falsification', in Antony Flew and Alasdair MacIntyre (eds), *New Essays in Philosophical Theology*, London: SCM, pp.96–9, 106–8.

Flew, Antony (1989), *An Introduction to Western Philosophy: Ideas and Argument from Plato to Popper*, London: Thames and Hudson.

Fricker, Miranda (1998), 'Rational Authority and Social Power: Towards a Truly Social Epistemology', *Proceedings of the Aristotelian Society*, **98**, 159–77.

Fricker, Miranda (2000), 'Feminism in epistemology: pluralism without postmodernism', in Miranda Fricker and Jennifer Hornsby (eds), *The Cambridge Companion to Feminism in Philosophy*, Cambridge: Cambridge University Press, pp.146–65.

Fricker, Miranda (2002), 'Power, Knowledge and Injustice', in Julian Baggini and Jeremy Stangroom (eds), *New British Philosophy: The Interviews*, London: Routledge, pp.76–93.

Geivett, R. Douglas and Sweetman, Brendan (eds) (1992), *Contemporary Perspectives on Religious Epistemology*, New York and Oxford: Oxford University Press.

Gellman, Jerome (1993), 'Religious Diversity and the Epistemic Justification of Religious Belief', *Faith and Philosophy*, **10** (3), 345–64.

Gier, Nicholas F. (1981), *Wittgenstein and Phenomenology: A Comparative Study of the later Wittgenstein, Husserl, Heidegger and Merleau-Ponty*, New York: State University of New York Press.

Goodman, Nelson (1978), *Ways of Worldmaking*, Indianapolis: Hackett Publishing Company.

Greenburg, Clement (1992), 'Towards a Newer Lacoon', in Charles Harrison and Paul Wood (eds), *Art Theory 1900–1990: An Anthology of Changing Ideas*, Oxford: Blackwell.

Gregory of Nyssa (1893), *Selected Writings of Gregory of Nyssa*, trans. W. Moore and H.A. Wilson, Oxford: Parker and Co.

Griffiths, Paul J. (1997), 'Comparative Philosophy of Religion', in P.L. Quinn and C. Taliaferro (eds), *A Companion to Philosophy of Religion*, pp.615–20.

Haack, Susan (1993), *Evidence and Inquiry: Towards Reconstruction in Epistemology*, Oxford: Blackwell.

Haack, Susan (1998), *Manifesto of a Passionate Moderate: Unfashionable Essays*, Chicago and London: University of Chicago Press.

Habermas, Jürgen (1987), *Philosophical Discourse of Modernity: Twelve Lectures*, trans. Frederick Lawrence, Cambridge: Polity, in Association with Basil Blackwell.

Hadot, Pierre (1995), *Philosophy as a Way of Life: Spiritual Exercises from Socrates to Foucault*, trans. Michael Chase, ed. Arnold I. Davidson, Oxford and New York: Blackwell.

Haldane, John (1999), 'Thomism and the Future of Catholic Philosophy', *New Blackfriars*, **80** (938), 158–71.

Harding, Sandra (2000), 'Comment on Hekman's "Truth and Method: Feminist Standpoint Theory Revisited": Whose Standpoint Needs the Regimes of Truth and Reality?', in Carolyn Allen and Judith A. Howard (eds), *Provoking Feminisms*, Chicago: University of Chicago Press, 50–57.

Hare, R.M. (1981), *Moral Thinking: Its Levels, Method and Point*, Oxford: Clarendon Press.

Hare, R.M. (1992), *Essays on Religion and Education*, Oxford: Oxford University Press.

Harris, Harriet A. (2000a) 'Fundamentalism and Warranted Belief', *Journal of Education and Christian Belief*, **4** (1), 67–76.

Harris, Harriet A. (2000b), 'Divergent Beginnings in "Feminist Philosophy of Religion"', *Feminist Theology*, **23**, January, 103–18.

Harris, Harriet A. (2001), 'Struggling for Truth', *Feminist Theology*, **28**, September, 40–56; revised and reprinted in P.S. Anderson and B. Clack (2004), *Feminist Philosophy of Religion*, pp.73–86.

Harris, Harriet A. (2002), 'Teaching Theology in a Secular University: Reflections on the Spirituality of Learning', *Journal of Education and Christian Belief*, **6** (1), Spring, 27–40.

Harris, Harriet A. (2004), 'On understanding that the struggle for truth is moral and spiritual', in Ursala King and Tina Beattie (eds), *Gender, Religion and Diversity: Cross-Cultural Perspectives*, London and New York: Continuum, pp.51–64.

Harrison, Charles and Wood, Paul (eds) (1992), *Art Theory 1900–1990: An Anthology of Changing Ideas*, Oxford: Blackwell.

Hart, Hendrik, Van Der Hoeven, Johan and Wolterstorff, Nicholas (eds), (1983), *Rationality in the Calvinist Tradition*, Lanham, MD: University Press of America.

Hebblethwaite, Brian and Henderson, Edward (eds) (1990), *Divine Action: Studies Inspired by the Philosophical Theology of Austin Farrer*, Edinburgh: T. & T. Clark.

Hebblethwaite, Brian and Sutherland, Stewart (eds) (1982), *The Philosophical Frontiers of Christian Theology: Essays Presented to D.M. MacKinnon*, Cambridge and New York: Cambridge University Press.

Hedley, Douglas (2000), 'Should Divinity Overcome Metaphysics? Reflections on John Milbank's Theology Beyond Secular Reason and Confessions of a Cambridge Platonist', *Journal of Religion*, **80** (2), 271–98.

Heller, Erich (1988), *The Importance of Nietzsche: Ten Essays*, Chicago: University of Chicago Press.

Helm, Paul (ed.) (2000), *Referring to God: Jewish and Christian Philosophical and Theological Perspectives*, Richmond: Curzon.

Hemming, Laurence P. (ed.) (2000), *Radical Orthodoxy? A Catholic Enquiry*, Aldershot and Burlington, VT: Ashgate.

Hewitt, Harold (ed.) (1991), *Problems in the Philosophy of Religion: Critical Studies of the Work of John Hick*, New York: St Martin's.

Hick, John (1966), *Faith and Knowledge*, Glasgow: Collins.

Hick, John (ed.) (1977), *The Myth of God Incarnate*, London: SCM Press.

Hick, John (1993), *Disputed Questions in Theology and the Philosophy of Religion*, New Haven: Yale University Press.

Hollywood, Amy (2004), 'Practice, Belief and Feminist Philosophy of Religion', in P.S. Anderson and B. Clack (2004), *Feminist Philosophy of Religion*, pp.225–40.

Holmes, Stephen, (2001), 'Review of Douglas Hedley, *Coleridge, Philosophy and Religion*', *Religious Studies*, **37** (4), 491–4.

Hughes, Gerard J. (1995), *The Nature of God*, London: Routledge.

Ignatius (1968), 'Epistle to the Smyrnaens', trans. M. Staniforth, *Early Christian Writings*, Harmondsworth: Penguin.

Insole, Christopher J. (2004), *The Politics of Human Frailty: a Theological Defence of Political Liberalism*, London: SCM Press.

Irenaeus (1868), 'Against Heresies', in *The Writings of the Fathers*, **5**, trans. A. Roberts and W.H. Rambault, Edinburgh: T. & T. Clark.

James, William (1977), *A Pluralistic Universe*, Cambridge, MA: Harvard University Press.

Jantzen, Grace M. (1995), *Power, Gender and Christian Mysticism*, Cambridge: Cambridge University Press.

Jantzen, Grace M. (1996), 'What's the Difference? Knowledge and Gender in (Post) Modern Philosophy of Religion', *Religious Studies*, **32** (4), 431–48.

Jantzen, Grace M. (1998), *Becoming Divine: Towards a Feminist Philosophy of Religion*, Manchester: Manchester University Press.

Kant, Immanuel (1960), trans. Theodore M. Green and Hoyt H. Hudson, *Religion Within the Limits of Reason Alone*, La Salle, IL: Open Court Publishing Company.

Kant, Immanuel (1974), *Fundamental Principles of the Metaphysics of Ethics*, trans. T.K. Abbott, London and New York: Longmans, Green & Co.

Kant, Immanuel (1997), *Critique of Practical Reason*, trans. and ed. Mary Gregor, with an Introduction by Andrews Reath, Cambridge: Cambridge University Press.

Kant, Immanuel (2000), *Critique of Judgment*, trans. Paul Guyer and Eric Matthews, ed. Paul Guyer, Cambridge: Cambridge University Press.

Katz, Stephen T. (1978), *Mysticism and Philosophical Analysis*, London: Sheldon Press.

Kee, Alasdair (1985), *The Way of Transcendence: Christian Faith Without Belief in God*, London: SCM Press.

Keller, Evelyn Fox and Grontkowski, Christine R. (1983), 'The Mind's Eye', in Sandra Harding and Merrill B. Hintikka (eds), *Discovering Reality: Feminist Perspectives in Epistemology, Metaphysics, Methodology and Philosophy of Science*, Dordrecht: D. Reidel, pp.207–24.

Kenny, Anthony (1985), *A Path from Rome: An Autobiography*, Oxford: Oxford University Press.

Kenny, Anthony (1987), *Reason and Religion: Essays in Philosophical Theology*, Oxford: Blackwell.

Kenny, Anthony (1992), *What is Faith? Essays in the Philosophy of Religion*, Oxford: Oxford University Press.

Kerr, Fergus (1986), *Theology After Wittgenstein*, Oxford: Blackwell.

Kretzmann, Norman (1999), *The Metaphysics of Creation: Aquinas's Natural Theology In Summa Contra Gentiles 11*, Oxford: Clarendon.

Kretzmann, Norman and Stump, Eleonore (eds) (1993), *The Cambridge Companion to Aquinas*, Cambridge: Cambridge University Press.

Kretzmann, Norman and Stump, Eleonore (eds) (2001), *The Cambridge Companion to Augustine*, Cambridge: Cambridge University Press.

Kuhn, Thomas S. (1962), *The Structure of Scientific Revolutions*, Chicago: University of Chicago Press.

Kvanvig, J.L. (ed.) (1996), *Warrant in Contemporary Epistemology: Essays in Honor of Plantinga's Theory of Knowledge*, Lanham, MD: Rowman & Littlefield.

La Caze, Marguerite (2002), *The Analytic Imaginary*, Ithaca: Cornell University Press.

Leaman, Oliver (1997), *Moses Maimonides*, Richmond: Curzon.

Leaman, Oliver (1998), *Averroes and His Philosophy*, Richmond: Curzon.

Le Doeuff, Michele (1991), *Hipparchia's Choice: An Essay Concerning Women, Philosophy, Etc.*, trans. Trista Selous, Oxford: Blackwell.

Le Poidevin, Robin (1996), *Arguing for Atheism: An Introduction to the Philosophy of Religion*, London: Routledge.

Lewis, Clarence I. (1946), *An Analysis of Knowledge and Valuation*, La Salle, IL: Open Court.

Lewis, H.D. (1963), 'Clarity is Not Enough', in H.D. Lewis (ed.), *Clarity is Not Enough: Essays in Criticism of Linguistic Analysis*, London: George Allen and Unwin.

Locke, John (1901), *Conduct of the Understanding*, 5th edn, ed. Thomas Fowler, Oxford: Clarendon Press.

Locke, John (1975), *An Essay Concerning Human Understanding*, ed. Peter H. Nidditch, Oxford: Clarendon Press.

Locke, John (1991), *An Essay Concerning Human Understanding*, ed. John Yolton, London: Everyman.

Lucas, J.R. (1955), 'The Lesbian Rule', *Philosophy*, **30** (114), 195–213.

Lucas, J.R. (1973), *A Treatise on Time and Space*, London: Methuen.

Lucas, J.R. (1976), *Freedom and Grace*, London: SPCK.

Lucas, J.R. (1995), 'The Restoration of Man', *Theology*, **98**, 445–56.

Lugones, Maria and Spelman, Elizabeth V. (1983), 'Have We Got a Theory for You! Feminist Theory, Cultural Imperialism and the Demand for "The Woman's Voice"', *Women's Studies International Forum*, **6** (6), 573–81.

MacDonald, Scott and Stump, Eleanor (eds) (1998), *Aquinas's Moral Theory: Essays in Honor of Norman Kretzmann*, Ithaca: Cornell University Press.

McGhee, Michael (ed.) (1992), *Philosophy of Religion and Spiritual Life*, Cambridge: Cambridge University Press.

McGhee, Michael (2000), *Transformations of Mind: Philosophy as Spiritual Practice*, Cambridge: Cambridge University Press.

McLeod, Mark S. (1993), *Rationality and Theistic Belief: An Essay on Reformed Epistemology*, Ithaca: Cornell University Press.

Mackie, J.L. (1977), *Ethics: Inventing Right and Wrong*, Harmondsworth: Penguin.

Mackinnon, Donald M. (1966), 'Discussion of Braithwaite's lecture', in Ian T. Ramsey (ed.), *Christian Ethics and Contemporary Philosophy*, London: SCM Press.

Macquarrie, John (1967), *God-Talk: An Examination of the Language and Logic of Theology*, London: SCM Press.

Macquarrie, John (1988), *Twentieth-Century Religious Thought*, London: SCM Press.

Magee, Bryan (1987), *The Great Philosophers: An Introduction to Western Philosophy*, Oxford: Oxford University Press.

Malcolm, Norman (1994), *Wittgenstein: A Religious Point of View?*, Ithaca: Cornell University Press.

Martin, David (2002), *Christian Language and its Mutations. Essays in Sociological Understanding*, Aldershot and Burlington, VT: Ashgate.

Martin, Michael (1990), *Atheism: A Philosophical Justification*, Philadelphia: Temple University Press.

Martyr, Justin (1868), 'On the Resurrection', in *The Writings of the Fathers*, **2**, trans. M. Dodds, G. Reith and B.P. Pratten, Edinburgh: T. & T. Clark.

Mascall, E.L. (1943), *He Who Is*, London: Longmans, Green.

Mascall, E.L. (1949), *Existence and Analogy*, London: Longmans, Green.

Mascall, E.L. (1957), *Words and Images*, London: Longmans, Green & Co.

Menand, Louis (2002), *The Metaphysical Club*, New York: Flamingo.

Milbank, John (1990), *Theology and Social Theory: Beyond Secular Reason*, Oxford: Blackwell.

Milbank, John, Pickstock, Catherine and Ward, Graham (eds) (1990), *Radical Orthodoxy*, London and New York: Routledge.

Miller, Perry (1956), *Errand into the Wilderness*, Cambridge, MA: Harvard University Press.

Mitchell, Basil (ed.) (1957), *Faith and Logic: Oxford Essays in Philosophical Theology*, London: Allen & Unwin.

Mitchell, Basil (1967), *Law, Morality and Religion in a Secular Society*, London: Oxford University Press.

Mitchell, Basil (1973), *The Justification of Religious Belief*, London & New York: Macmillan.

Mitchell, Basil (1980), *Morality, Religious and Secular: The Dilemma of the Traditional Conscience*, Oxford: Clarendon.

Mitchell, Basil (1990a), *How to Play Theological Ping-Pong*, London: Hodder and Stoughton.

Mitchell, Basil (1990b), 'How to Play Theological Ping-Pong', in Basil Mitchell, *How to Play Theological Ping-Pong*, London: Hodder and Stoughton.

Mitchell, Basil (1990c), 'The Place of Symbols in Christianity', in Basil Mitchell, *How to Play Theological Ping-Pong*, London: Hodder and Stoughton.

Mitchell, Basil (1993), 'War and Friendship', in Kelly James Clark (ed.), *Philosophers Who Believe*, Downers Grove, IL: InterVarsity Press.

Mitchell, Basil (1994), *Faith and Criticism*, Oxford: Clarendon.

Moore, A.W. (1997), *Points of View*, Oxford: Oxford University Press.

Moore, A.W. (2003a) 'Williams on Ethics, Knowledge and Reflection', *Philosophy*, **78**, 337–54.

Moore, Andrew (2003b), *Noble in Reason, Infinite in Faculty: Themes and Variations in Kant's Moral and Religious Philosophy*, London: Routledge.

Moore, G.E. (1903), *Principa Ethica*, Cambridge: Cambridge University Press.

Moreland, J.P. and Craig, William Lane (2003), *Philosophical Foundations for a Christian Worldview*, Downers Grove, IL: InterVarsity Press.

Mulhall, Stephen (1994), *Stanley Cavell: Philosophy's Recounting of the Ordinary*, Oxford: Clarendon.

Murdoch, Iris (1966), 'Vision and Choice in Morality', in Ian T. Ramsey (ed.), *Christian Ethics and Contemporary Philosophy*, London: SCM Press, pp.195–218.

Murdoch, Iris (1970a), 'Existentialists and Mystics: A Note on the Novel in the New Utilitarian Age', in W.W. Robson (ed.), *Essays and Poems Presented to Lord David Cecil*, London: Constable, pp.169–83.

Murdoch, Iris (1970b), *The Sovereignty of Good*, London: Routledge & Kegan Paul.

Murdoch, Iris (1999a), 'Metaphysics and Ethics', in Peter Conradi (ed.), *Existentialism and Mystics: Writings on Philosophy and Literature*, London: Penguin Books, pp.59–75.

Murdoch, Iris (1999b), 'Vision and Choice in Morality', in Peter Conradi (ed.), *Existentialism and Mystics: Writings on Philosophy and Literature*, London: Penguin Books, pp.76–98.

Murphy, Nancey (1996), *Beyond Liberalism and Fundamentalism: How Modern and Postmodern Philosophy Set the Theological Agenda*, Valley Forge, PA: Trinity Press International.

Murphy, Nancey (1997), *Anglo-American Postmodernity: Philosophical Perspectives on Science, Religion and Ethics*, Boulder, CO: Westview.

Murray, Paul D. (2004), *Reason and Truth in Pragmatist Perspective*, Louvain: Peeters.

Nagel, Thomas (1986), *The View From Nowhere*, Oxford: Oxford University Press.

Nagel, Thomas (1987), 'Moral Conflict and Political Legitimacy', *Philosophy and Public Affairs*, **16** (3), 21–40.

Newman, Barnett (1992), 'The Sublime is Now', in Charles Harrison and Paul Wood (eds), *Art Theory 1900–1990: An Anthology of Changing Ideas*, Oxford: Blackwell.

Nielsen, Kai (1982), *An Introduction to the Philosophy of Religion*, London: Macmillan.

Nussbaum, Martha C. (2001), *Upheavals of Thought: The Intelligence of Emotions*, Cambridge: Cambridge University Press.

O'Donovan, Oliver (1987), 'The Reasonable Man: An Appreciation', in W.T. Abraham and S.W. Holtzer (eds), *The Rationality of Religious Belief*, pp.1–15.

O'Grady, P. (2000), 'Anti-Foundationalism and Radical Orthodoxy', *New Blackfriars*, **81** (950), 160–76.

O'Hara, C.W. (1931), *Science and Religion: A Symposium*, London: Gerald Howe Ltd, pp.107–16.

O'Neill, Onora (2000), *Bounds of Justice*, Cambridge: Cambridge University Press.

O'Neill, Onora (2002), *Autonomy and Trust in Bioethics*, Cambridge: Cambridge University Press.

Origen (1869), 'Against Celsus', in *The Writings of Origen*, **I**, trans. Frederick Crombie, Edinburgh: T. & T. Clark.

Padgett, Alan G. (ed.) (1994), *Reason and the Christian Religion: Essays in Honour of Richard Swinburne*, Oxford: Clarendon.

Passmore, John (1957), *A Hundred Years of Philosophy*, London: Duckworth.

Pears, David F. (1971), *Wittgenstein*, London: Fontana.

Peterson, Michael, Hasker, William, Reichenbach, Bruce and Basinger, David (1996), *Philosophy of Religion: Selected Readings*, New York and Oxford: Oxford University Press.

Phillips, D.Z. (1965), *The Concept of Prayer*, London: Routledge & Kegan Paul.

Phillips, D.Z. (1970), *Death and Immortality*, London and New York: Macmillan and St Martin's.

Phillips, D.Z. (1982), *Through a Darkening Glass: Philosophy, Literature and Cultural Change*, Oxford: Blackwell.

Phillips, D.Z. (1986), *Belief, Change and Forms of Life*, London and Basingstoke: Macmillan.

Phillips, D.Z. (1988), *Faith After Foundationalism*, London and New York: Routledge.

Phillips, D.Z. (1991), *From Fantasy to Faith: The Philosophy of Religion and Twentieth-Century Literature*, Basingstoke: Macmillan.

Phillips, D.Z. (1993), *Wittgenstein and Religion*, Basingstoke and New York: Macmillan and St Martin's.

Phillips, D.Z. and Tessin, Timothy (eds) (1997), *Religion Without Transcendence*, Basingstoke: Macmillan.

Phillips, D.Z. and Tessin, Timothy (eds) (2001), *Philosophy of Religion in the 21st Century*, Basingstoke: Palgrave.

Pickstock, Catherine (1993), 'Liturgy and Language: The Sacred Polis', in Paul Bradshaw and Bryan Sparks (eds), *Liturgy in Dialogue: Essays in Honour of Roland Jasper*, London: SPCK, pp.115–37.

Pickstock, Catherine (1998), *After Writing: On the Liturgical Consummation of Philosophy*, Oxford and Cambridge, MA: Blackwell.

Plantinga, Alvin (1967), *God and Other Minds*, Ithaca: Cornell University Press.

Plantinga, Alvin ([1982] 1996), 'The Reformed Objection to Natural Theology', *Christian Scholar's Review*, **11** (3), 187–98, reprinted in M. Peterson, W. Hasker, B. Reichenbach and D. Basinger (eds), *Philosophy of Religion*, pp.330–36.

Plantinga, Alvin (1982) 'On Reformed Epistemology', *The Reformed Journal*, January, 13–17; reprinted in M. Peterson, W. Hasker, B. Reichenbach and D. Basinger (eds), *Philosophy of Religion*, pp.330–35.

Plantinga, Alvin (1983), 'Reason and Belief in God', in A. Plantinga and N. Wolterstorff (eds), *Faith and Rationality*, pp.16–93.

Plantinga, Alvin (1993a), *Warrant: The Current Debate*, New York and Oxford: Oxford University Press.

Plantinga, Alvin (1993b), *Warrant and Proper Function*, New York and Oxford: Oxford University Press.

Plantinga, Alvin (2000), *Warranted Christian Belief*, New York and Oxford: Oxford University Press.

Plantinga, Alvin and Wolterstorff, Nicholas (eds) (1983), *Faith and Rationality: Reason and Belief in God*, Notre Dame: University of Notre Dame Press.

Pojman, L.P. (1986), *Religious Belief and the Will*, London and New York: Routledge and Kegan Paul.

Putnam, Hilary (1978), *Meaning and Moral Sciences*, London: Routledge and Kegan Paul.

Putnam, Hilary (1984), *Objectivism, Relativism and Truth*, London: Blackwell.

Putnam, Hilary (1992), *Renewing Philosophy*, Cambridge, MA and London: Harvard University Press.

Putnam, Hilary (1994), *Words and Life*, Cambridge, MA: Harvard University Press.

Putnam, Hilary (2000), 'From Darkness to Light? Two Reconsiderations of the Concept of Idolatry', *Harvard Divinity Bulletin*, **29** (2).

Quine, W.V. and J.S. Ullian (1970), *The Web of Belief*, New York: Random House.

Quinn, Philip L, and Taliaferro, Charles (eds) (1997), *A Companion to Philosophy of Religion*, Oxford and Cambridge, MA: Blackwell.

Ramsey, Ian (1957), *Religious Language*, London: SCM.

Ramsey, Ian (ed.) (1961), *Prospect for Metaphysics*, London: Allen & Unwin.

Raphael, Melissa (1997), *Rudolf Otto and the Concept of Holiness*, Oxford: Clarendon.

Rawls, John (1971), *A Theory of Justice*, Cambridge, MA: Harvard University Press.

Rawls, John (1993), *Political Liberalism*, New York: Columbia University Press.

Reid, Thomas (1863), *Works*, 6th edn, ed. William Hamilton, Edinburgh: Maclachan & Stewart.

Rhees, Rush (1969), *Without Answers*, London: Routledge & Kegan Paul.

Rhees, Rush (2000), *Discussions of Simone Weil*, ed. D.Z. Phillips, Albany: SUNY.

Rogers, B. (1999), *A.J. Ayer. A Life*, London: Chatto & Windus.

Rorty, Richard (1980), *Philosophy and the Mirror of Nature*, Princeton: Princeton University Press.

Rorty, Richard (1982), *Consequences of Pragmatism*, Minneapolis, MN: University of Minnesota.

Rorty, Richard (1988), *Truth and Progress: Philosophical Papers, Volume 3*, Cambridge: Cambridge University Press.

Rorty, Richard (1991), 'The Priority of Democracy over Philosophy', in *Objectivity, Relativism, and Truth: Philosophical Papers 1*, Cambridge: Cambridge University Press.

Rorty, Richard (1997), 'Religious Faith, Intellectual Responsibility, and Romance', in Ruth Anna Putnam (ed.), *The Cambridge Companion to William James*, Cambridge: Cambridge University Press, 1997.

Rorty, Richard (1998a), *Achieving Our Country*, London: Harvard University Press.

Rorty, Richard (1998b), 'Pragmatism as Romantic Polytheism', in Morris Dickstein (ed.), *The Revival of Pragmatism: New Essays on Social Thought, Law, and Culture*, Durham, NC: Duke University Press, pp.21–36.

Rorty, Richard (1999), *Philosophy and Social Hope*, London: Penguin Books.

Rosenzweig, F. (1999), *Understanding the Sick and the Healthy: A View of World, Man and God*, trans. N. Glatzer, London: Harvard University Press.

Royal Institute of Philosophy (1969), *Talk of God*, London: Macmillan.

Ruskin, John (1920), *Modern Painters*, London: Waverly.

Russell, Bertrand (1945), *A History of Western Philosophy*, New York and London: Simon and Schuster and George Allen and Unwin.

Russell, Bertrand (1957), *Why I am not a Christian; and other essays on religion and related subjects*, New York: Simon and Schuster.

Russell, Bertrand (1975), 'My Mental Development', in Paul Arthur Schilpp (ed.), *The Philosophy of Bertrand Russell*, La Salle, IL: Open Court.

Ryan, Alan (1992), 'Princeton Diary', *London Review of Books*, 26 March, **14** (6), p.21.

Sarot, Marcel (1999), *Living a Good Life in Spite of Evil*, Frankfurt: Lang.

Sarot, Marcel and van den Brink, Gysbert (eds) (1999), *Identity and Change in the Christian Tradition*, Frankfurt: Lang.

Sartre, Jean-Paul (1956), *Being and Nothingness*, trans. H. Barnes, New York: Philosophical Library.

Seeskin, Kenneth (2000), *Searching for a Distant God. The Legacy of Maimonides*, New York: Oxford University Press.

Seller, Anne (1994), 'Should the Feminist Philosopher Stay at Home?' in K. Lenon and H. Whitford (eds), *Knowing the Difference: Feminist Perspectives in Epistemology*, London: Routledge, pp.230–48.

Senor, Thomas D. (ed.) (1995), *The Rationality of Belief and the Plurality of Faith: Essays in Honor of William P. Alston*, Ithaca: Cornell University Press.

Sharma, Arvind A. (1993), *God, Truth and Reality: Essays in Honour of John Hick*, Basingstoke and New York: Macmillan and St Martin's.

Singer, Peter (ed.) (1991), *A Companion to Ethics*, Oxford: Blackwell.

Smith, Adam (1976), *The Theory of Moral Sentiments*, Oxford: The Clarendon Press.

Solomon, Robert C. (1977), *The Passions*, Garden City, NY: Anchor Books.

Solomon, Robert C. (1995), *A Passion for Justice: Emotions and the Origins of the Social Contract*, Lanham, MD: Rowman & Littlefield.

Solomon, Robert C. (1997), *Introducing Philosophy: A text with integrated readings*, 6th edn, Fort Worth, TX: Harcourt Brace.

Solomon, Robert C. (1999), *The Joy of Philosophy: Thinking Thin versus the Passionate Life*, Oxford and New York: Oxford University Press.

Solomon, Robert C. (ed.) (2004), *Thinking about Feeling: Contemporary Philosophers on Emotions*, New York and Oxford: Oxford University Press.

Solomon, Robert C. and Higgins, Kathleen M. (1997), *A Passion for Wisdom: a Very Brief History of Philosophy*, New York and Oxford: Oxford University Press.

Sosa, Ernest (1991), *Knowledge in Perspective*, Cambridge: Cambridge University Press.

Soskice, Janet Martin (1985), *Metaphor and Religious Language*, Oxford: Clarendon.

Soskice, Janet Martin (1987), 'Theological Realism' in W.J. Abraham and S.W. Holtzer (eds), *The Rationality of Religious Belief*, pp.105–19.

Soskice, Janet Martin (1992), 'Love and Attention', in Michael McGhee (ed.), *Philosophy of Religion and the Spiritual Life*, Cambridge: Cambridge University Press, pp.59–72.

Stiver, Dan R. (1996), *The Philosophy of Religious Language: Sign, Symbol and Story*, Cambridge, MA: Blackwell.

Stiver, Dan R. (2001), *Theology After Ricoeur: New Directions in Hermeneutical Theology*, Louisville: Westminster John Knox.

Strawson, Peter (1966), *Bounds of Sense*, London: Methuen.

Stump, Eleanor (ed.) (1993), *Reasoned Faith: Essays in Philosophical Theology in Honor of Norman Kretzmann*, London and Ithaca: Cornell University Press.

Stump, Eleanor and Flint, Thomas (eds) (1993), *Hermes and Athena: Biblical Exegesis and Philosophical Theology*, Notre Dame, IN: University of Notre Dame.

Sutherland, Stewart (1984), *God, Jesus and Belief*, Oxford: Blackwell.

Swinburne, Richard, (1970), *The Concept of Miracle*, London: Macmillan.

Swinburne, Richard (1977), *The Coherence of Theism*, Oxford: Clarendon.

Swinburne, Richard (1979), *The Existence of God*, Oxford: Clarendon.

Swinburne, Richard (1981), *Faith and Reason*, Oxford: Clarendon.

Swinburne, Richard (1989), *Responsibility and Atonement*, Oxford: Clarendon.

Swinburne, Richard (1992), *Revelation: From Metaphor to Analogy*, Oxford: Clarendon.

Swinburne, Richard (1993), *The Coherence of Theism*, Oxford: Clarendon.

Swinburne, Richard (1994), *The Christian God*, Oxford: Clarendon.

Swinburne, Richard (1996), *Is there a God?* Oxford and New York: Oxford University Press.

Swinburne, Richard (1997), *The Evolution of the Soul*, Oxford: Clarendon.

Swinburne, Richard (1998), *Providence and the Problem of Evil*, Oxford: Clarendon.

Swinburne, Richard (2001), *Epistemic Justification*, Oxford: Clarendon.

Swinburne, Richard (2003), *The Resurrection of God Incarnate*, Oxford: Clarendon.

Taliaferro, Charles (1988a), 'Relativizing the Ideal Observer Theory', *Philosophy and Phenomenological Research*, **1** (49), Sept., 123–38.

Taliaferro, Charles (1988b), 'The Environmental Ethics of an Ideal Observer', *Environmental Ethics*, **3** (10), Fall, 233–50.

Taliaferro, Charles (1989), 'Does God Violate Your Right to Privacy?', *Theology*, May, 190–96.

Taliaferro, Charles (1990), 'The Ideal Aesthetic Observer', *British Journal of Aesthetics*, **1** (30), Jan., 1–13.

Taliaferro, Charles (1992), 'God's Estate', *Journal of Religious Ethics*, **20** (1), Spring, 69–92.

Taliaferro, Charles (1994), *Consciousness and the Mind of God*, Cambridge: Cambridge University Press.

Taliaferro, Charles (1997), *Contemporary Philosophy of Religion*, Oxford: Blackwell

Taliaferro, Charles (1998), *Contemporary Philosophy of Religion*, Oxford: Basil Blackwell.

Taliaferro, Charles (1999), 'The Ideal Observer's Philosophy of Religion', *Proceedings of the 20th World Congress of Philosophy*, vol. IV, Philosophy Documentation Center. Bowling Green: Bowling Green State University.

Taliaferro, Charles (2003), 'The God's Eye Point of View: A Divine Ethic', in Harriet A. Harris and Christopher J. Insole (eds), *Faith and Philosophical Analysis: the Impact of Analytical Philosophy on the Philosophy of Religion*, Aldershot: Ashgate.

Taylor, Charles (1999), *Philosophy and the Human Sciences: Philosophical Papers 1&2*, Cambridge: Cambridge University Press.

Taylor, Charles (2002), *Varieties of Religion Today: William James Revisited*, Cambridge, MA: Harvard University Press.

Taylor, Mark C. (1992), 'Reframing Postmodernism', in Phillippa Berry and Andrew Wernick (eds), *Shadow of Spirit: Postmodernism and Religion*, London: Routledge.

Tilghman, B.R. (1994), *An Introduction to the Philosophy of Religion*, Oxford: Blackwell.

Trigg, Roger (1989), *Reality At Risk*, London: Harvester Wheatsheaf.

Turner, Denys (1995), *The Darkness of God: Negativity in Christian Mysticism*, Cambridge and New York: Cambridge University Press.

Van Buren, Paul (1963), *The Secular Meaning of the Gospel*, London: SCM Press.

van den Brink, Gijsbert, van den Brom, Luco J. and Sarot, Marcel (eds) (1992), *Christian Faith and Philosophical Theology: Essays in Honour of Vincent Brummer*, Kampen: Kok Pharos.

Vanhoozer, Kevin J. (2003), *The Cambridge Companion to Postmodern Theology*, Cambridge and New York: Cambridge University Press.

Vesey, Godfrey (ed.) (1989), *The Philosophy in Christianity*, Cambridge: Cambridge University Press.

von Balthasar, Hans Urs (1982), *The Glory of the Lord: A Theological Aesthetics*, trans. Leiva-Marikakis, Edinburgh: T&T Clark.

Von Wright, G.H. (1982), *Wittgenstein*, Oxford: Basil Blackwell.

Wainwright, William J. (1995), *Reason and the Heart: A Prolegomenon to a Critique of Passional Reason*, Ithaca: Cornell University Press.

Wainwright, William J. (ed.) (1996), *God, Philosophy and Academic Culture: A Discussion between Scholars in the AAR and the APA*, Atlanta, GA: Scholars.

Waismann, Frederich (1979), *Ludwig Wittgenstein and the Vienna Circle*, Oxford: Basil Blackwell.

Ward, Graham (1996), *Theology and Critical Theory*, London: Macmillan.

Ward, Keith (1982), *Holding Fast to God*, London: SPCK.

Ward, Keith (1994), *Religion and Revelation: A Theology of Revelation in the World's Religions*, Oxford: Clarendon.

Ward, Keith (1995), 'The Concept of God', in Peter Byrne and Leslie Houlden (eds), *Companion Encyclopedia of Theology*, London: Routledge.

Ward, Keith (2000), *Religion and Community*, Oxford: Clarendon.

Warner, Martin (ed.) (1992), *Religion and Philosophy*, Cambridge: Cambridge University Press.

West, Cornel (1982), *The American Evasion of Philosophy*, Madison, WI: University of Wisconsin Press.

Wheeler, Samuel J. (2000), *Deconstruction as Analytical Philosophy*, Stanford: Stanford University Press.

Whittaker, John H. (ed.) (2002), *The Possibilities of Sense: Essays in Honour of D.Z. Phillips*, New York: Palgrave.

Wilenski, Reginald Howard (1993), *John Ruskin: an Introduction to the Further Study of his Life and Works*, London and New York: Faber and Faber.

Wiles, Maurice (1987), 'The Reasonableness of Christianity', in W.J. Abraham and S.W. Holtzer (eds), *The Rationality of Religious Belief*, pp.39–51.

Williams, Bernard (1985), *Ethics and the Limits of Philosophy*, London: Fontana.

Williams, Bernard (2000), 'Philosophy as a Humanistic Discipline', *Philosophy: The Journal of the Royal Institute of Philosophy*, **75**, October, 477–96.

Williams, Bernard (2002), *Truth and Truthfulness: An Essay in Genealogy*, Princeton: Princeton University Press.

Wittgenstein, L. (1953), *Philosophical Investigations*, trans. G.E.M. Anscombe, Oxford: Blackwell.

Wittgenstein, Ludwig (1958), *The Blue and Brown Books*, Oxford: Blackwell.

Wittgenstein, Ludwig (1961), *Tractatus Logico-Philosophicus*, trans. D.F. Pears and B.F. McGuinness, London: Routledge and Kegan Paul.

Wittgenstein, Ludwig (1965), 'A Lecture on Ethics', *Philosophical Review*, **74** (1), 3–12.

Wittgenstein, Ludwig (1966), *Lectures and Conversations on Aesthetics, Psychology and Religious Belief*, ed. Cyril Barrett, Oxford: Blackwell.

Wittgenstein, Ludwig (1969), *On Certainty*, Oxford: Blackwell.

Wittgenstein, Ludwig (1972), *Tractatus Logico-Philosophicus*, trans. D.F. Pears and

B.F. McGuinness, New York: Humanities Press and London: Routledge and Kegan Paul.

Wittgenstein, Ludwig (1979), *Remarks on Frazer's 'Golden Bough'*, trans. A.C. Miles, ed. R. Rhees, Retford: Brynmill.

Wittgenstein, Ludwig (1980), *Selections: Culture and Value*, trans. P. Winch, Oxford: Blackwell.

Wolterstorff, Nicholas ([1980]1997), *Art in Action*, Grand Rapids: Eerdmans, 1980; Cumbria: Solway, 1997.

Wolterstorff, Nicholas (1983), 'Thomas Reid on Rationality', in H. Hart, J. Van Der Hoeven and N. Wolterstorff (eds), *Rationality in the Calvinist Tradition*.

Wolterstorff, Nicholas (1987), 'Hume and Reid', *Monist*, **70** (4), 398–417.

Wolterstorff, Nicholas ([1987]1997), *Lament for a Son*, Grand Rapids: Eerdmans, 1987; London: SPCK, 1997.

Wolterstorff, Nicholas (1992), 'Is Reason Enough?', in R.D. Geivett and B. Sweetman (eds), *Contemporary Perspectives on Religious Epistemology*, pp.142–9.

Wolterstorff, Nicholas (1995), *Divine Discourse: Philosophical Reflections on the Claim that God Speaks*, Cambridge and New York: Cambridge University Press.

Wolterstorff, Nicholas (1996a), *John Locke and the Ethics of Belief*, Cambridge: Cambridge University Press.

Wolterstorff, Nicholas (1996b), 'Sacrament as Action, not Presence', in David Brown and Anne Loades (eds), *Christ the Sacramental Word. Incarnation, Sacrament and Poetry*, London: SPCK.

Wolterstorff, Nicholas (1998), 'Is it Possible and Desirable for Theologians to Recover From Kant?', *Modern Theology*, **14** (1), January, 1–18.

Wolterstorff, Nicholas (2001), *Thomas Reid and the Story of Epistemology*, Cambridge and New York: Cambridge University Press.

Wood, W.J. (1998), *Epistemology: Becoming Intellectually Virtuous*, Leicester: Apollo.

Wright, Crispin (1992), *Truth and Objectivity*, Cambridge MA: Harvard University Press.

Wykstra, Stephen J. (1989), 'Toward a Sensible Evidentialism: On the Notion of "Needing Evidence"', in William L. Rowe and William J. Wainwright (eds), *Philosophy of Religion: Selected Readings*, 2nd edn, San Diego: Harcourt Brace Jovanovich, pp.426–37.

Wynn, Mark (2002), 'Valuing the world: the emotions as data for the philosophy of religion', *International Journal for Philosophy of Religion*, **52**, 97–113.

Wynn, Mark (2003), 'Saintliness and the Moral Life: Gaita as a Source for Christian Ethics', *Journal of Religious Ethics*, **31** (3), 463–86.

Young, Iris Marion (1997), 'Asymmetrical Reciprocity: On Moral Respect, Wonder and Enlarged Thought', *Intersecting Voices: Dilemmas of gender, political philosophy and policy*, Princeton: Princeton University Press, 38–59; reprinted

(2001) in R. Beiner and J. Nedelsky, *Judgment, Imagination and Politics*, Lenham, Md.: Rowman and Littlefield, pp.205–28.

Zagzebski, Linda (ed.) (1993), *Rational Faith: Catholic Responses to Reformed Epistemology*, Notre Dame, IN: University of Notre Dame.

Zagzebski, Linda (1996), *Virtues of the Mind: An Inquiry into the Nature of Virtue and the Ethical Foundations of Knowledge*, Cambridge: Cambridge University Press.

Zizioulas, John (1987), 'The Early Church Community', in Bernard McGinn, John Meyendorff and Jean Leclerque (eds), *Christian Spirituality: Origins to the Twelfth Century*, London: SCM.

Index